SPITFIRE SAGA

– with a Spell on Wellingtons

Spitfire Saga

– with a Spell on Wellingtons

ROGER HENSHAW WHITE

WILLIAM KIMBER · LONDON

First published in 1981 by
WILLIAM KIMBER & CO. LIMITED
Godolphin House, 22a Queen Anne's Gate,
London, SW1H 9AE

ISBN 0-7183-0058-0

Photoset by
Specialised Offset Services Liverpool,
and printed and bound in Great Britain by
Redwood Burn Limited, Trowbridge and Esher

Contents

List of Illustrations

For my mother,
Jennie Henshaw White

Acknowledgements

My thanks are due to all those who gave me their help either directly or indirectly while I was preparing this book for publication. In particular there is Kenneth Woolley, for his undying enthusiasm and encouragement, and for his painting which appears on the jacket of this book.

R.H.W.

Preface

If a preface is required at all for this book I am sure that it must stress my gratitude to all those unknown and mostly unseen, by me at any rate, who made our crusade possible, and more often than not, enjoyable.

The whole assembly of a war machine, with all its intricacies of spare parts, telecommunications, food and water, often delivered to us after battles with all the elements, and the enemy himself, deserves the highest of praise; for those whose thoughtfulness very rarely left us wanting anything, and particularly for those who delivered the goods.

In a roundabout sort of way, all of us who had the undoubted pleasure of flying Spitfires, owe a debt of gratitude to my maternal grandfather, whose hobby was building model steam engines, avidly followed by his son, my uncle, together with another lad of the same age, one Reginald Mitchell, the son of the Rector. This was in the village of Talke-o'-the Hill, in Staffordshire, very tiny in the early 1900s.

Virtually the only source of income for the village was the small coal mine, of which my grandfather was managing director. Though young Mitchell went to his elementary school in nearby Laughton, and high school in Hanley, there was little chance of his going to high educational levels on his father's stipend. Nonetheless, my grandfather recognised the boy's ability towards machine drawing and draughtsmanship generally, and gave him a place in the colliery drawing office where he could practise his skills, under very expert guidance. It is probably well known that Mitchell's first job was building real steam engines, as an apprentice of Messrs Kerr, Stuart & Co in Stoke on Trent.

Following years of effort at night school and local technical colleges, he joined Supermarine at Southampton in 1916, at the age of twenty-one. His development of the Schneider Trophy winner and subsequently the Spitfire are to be revered throughout our future history.

In this day of technological advance when every flying machine is largely impersonal, I would like to recapture the activities and feelings of one who flew aeroplanes in those last war days before jets, turbo-props and silicon chips ruled the air.

During my time in the Western Desert and Italy with the Eighth Army and Desert Air Forces, I kept a daily record of events which, with very little editing, form the major part of this book.

Reading these notes for the first time since they were written some thirty-five years ago, I blush at the youthful ebullience of the adjectival phrases: everything seems to be lovely, beautiful, gorgeous or glorious. The truth is that we were all bubbling over, like pop out of a bottle, as one of us put it; so much was new to us and everything exciting.

If you ask, why did we so enjoy our war, the 91st Psalm says it all.

R.H.W.

CHAPTER ONE

How it all Began

Those of you who were around and listened to the wireless in the days of the 'phoney war' of late 1939 and early 1940, will recall that by early summer it was known that the German air force, the Luftwaffe, was preparing for an enormous onslaught of Britain. By comparison in numbers, our air force and strength in terms of trained crews and available machines were seen as no match for the enemy's, and every effort therefore had to be made to rectify the balance of power; like all good Boy Scouts, we had to 'Be Prepared'.

So, every night on the nine o'clock news came the request for anyone with such and such schooling and normal health to visit his local RAF recruiting office for an interview. There were twelve men on the ground for every one who flew, so *everyone* was needed, potential air-crew or not.

Soon after the war had been declared I was enrolled into the University of Cambridge, as a student at the school of Agriculture, under the directorship of Wilfred Mansfield, a man for whom we all had the greatest respect, and tremendous affection.

A strict ruling of the university was that there were to be no volunteers for the armed services but just how strict we wondered? By the end of the summer term of 1940, Cambridge had lost much of its sparkle so, at the end of term, we decided, one and all to join up and the Devil take the Hindmost.

A few paper-backs about the war had started to appear, and after reading *I was Hitler's prisoner* I couldn't wait to get at the bastards, so without hesitating I left my grandfather's house at Deganwy, in North Wales, where I was then living, and took the train to Chester and joined the RAF.

I say joined, but it was not all that simple. Firstly, there were various tests and a long wait for an interview. After that, I was told

– not *asked* I noted – to take the train to Padgate, near Warrington and report to the RAF recruitment depot there.

It was nearly five o'clock by then but luckily I found a chemist open on my way to the station and bought the requisite toothbrush and paste, plus razor. Having telephoned home to let them know of my movements, I started to wonder what on earth would happen if I were sacked from the university for breaking the rules?

Arriving at Padgate, I was too busy being dragooned to worry about it and, after a very reasonable supper, was ushered into a barrack room with beds and 'biscuits' – that is what they are called. Horse-hair mattresses, three foot square, and some three inches deep, to fit the six foot three inch bed. Result? Your hip soon forces the biscuits apart, so that you lie on the piano wires strung below. Branded for life, I thought, and felt, when I caressed the indentations in the morning.

Sixty of us went before a selection committee, and ten were passed through. Of those ten, after a medical, four passed through. At the end of it all, with little more than a nod or a cough in response to a question or command, I was IN. I wrote to my tutor at the university to tell him, and kept my fingers crossed. A week later, I received a letter from him full of compliments; evidently he had done much the same thing twenty-five years before!

I had been told to go home and wait for movement orders so I returned to Deganwy, where my father and mother now lived. (Our house in Hampstead had been surrounded with unexploded or possibly time bombs and had to be evacuated. The orders to exit were given by the local chief fire officer, who promptly asked if he could occupy it and look after it for us. We let him do this gladly and never had any regrets for so doing).

My father had been living throughout the blitz in the basement of the Air Ministry, sleeping on a Lilo, teaching those in need all they needed to know about radar, Asdic etc. He had worked all his life in the Marconi Company, starting as PA to Signor Marconi, and doing all his ghost-writing in the *Sphere, Illustrated London News* etc.

On hearing the news about Hampstead, he told my mother to pack all that she wanted into the car and drive it to North Wales, where he was able to join her shortly afterwards, as his job at the Air Ministry had come to an end.

The summer of 1940 was, and we knew it, a brief respite giving us a chance to evaluate the situation. The war *had* to be won by us, in the name of freedom, and thereby, God's will; 'So let's get on with it' ... we heard that said so many times.

We were all filtered away by the war machine into training and re-training depots so that we could play our fullest possible parts wherever we were sent. In my case, my initial training was slightly postponed by a rumbling appendix. It had troubled me for years as a pain which occasionally woke me in the night, and sent me shivering from head to foot uncontrollably, to the lavatory where I was violently sick. I asked our local Aussi surgeon friend about it, and he had a feel.

Making me jump, he said, 'Yep, it's there all right. Doctor wouldn't find it, but we do, sometimes. It's retrosaecal, that is wrapped around behind your saecum. Have it out tomorrow for you; better that than you risk the lives of your crew if you go on bombers.' And so it was to be and my actual entry into the RAF proper was delayed by some three months.

At Newquay, my initial training camp, where I remember sunning myself on the cliff top outside our hotel in shirt sleeves on 1st January 1941, it was that hot, we were taught the rudiments of flying and navigation, and had exams to pass. Then we went to North Luffenham in Rutland for initial flying training. This was shortly to become a heavy bomber base, and while our accommodation was superb – possibly RAF peacetime standards? – the runways had not yet been built.

We learned to fly Tiger Moths at North Luffenham and loved every minute of it. Then it was on to the service flying training school at Montrose in Scotland where we flew Miles Master Is and soon after, Hurricanes – ex-Battle of Britain, covered with patches in the fabric, and even with fabric-covered wings which were later superseded by metal-covered ones for squadron use. Finally I went to No 57 Operational Training Unit at Hawarden, close to Chester and almost overlooking the Dee estuary. It was over that flat expanse of sand, mud and water that we practised low flying, much to the chagrin of the local fishermen, who sometimes lost a mast, while we suffered a bent propeller and severe reprimand for so doing.

I used to hear of other low level tactics being practised in Chester but we were only new boys, who could not afford the taxis to and fro, let alone the drinking which participated in flooring our older comrades in arms.

It was at Hawarden where we first learned to fly the already revered Spitfire, firstly in a mock-up on the ground in which we were shown how to operate all the tabs, tits and switches in the right order and at the right time; then came our first take-off. The early Spitfires used a long-handled lever to pump the oil necessary to raise and lower the undercarriage legs, and lock them in their respective positions. (A little finger protruded through the top of each wing as the wheels went down, and a thin red line appeared flush with the wing surface when locked down; this finger disappeared from sight when the wheels were up; if it didn't, your wheels were not tucked up as they should be.)

Everyone watched your first take-off in one of these, expecting you to push the control column back and forth with your left hand as fast as you pumped with your right. Naturally enough we made a point of hardly touching the 'stick' until the right hand had done its job, so as to ensure a smooth take-off and a steady climb. Properly trimmed, a Spitfire would fly Hands Off at all normal speeds, hence its delight to us all.

With exams passed, and fully medically fit, we were selected for operational squadron duties, according to our abilities. The two plums were Biggin Hill and North Weald, if you were to be regarded as a worthwhile fighter pilot capable of going into (possibly) deathly combat on your first encounter with the enemy. Biggin Hill took the brunt of the attacks over south-eastern England during the Battle of Britain, which had fizzled out like a damp fire-work some fourteen months before, and North Weald, which had had the most to do since then, protecting our East Coast convoys bringing coal from the northern pits to southern power stations, and manufactured goods from the south to relatively safe assembly factories up north. Between such protective umbrella jobs, we 'swept' the Low Countries riding on our broomsticks (many such emblems adorned the cockpit sides of those who felt so inclined) but our Black Cats (our Spitfire Vs) were no match for the FW190s.

Without any justification, as far as I know, I was posted to No 222 Squadron, at North Weald, just before Christmas 1941. The squadron had been badly mauled during its sweeps and

ne birthplace of the
itfire. Mitchell's first
awing office classroom at
alk o'th'Hill Colliery,
oke-on-Trent.

ur first efforts at flying:
ger Moths at North
uffenham.

o 8 Group, Z Flight,
orth Luffenham, during
itial flying training. I am
xth from the left in the
ack row.

The Miles 'Master' I, in use at the Service Flying Training School, Montrose

(*far left*)
Our first Hurricanes Montrose, 1941.

Air Cadet LAC White at Montrose July 1941.

Rosemount, the officers' mess near Montrose; we camped in the garden as very NCOs.

'Rhubarbs' (low level straffing attacks on enemy installations) of France and further east, losing too many pilots and machines, so it was decided that the whole unit should be sent to Peterhead in the frozen north of Scotland, to re-form. An advance party went off early in January, to establish a base for us when news came through that my flight commander had been killed there.

As the sirens wailed their warning of an approaching enemy, the pilots on duty raced to their aircraft, but the enemy was already straffing the huts. My boss fell in the passage with those simple but finite words to someone who went to his aid, 'They've got me', and died on the spot.

The notice board in the mess blossomed with fresh flowery invitations to volunteer for all and sundry jobs. Some of our instructors at Hawarden had served in the Middle East and had great 'sport' as they put it, clobbering the Machis and other Italian craft over the Western Desert and when the door to that warm and sunny climate opened for me, I put my name down for selection, which was duly granted.

The trip to the Middle East took a long time, but was hardly what one could call eventful, thank God. Something like three weeks were spent in Blackpool, which emptied our pockets, and the local bars. Almost at dead of night (whenever that is) we were called out of our billets and loaded into three-ton lorries with canvas sides and back-cloth – to hide us from prying eyes – to be taken to the station.

Early morning saw us embarking on the SS *Alcantara*, an armed merchantman which had previously been one of the luxury liners on the South American run. As always in those times, ours was the largest convoy to sail to date. There were about 40 of us, including enormous cruisers and destroyers.

During daylight hours, which were thankfully few at that time of year, we, the RAF pilots – about sixty of us – had to be the Navy's 'Observer Corps', on the bridge. I like to think that the ship's staff had better things to do than scan the sky for aircraft, and this is why we were asked to do it. That thought of mine did not ring quite so true when I learned that nobody aboard could tell a Spitfire from a Sunderland, and that *any* aircraft that came within range was to be shot at.

Cecil Beaton had been appointed as official RAF photographer to the Middle East and came with us; a most amusing and entertaining companion. So as not to inflict camera shyness upon his unwitting subject, he aimed his Rolleiflex Reflex type camera sideways, without his subject knowing the fact. His knowledge of the Dunkirk fiasco (when the Navy admittedly shot down almost as many Spitfires as those which survived) made him grateful for our long stints on the bridge, where he spent much of his time in case of action.

A funny little coaster took us from Lagos down to Takoradi, about a week's voyage, and we had no escort. We thanked the Lord in our prayers each night that we could not be worth a single torpedo from such an atheistic race as Hitlerite Germany, and he agreed, so we were not attacked.

The boring days dragged on, and every morning when our little cabin boy brought us our morning tea, we asked, 'When are we going to get there, Sambo?'

Every day came the same reply, 'Next week maybe, sometime, perhaps', with a grin from ear to ear. With such faith, he was surely one of God's chillun.

Once we had landed, it seemed to take no time before Pan Am Airways took twenty-two of us across Africa via Kano and Khartoum, to Heliopolis in Cairo in a DC3 Dakota. The aluminium bench type seats along the sides got very hard. Nonetheless, the pilot (an American civilian of course) took us down to take closer looks at the herds of elephant etc, whenever he saw something of interest for us.

Having landed in Cairo, we all went to the transit camp in the suburbs called Almaza, just a mass of tents half buried in loose sand, where the desert meets the town. The lower half of each tent had to be below ground level, to stop it blowing away. The only two concrete block-built buildings were the orderly room and the cook-house dining area. It was the first time I had met Egyptian tomatoes, which we had for every meal, hot or cold; the size of grapefruit, they were delicious in every way.

There was no chance of being posted to a squadron immediately, for as yet there were no Spitfires. A few had arrived by sea to Takoradi, and with large 'slipper' tanks under their bellies (to give them extra range) had been flown to Egypt, the way we had come. Unfortunately these were few, and were desperately needed for the high-level photographic reconnaissance job, and could not be spared for fighting.

My sister, Bay White, had arrived in Egypt some time before me having had a wonderful trip round the Cape. She came out with an ENSA party to play *George and Margaret*, in which she had the juvenile lead. I telephoned the ENSA office in Cairo, who gave me her pension address and number in Ismailia, a beautiful little French town, the home of the Suez Canal pilots, halfway along its length from Port Said in the north to Suez in the south.

There was no difficulty in hitching a hike anywhere, for there were masses of military vehicles going in all directions. By tea time I had arrived and we had a wonderful weekend together, on the shore of Lake Timsa, spent mostly at the French Club, with its glorious little beach, sailing club attached, and excellent restaurant.

Something like three weeks of boredom passed by at the transit camp, by which time I had made myself known to the Personnel Department at Air Headquarters, Middle East, and very probably quite a bit of a nuisance too.

There were a few Hurricane squadrons operating in the Western Desert, mostly to give top cover to our ground troops, trying to protect them from attack by Stuka dive bombers. With great joy I was posted to No 73 Squadron which I discovered had one of the highest scores in the RAF, and had been the first, together with No 1 Squadron to be flown into France in 1939 at the outbreak of war.

The simplicity of life in the desert seemed to suit everyone, but being constantly on the move we lived in tiny little 'bivouac' tents, just big enough to crawl into, except for the mess tents and orderly room, which were known as EPIs, though I never discovered what the initials meant, or why they were so called.

We all had to dig slit trenches immediately adjacent to our tents because air raids at night were frequent. Jerry knew the location of all the aerodromes and it was easy for him to illuminate them with parachute flares and bomb them more or less at will; our defence force of Bofors guns made a lot of noise, but – like the Jerry's – were pretty ineffective.

Few of the bombing raids did much material damage except perhaps the Butterfly Bombs, which one night destroyed our cook-house. Another menace was the scattering of pressed-steel three sided pyramids, measuring some two inches from point to point, with barbed hooks stamped into the scalloped edges. These were designed to puncture the tyres of course, but at sunrise everyone lined up like a troop of potato pickers, collected them all, and dumped them into the bomb craters, which would soon be filled anyway. The cleverest thing about them was their colour, absolutely exact for that particular patch of desert, which varies in colour every few miles. At dawn and early sunrise, their little shadows made them easy enough to see.

By late August 1942 Jerry was being a bit troublesome in the Suez Canal zone, night after night dropping mines into the vital passage-way. This meant that the few night-fighting Beaufighters we had to give top-cover to our desert troops at night had to be sent down to the canal, where they were very successful in shooting down many of the raiders. There was so little daytime activity for us to combat so it was decided that 73 Squadron should go back to the Nile/Delta aerodromes and practise night-flying to replace the Beaufighters on the Western Front.

By this time, more Spitfires were being delivered, though an awful lot had been sunk while being sent to the Gold Coast as deck cargo. Nonetheless, I did not much like the idea of night flying, Hurricanes or anything else, and I did not think that my eyesight would be good enough anyway; the glare on blue-eyed people strains the eyes terribly. My CO (Robin Johnston) agreed to release me and gave me a recommendation to that effect, so that I could call on our Air Officer Commanding, Maori Coningham, and happily he agreed also. (I learned later that he had been a First World War CO of No 92 Squadron, currently being shipped to the Middle East with their Spitfires, so perhaps he kept his fingers crossed, just as I did.)

Back in the Delta, I found that things had not gone as well as expected with Spitfire deliveries; three complete squadrons were queueing up for their aircraft to arrive, leaving me no chance at all. When I visited Air Headquarters Middle East my fears were confirmed:

'No chance at all, old man ... How about flying twins?'

Feeling as shrivelled as a Bateman drawing, I winced and asked, 'What twins, sir?' as bravely as I could from my crumpled ego.

'How about Blenheims?' (Flying coffins most of us called them.) 'Beaufighters perhaps?' (That meant night fighting again, and not that which I have been expensively trained to do.) 'We're very short of Wellington pilots; most of those have gone home to convert to

Atop the Great Pyramid, with my sister Bay White in May 1942.

The first ENSA Play Unit to the Middle East. Harry Compton-Wilkins as Roger and Bay White as Frankie in *George and Margaret* with producer Noel Howlett.

Pilot Officer White plus Home Guard father September 1941.

Halifaxes you know. Think you could give them a hand?'

If ever I felt deflated it was just then; I had come all this way to be a bus driver ... so be it, it might be fun after all.

I was posted to Lydda Airport, feeling very much a new boy among the bomber types, whose temperament was known to be so different; why else, was one selected for Fighter or Bomber Command so early on in one's training? To my delight, I discovered one other fighter pilot, one Squadron Leader Micky Mount who had been on fighters for nine years! How had he survived, I wondered?

In the first few days of my stay there, two peacetime friends turned up, both of whom had been flying instructors at home unbeknown to me: Dick Lawrence who had lived a few doors away in Totteridge before we moved to Hampstead, and Ivan Strutt who lived in a glorious Elizabethan mansion near Bath. Much to my regret, both were shot down and killed not long afterwards.

Micky and I had great fun virtually teaching ourselves to fly these monstrous – or so they seemed to us – great Wellingtons. Once we had been shown all the bits and pieces to push and pull, and read the instruction book on when to do them, we were sent off on our own after a circuit or two with an instructor.

Soon came the night flying, which was more more fun than I had anticipated. Being built for night work, the instrument illumination lights were controllable for brightness, and there was plenty of room to move about in your seat, which made for gracious comfort, armchair flying!

There were trainee wireless operators and navigators with us, having enjoyed their initial training in South Africa mostly. One of the instructors took two crews down to Habbaniya, a vast peacetime camp close to Baghdad, to collect a re-built Wellington from the Maintenance Unit there.

Micky and I were to take the return trip, but the new one was not quite ready. Our instructor had a full-time programme to fulfil, day and night, so he bogged-off and left us to it. (This was the first of many future occasions when I felt that just because we were 'fighter types' [we were expected to be the Whizz Kids of the force], and could be expected to do anything; nothing could be further from the truth, we felt.)

It wasn't long before our kite was ready and we set off, complete with trainee wireless operator and navigator. Micky wanted to take some photographs or simply admire the view perhaps, but left me to do the flying.

Suddenly our trainee navigator (with his head in the Astro-Dome in the top of the fuselage) shouted that smoke was pouring out of the starboard engine. Within seconds the oil pressure started to drop which meant that the engine's own oil tank was already empty. The Wimpy carries something like 40 gallons of oil in a tank in the fuselage, fitted with a hand-operated wobble pump and selector cock with which to top-up each engine tank. This we used like mad, but to no avail.

We had crossed the Habbaniya Pipe line some five minutes before, glistening under the sun in its silver-aluminium paint. When I asked our navigator for our position he was obviously in a flat spin about it so I turned through 180 degrees and waited for the pipe line to appear again, as I throttled back on the blown engine to rest it as well as I could.

On those early Wimpys, we could not feather the propellers to reduce the drag on the aircraft when one engine went dead. We had a drill to overcome the problem which was simple enough. You put the propeller into fine pitch, allowing maximum revs, and watched your cylinder head temperature gauge as it rose to around 400 degrees (at which the engine was about to seize solid). At that point, you pulled the pitch lever back into coarse position giving it as much work as possible to do. Hopefully, the engine would seize at that precise moment and the prop would shear its shaft, and go wind-milling happily before you. (Sometimes it came sideways through the cockpit onto the driver's lap, but few lived to tell that tale.)

We found the 'H' pipe line soon enough and followed it south in order to find one of its many pumping stations, with their nearby landing strips for the mail plane and supplies. Micky did that which I consider was a very brave thing. Instead of taking over, which, with all his experience, I certainly expected him to do, he gathered the crew into the crash-landing position, sitting on the floor just behind the main spar of the wing which runs through the fuselage, a very safe place.

My altimeter showed something like 2,000 feet, though I could see we were at more like only 800 feet. It made no difference because I am not the type to fly with my head 'in the office' which I suppose most night flying bomber boys probably do. I selected 'wheels down', and they took an age to lock, for the starboard engine drives the hydraulic pump and it was only wind-milling; nonetheless, they did lock, so one worry had passed. I spiralled down adding a little flap at a time, to a peach of a glide approach from 300 feet and a three point touch-down.

Micky was amazed, he had quite expected me to belly-land the thing so we were all very much relieved. There we stuck, on 'H2' as the pumping station is called. The station crew looked after us extremely well, despite one or two of them being completely 'sand-happy'; hardly surprising I suppose on a couple of bottles of the hard stuff every day. Worst of all they insisted that we play tennis with them, on their oil-soaked (therefore hard) court. The shade temperature was around 100 degrees F and more like 140 in the sunshine, while we played.

I was falling fast with sand-fly fever and was almost a walking corpse by the end of the week, when we were collected in another Wimpy: a big-end had gone on our starboard engine, so another complete engine plus crane etc would have to be brought by road from Habbaniya before she would fly again.

Then it was back to Palestine, a week or so in hospital to get rid of the fever and a few days in Jerusalem on sick-leave; most enjoyable. When I returned to Lydda, there was a need for someone to take an overhauled Wimpy up to 70 Squadron in the Western Desert. Luckily I was given the job. This meant landing at Heliopolis in Cairo to collect as much beer as I could from the Naafi and as many Western Desert air force types as needed to get back from leave in Cairo.

Somewhat to my dismay, the only types there were ground staff; no navigators or wireless operators. The very fact that at last I was on my way back to the Desert denied any feelings of apprehension that such a trip should have provoked. Everyone in the Middle East campaign had been issued with a silk handkerchief measuring some two feet square on which was printed the map of the North African coast, running as far east as one was likely to need. Spreading this on my lap I simply set an approximate course on the compass and sailed away.

The coastline was familiar to me and though we ran into a sand storm for a hundred miles or so, it had cleared by the time we hit the coast at Derna. A simple matter then to fly on for a few more miles

Convalescent at Jerusalem after sand-fly fever.

to the drome, and with all that beer on board, be welcomed with open arms.

When I'd handed over the requisite papers to the Adjutant – and got a receipt for the aircraft – the CO asked me my plans, of which I had none other than being posted to a Spitfire Squadron as and when possible. He explained that many of his crews were tour-expired (having done something like 100 operational sorties) and were being returned to the UK for conversion courses onto Halifaxes, Lancasters etc, leaving him very short of pilots. I agreed to join him if it would help, so flew back to Cairo for my kit with one of the tour-expired crews.

There were no other aircraft going west when the paper work at HQME had been done, so I decided to see the country from the army's view point, by hitch-hiking.

CHAPTER TWO

Wellingtons – Good for Water

To hitch-hike one thousand miles is not a problem when there is only one road, and the company you expect to find and keep, is all friendly.

The first leg of the journey to Alex was easy enough, as was the next to some camp just east of El Alamein. I was introduced to some RAF types who were going all the way to Tripoli (West), they hoped. Even in the light of hurricane lamps in the mess there seemed to be something odd about them. They talked of 'flying through 10/10ths cloud, and terrible freezing conditions which could well be 'curtains for them all' ... 'Gale force winds which made landing impossible' etc etc. When I finally had the strength after carrying my gear to lift a glass at the bar, they turned to greet me; they had no wings as we knew them, they *flew* balloons!

My diary describes the hazardous journey from there to our destination ... at many times I felt that we were well on our way to Eternity, but the Almighty had other plans for us, obviously.

January 20th 1943: Derna was out of bounds, being an Eighth Army rest camp. We rang up the Town Major, but luckily he was out so we went in to find him. Here, for fifteen miles, no traffic; a lovely sight, the view of the town and sea from the top of the zig-zag pass. My unexposed films were buried somewhere in my kit. What a pity, I felt, as we hit one cliff face and slid the wrong way round; just the opportunity to take a snap.

There was one solitary merchantman sunk in the pond of a harbour. The Town Major was very annoyed that we had got in, but gave us a house behind the Bar Ristorante Milano; very comfortable and comparatively draught-free. Dinner at the officers' mess was very dull. Pongoes (army types) were everywhere, and we had as little as possible in common – who wants to start an argument at that time of night anyway? Happily there were three very good-lookers from a local ENSA show present, and they helped to brighten (Brighton?) the surroundings.

Awoke at 7.45, a warm morning, dressed and walked round to breakfast, not bad at all. Packed up and at 10.30, having parked the lorry, mooched round the bazaar. All the loot of the desert was there and our poor Tommies pay fantastic prices for everything. I bought a pair of rubber-soled desert boots at the officers' shop for 24s. (or £1.20 today); all the wog shops charged £3.00.

After Derna the country changed completely, to small rounded hills of unending limestone covered shallowly with soil. Here it was deep blood-red, the brilliance of colour was astounding. Every now and then we passed a sham castle; it seems that the Italians love to cover their houses with castellations and fort-like walls. It was lovely to see hundreds of starlings on the telephone wires about to migrate; hope they take my good wishes with them to England.

Strongly worded road signs keep us company, such as: 'This road is MINED, keep 100 yard intervals:' 'One mine = one vehicle, NOT TEN; keep 100 yard intervals:' 'Don't be a bloody fool, KEEP IT.'

We arrived at Benghazi about five and caught the main 70 Squadron convoy to Benina, (a few miles south). The town is pretty broken, Arab children float and punt about on rafts of Jerrycans on the ponds which abound in the bomb craters. I arrived on the drome around 5.30. A New Zealand air gunner pilot officer made friends immediately and with the help of various rations we made a very fair supper. Only one tent, so Tubby, Mac – who came by road this morning – plus two others, camped in the one EPI to arrive, which is to become our future mess tent. Very cold.

Sunday, January 24th: Woke-up at 8.15 and at about 9.00 got up and went over to Elliot's tent. There, on sand and petrol-stove fire we made a very good breakfast; tea, fried bacon and bread. After that, we went back to the EPI tent, where things were getting organised, such as hot water with which to shave, so I began to feel comfortable again.

There was about 5/10ths cloud, but when the sun shone it burned like an English July, so, having already discarded battle-dress top, I changed into shorts and shirt. Amazing, the comfort and freedom of just shirt and shorts again.

The aircraft started to arrive and brought the CO, Micky Mount, Crossley and Lawson, to whom I was introduced as my flight commander, A Flight. Lunch was brought over from the airmen's mess out onto a table beside the other EPIs in the process of erection. Bully beef, potatoes (cold, tinned) and beetroot likewise.

The bar was placed at one end of the three tents and the cookhouse, which was housed and partitioned off at the opposite end. All was very quiet all afternoon, people collecting their kit off various lorries and putting up their tents. Mount and I strolled away from the tents and talked of various things; he has now done six ops, three of them as captain.

We returned to help put up the EPIs. Tonight was the first for about ten days when the whole squadron was together so there was quite a lot of drinking and singing going on. Everyone seemed to want to exhibit his voice, or sing a different song from the one in use at the time and the noise was horrible.

At last there was some unity of effort when to the tune of 'Clementine', the following brought a happy glow over everyone:

70 Squadron, 70 Squadron, though we sing it with a sigh,
We must do that bloody mail run ev'ry night until we die.

Down to Flights each ruddy morning,
Sitting waiting for a clue,
Same old notice on the flight board,
'Maximum Effort', guess where to.

70 Squadron, 70 Squadron etc.

'Have you lost us, navigator?'
'Come up here and have a look,'
'Someone's shot our starboard wing off,'
'We're all right then, that's Tobruk.'

70 Squadron, 70 Squadron etc.

Oh to be in Piccadilly,
Selling matches by the score,
Then we'll do this bloody mail run,
Not tonight, nor evermore.

Each month, it seemed, some smarty would compose an

acceptable verse of the song so it went on for hours. It all began when the squadron was based down on the Suez canal, and were sent to Benghazi night after night to bomb the material being landed there from Brindisi, or Taranto, even Greece and Crete. Got to bed at 11.40 in the mess, feeling very cold.

January 25th: Up at 8.15 after the cooks had brought me some tea from the far end of the mess. I went round to the Orderly Room after breakfast, filled in various cards and forms then went over to A Flight office where Lawson told me that he'd have a flying programme out tomorrow after lunch. I took my pipe to the Signals trailer, where they have all the small tools and did a fair job on cutting down my pipe stem which had been broken.

Went back to A Flight in the hope of getting something to fly; Lawson was not there, but his flying kit was on his desk. Looking at the programme I see that I am down for 2 hour dual and 2 hour solo tonight, 9pm-11pm and the same tomorrow but 8pm-10pm. Had a good look round the CO's Lysander. Quite a nice aeroplane. Two pitch prop operated by push-pull knob on the dash board. Unserviceable at the moment due to a cracked exhaust ring; could be important on a fabric-covered fuselage, but its battery is flat also.

Got hold of a good tent and quickly dug it in at the edges to anchor it against the wind and make a trench to catch the rain. Tubby Fieldhouse and Flying Officer Tate (NZ) sharing it. Made Nescafe on Tate's petrol stove; eventually to bed at 11.30.

January 26th: Woke up at 8.00, a very good breakfast of porridge, bacon and fried bread, then dashed down to the flight at 8.45. Sergeant Frazer, another NZ, was to take me up on a few circuits and bumps. We went out to the aircraft *when* the ground crew arrived; appalling lack of discipline everywhere, it seems to me. The kite was to have a wheel change and the Sergeant in charge said that it ought to have been done the day before. Anyway, we waited all morning in the midst of which Lawson told me that I was operating tonight.

I was to be second dickie to a Flight Lieutenant Milburn, DFC, an excellent lad on his second tour. The trip was to be to Catania airfield on Sicily, about the hottest target out there at the moment, so we'd have to climb to 13,000 feet using oxygen.

Two Hercules Wimps arrived; the first in Egypt, I gather. They took off without a sound. The Group Captain flew one round with the CO. At 11.15 we decided to scrub the flying (circuits and bumps), as the aircraft was still unfit to fly. I tested my helmet on the way to the mess, all OK. Got parachute harness from the store – a horrible thing you wear like a corset because the canopy is left in the cockpit and it has to be clipped to your corset on the way out! Charming, I'm sure.

Wing phoned to say the ops were off; the weather over the Med was too dicey. It would have been a very long trip, and honestly not worthwhile for 2,500 lbs of bombs; a little over a ton was all we could carry due to the weight of petrol load required. It is about 525 miles from here, and that with the return trip would take us about 8½ hours.

This afternoon, I did manage to get a serviceable kite and did an hour's circuits and bumps with Frazer. All very successful though the flaps would only come down 30 degrees. Frazer cut the port engine while I was coming in to land (on the regular left handed circuit) just to see how I would cope, and it went off fine; very glad he tried it.

Bags of mail arrived today; only a telegram for me dated December 18th, wishing Happy Christmas and New Year! Family all well.

January 27th: A dull morning with heavy cloud and rain. It's horrid trying to fly before 10.30, the ground crews are never there! The aircraft seem to be perpetually without their daily inspection, and no petrol. Anyway, at 11.15 Sergeant Frazer and I took off and did an hour of circuits and bumps, flapless, one engine and so on.

After lunch I went over to B Flight to borrow their aircraft 'M' which I was told was available (and serviceable): this at 1.45 p.m. The ground crews go to lunch at 12.00 and still no one had returned. There was only one fellow there. He plugged in the starter trolley batteries to boost mine, and came along for a couple of circuits. (It appears that these chaps are not made to feel part of the team; they are never asked to fly ... the one thing they joined for; no wonder they lack interest.)

At 6.30 I was to have done some check circuits followed by two hours solo in 'U', but Crossley took up our only dual control kite on test and on the runway the port engine just stopped. Verdict? An engine change required, so that too was scrubbed.

Our dinner tonight was a rather special occasion, and it was delicious. Chicken pie with a lovely puff pastry, mashed potatoes and beans, (tinned runner jobs). I went back to my tent to write some letters when Mount came round to tell me that Ivan Strutt had bought it. (He got to know him quite well at Lydda and liked him as much as we all did.) He says that he was found dead in his dinghy, but others have told me that he got a direct hit over Sfax from flak.

Sewed on some buttons to my battle-dress trousers which had practically gone. Took the top off my hurricane lamp and boiled some water for some Nescafe; it took remarkably little time to boil and was very welcome.

January 28th: Tubby woke me at about 7.00; he was appointed Messing Officer yesterday and had to dash off to Benghazi for rations. The lorry goes every other day and brings back the mail. I got up at 7.30, using the hurricane lamp to warm my clothes; it worked very well. Same old breakfast of porridge, fried bacon and bread. Lawson sat next to me and told me that I had better go down to A Flight office in case he had something for me to fly. He's a bit like that; he seems to love keeping people on tap.

Met Micky Mount by chance, he's still trying to get away to 104 Squadron on LG (Landing Ground) 237. I told him that Lawson was sending a plane down there tomorrow and he said, 'Oh, they always say tomorrow' – almost as disenchanted with these types as I am perhaps? Nothing for me to fly of course but the CO wanted to see me at 10.00. Rushed back and shaved and arrived on time to find the AOC (Air Officer Commanding) in his office. 70 Squadron is to be the first to be equipped with the Wimpy Mk III. Their extra power will be a great help, but why tell me I wonder?

I'm on ops tonight; weather reported to be OK. Rather hope I go. Lawson keeps telling me I'll be a captain after seeing what flak looks like on 30 trips – though I understand that this is the minimum when flying as a second dickie.

Rainstorms and a cold wind hit us all day. Quite a squall arrived at five to eleven; luckily the rain followed so there is little dust. Advised of briefing at 10.15, so there was no time for a sleep before

My first aeroplane in the desert, Hurricane No BN403 of 73 Squadron.

My first Wellington in the desert (unbeknown to The Princess Margaret, my idol at that time).

take-off. If this rain goes on, none of us will get off, for the drome will become a bog.

Ops were scrubbed at 3.30, but I have to witness a pay parade, darn it, one of the chores of being Orderly officer.

January 29th: Didn't wake until 8.20, had a very quick breakfast and dashed to the Adjutant's office to sign-off being Orderly dog, only to find that the job goes on until 2.00 so I walked down to flights, read and signed the order book. Raining hard in heavy storms.

Dickie Milburn and I went over the operation of George the automatic pilot and all the tits in 'M', being the nearest aircraft. Drome is still unserviceable at the moment, but never mind.

After lunch, I collected parachute harness and took six rolls of film to be developed. The section has so much work to do that they will not be taking in any more development work for a week. I collected some petrol and empty tins from the MT section and made a very good sand fire for my tent. (An empty tin split along its length measures some 15″ by 9″ by 4½″. Fill this trough with four inches of sand, or desert dust, pour in a pint of petrol, and the sand becomes a wick. The other split half of the tin rests on top with water, for shaving, bathing etc.)

The aircraft are being loaded with nine 250-lb bombs and 750 gallons of petrol, i.e. maximum load. Several kites used our drome this afternoon but being unladen, did not damage its surface. I hope it's not too boggy, for we take off very close to a mass of telephone wires. Briefing at 10.51, take-off at 11.45, I gather, so we land in daylight.

January 30th: It was a good still night, and Catania aerodrome and the port of Augusta were our first and second targets. The short briefing was at 10.45 and we took off in rain at 11.50. We stayed at 2,000 feet for about three hours under light patches of showery cumulo stratus at 2,500 feet. Then just as we wanted to climb towards our target area, the cloud ended like a sheet-end, and we were left in a grey haze.

I climbed up to 8,000 feet (plus 2 lbs boost and 2,150 rpm), levelled out and handed over to Dickie. Soon Italy came in sight. We went up the coast, it only being 3.30, then south to southern tip of Sicily. About twenty searchlights were sweeping our way; the master lights with a slightly blue or violet colour are said to be radar controlled. These caught us quite often but everyone on the ground seemed to be completely clueless; no one was interested in us, yet we were the first to go in and it was our job to illuminate the target for the rest.

The searchlights and guns were all sweeping the sky and firing in different directions. About the first shell was quite close and underneath us. It made a hell of a noise and bounced the kite quite a bit. We went north again and turned in over Catania, just short of Etna, towards the aerodrome where a flarepath was burning until we were quite close. It was so bright from 13,500 feet that nobody could believe it to be the drome, it was more likely to be a decoy drome, and so we turned south and then south-east towards Augusta.

All the flak was going out to sea. We had stooged about for twenty-five minutes over the land and bombed what looked like an aerodrome south-west of Augusta. One big fire on Catania is believed to have been McMichael, or one of 32 Squadron who is also missing. We saw one of 40 Squadron jettison his bombs and flares halfway to Malta; engine trouble, but he landed there OK.

To sleep at 10 a.m. till 4.30. A lovely sunny day, no wind. Crossley went out to search for McMichael in one of the Merc-engined Wimps (Mk IIIs). On the way back last night I used George; he behaved perfectly so I found it difficult to stay awake; in fact I fell asleep three times.

Sunday, January 31st: A lovely windless day again, hot sunshine. I went down to the flight and made up my log book, returned to do some clothes washing which went off quite well. Cloud began to form by 11.00 and at 1.00 there were 4/10ths cumulus, base 2,500 feet with their tops up to about 6,000 feet. I'm on ops again tonight, in the A Flight Mk III taking eighteen 250-pounders to be dropped in one stick, i.e. all at once. Squadron Leader Lawson, my flight commander, is first pilot. It will be very interesting to fly the kite; we are taking off at 5.15, three quarters of an hour after the others, owing to our increased speed.

MacNamara is going as second dickie to Squadron Leader Crossley, his flight commander, and he is very excited about it. Our 'blitz' period, i.e. 'time over target' is expected to be 8.30.

(News came through that Ivan Strutt went down in flames over a target near Sfax; he never had a chance to use his dinghy.) No news of the missing 40 Squadron kite, or ours, with McMichael as first pilot.

The weather looked not too bad, so after tea we went out to 'L'. On run-up, we found the artificial horizon was u/s (unserviceable). We had it changed for another, then found that the rubber connecting tube to its air supply was twisted! Took off at 5.45 instead of 5.15, and went straight up to 10,500 feet. Inversion over the cloud, 10/10ths at 4,000 feet so the temperature was plus half a degree all the way. Cockpit heating was good, but navigation bad; we steamed straight up the straits of Messina at 11.500 feet with flak from *both* sides!

From the light of the parachute flares we could see the Halifaxes bombing away hard. We turned south but could not pin-point our position anywhere, through the cloud. Flak and searchlights lined the coast and quite a concentration of light stuff was going very high over the drome. As they paid no heed to our presence we dropped nine of our eighteen bombs on the beach and came home. A very dull and disappointing trip. Landed at 12.45. Crossley went in *under* the cloud and did a very fair job. Supper and to bed.

February 1st: A cold miserable morning, had breakfast and went back to bed and continued reading Williamson's *So the Sun Shines.* Quite an interesting book but his style is very loose and after writing a flowery description of some beauty of nature, he goes on and describes it again and again to no purpose.

Shaved and washed at lunch time. Mess meeting after lunch, very dull. Cleaned the floor of my tent of rotting vegetation – mostly foliage – and burned the rubbish.

Tomorrow we go to Palermo, with overload tanks, 65 miles beyond Catania. Incidentally these last two raids we have done were the longest over water that the RAF have ever flown. The longest previously were those to Norway from the UK, i.e. about 400 miles each way, whereas ours are about 510 each way.

A Note for the History Books: Christmas dinner for everyone in the Middle East was 'M & V' which is tinned meat and vegetables, which we eat almost every day in any case, if we are lucky! Cheese and biscuits. 'That's your lot.' The Naafi are racketeering as ever, telling us that 'Of course you can buy turkey etc from us, *if* you pay the price!'

Middle East meals, as laid down:

Breakfast: Bacon, sausage, porridge, tea, biscuits, margarine and jam.

Lunch is *not* provided; you do your best out of biscuits, cheese and tea.

Tea is not provided, again you do your best out of the rations taken off the strength of the two meals given.

Dinner is provided; M & V or Bully beef, biscuits, margarine, cheese or jam and tea.

We as a squadron draw rations for 50 in the mess of about 25 and still we don't get sufficient to eat. In all fairness, if we are within something like 25 miles of a working bakery – or army bakehouse we do get bread. The bomber bases are so far back that this luxury is usually afforded us. Holding a slice up to the light you can count the weevils – and run a 'book' on it as some do – but if you get more than five per slice which is average, you praise the Lord for increasing your protein ration.

February 2nd: Wilson woke me at 8.15. A lovely day, cloudless and the sun quite hot, though a fair breeze.

Took my log book down to be signed. Ops tonight *are* Palermo on the north coast of Sicily, so you pass over Catania to get there. I asked if I could go, seeing that my name was not on the list, but Lawson said that he did not want me to pile up the hours as second dickie and he would rather wait until I could go as captain. (After all the bull about *having* to do so many as second dickie, his comments did not make sense, but then who can understand the mentality of these bomber types anyway?)

Returned to my tent and did some washing, polished my flying boots – now drying and cracking rather badly – and generally tidied my tent. Why did I write 'cracking rather badly', I wonder, when I obviously mean that they are cracking rather *well*, if I mean that they are 'badly cracked,' or do I mean '*well* cracked'? I must be going round the bend myself, or 'sand-happy' perhaps. I have often felt my hackles rise when the barber says, 'Yes Sir, you need your hair cutting badly.' I am always inclined to say – but as yet have never dared – 'No I don't: you did that last time, this time I want it cut well!'

After lunch, Ops were scrubbed, not that it mattered much to me so I cleaned my helmet again of congealed sweat and dust and washed my pyjamas.

The fire we have built in the mess is really excellent. Our standard petrol tins, measuring some 9 inches square by 15 inches deep, are filled with desert sand so can be stacked like bricks, one upon the other. With some twenty of these we have built a hearth and a chimney stack. Iti telephone poles provide the wood. It draws perfectly so after dinner I settled down by it reading *Harvest by Lamplight* and soaked in the warmth both from the fire and my memory of the warm English countryside, seeing the faces of old friends or farm-hands.

No mail today so I wrote to No 4 Air Formation Postal Unit to get them cracking on their job.

February 3rd: A wizard morning, a warm wind for a change and clear sunshine. Ops on again tonight and I'm going after all as second dickie to Sergeant Frazer. Tubby Fieldhouse is dropping flares to illuminate the target.

Up till the last minute, it was half cancelled owing to bad weather over the target, but we went after all, taking off at 6.15. It seemed to get dark very quickly tonight and both Frazer and I were terribly sleepy. I kept nodding over the stick and all the instruments became very blurred. Eventually I put on the oxygen and that wakened me. We went up to 7,000 feet over the top of strato-cumulus cloud. At 7.15 we saw quite a sea battle going on, or so it appeared. There was very rapid and heavy firing but nothing came our way and it was too dark to see the ships.

After an hour and a half, Frazer took over and shortly gave up again, saying that he felt too sleepy. We could only make 125 mph and she got very hot, so I put her into rich mixture. At the same moment, the starboard engine objected and stopped for about 10 seconds, but then happily got a grip on itself again. These overload tanks were a bit out of the normal and rather than suffer an air-lock on the way out – and so possibly waste a trip – we agreed to fly on our normal wing tanks and everything took on a normal performance thereafter.

As we saw the searchlights come up at Catania, I started to climb to 12,000 feet where I handed over to Frazer again. He wanted to go north of Mount Etna, then turn left along the north coast to Palermo, instead of following the undefended south coast and driving north to Palermo as I had suggested.

We stooged on, almost straight up the Straits, and just over Messina itself there was a break in the cloud. Before we could move out of the way, up came a 'box' barrage and a cone of searchlights, with us, slap in the middle. Evasive action while loaded like that is useless so we let go the three 500 lb bombs and dived like fun into the cloud at 4,000 feet below with about 16 heavy guns putting all they'd got in our way. I took over, put in George, and came home very easily. Landed at 1.30. Breakfast of porridge, sausage and fried bread. All planes returned safely.

February 6th: Two aircraft were missing after last night's raid but at 6.00 the news came through that both had landed safely at Malta. McNamara was one of them, as second dickie to Crossley. Evidently the target was very nasty last night, the blitz period being timed too late, plus bad weather and heavy icing in cloud. Everyone stooged over the place without knowing it and got shot-up pretty hotly.

McNamara left his pay book etc with me before he went; I advised him to take at least some money with him but he refused. Now he's stuck on Malta, he'll wish he had some. No wind and a very hot sun; no flying as the dual machine is not yet ready. Dispersed 'L' from where she had been left and came back to the tent for 11.00 tea, Dickie joined me.

Yesterday I killed a legged snake, a beautiful skin but only about five inches of it was any use, so I cleaned it and hope to stick it round my cigarette lighter.

Both Nos 37 and 462 Squadrons lost an aircraft last night; someone saw one of them, possibly, drop its bombs and turn for home only about 75 miles from Benghazi, but as far as I know, neither has been heard of since.

Went along the 65 miles of deep pot-holed road to Benghazi where Lawson, Dick Milburn and I had hot showers. Three EPI tents have been erected, two for changing and one with a marble-tiled slab floor where nine showers spout from two pipes, and a boiler outside. Nothing like as good as a bath, but well worth it for all that. The drive back was rather hectic. Lawson does not appear to like driving at night so he raced the daylight and we hit some of the potholes very hard, some up to 10″ deep. We passed one lorry with a broken stub-axle and were surprised that ours didn't break.

February 7th: After lunch the news came through that we move-up to Misurata presumably. I shall be flying up to Cairo the day after tomorrow in 'N', one of our machines, taking more tour expired crews and staying the night (or two if I can make it). It'll be quite good fun though Cairo and Heliopolis are very murky with clinging fog in the morning still.

February 8th: Down to flights, but no ops for me; they're awaiting the dual aircraft still. Went out to 'N' to do an air test, but the starboard engine plugs, on the bottom two cylinders, had oiled-up and the overload tank had not been removed. It was rather an exasperating morning helping the chaps to get it ready when all the time they had no real heart in the job. Eventually we finished it by 12.00 and they wanted to go away for lunch. At their request I fixed the time for the air test at 2.30, giving them two and a half hours for their lunch. I waited from 2.30 till 3.00 for the corporal fitter to arrive. The sloppiness of these people makes me really angry, but I did get off and flew round about the drome. I took off north-east to south-west across very bumpy ground. I didn't use any flap and had to pull her off at 90 mph; the speed only just built up to 105, even though I held her down, and only just cleared the telegraph wires which are a good three hundred yards off the landing ground. A very clapped-out old aeroplane.

The starboard constant speed unit is all to hell, the revs wandering about 250 rpm at any old time, but she flies okay so I landed and taxied her over to her place, ready for the morrow.

Woken up by Tubby when he came to bed at 2.30 a.m. It seems that they met three fronts and bad icing conditions which were responsible – more than anything else – for everyone arriving over the target at differing times so that every opponent on the ground feels that each arrival is *his* pigeon. 37 Squadron lost another kite; their losses are pretty heavy recently.

CHAPTER THREE

The Mecca of the RAF

February 9th 1943: Went down to the flight at 8.45. Wilson had woken me at 7.00 and I dressed in blue straightaway, to look more or less civilised for my arrival in Cairo. Johnson was there and his navigator arrived shortly afterwards. The aircraft was – of course – in pieces; something in my air test report must have giggered them up a bit perhaps, or were they just being meddlesome? We took off at 10.15 and cracked down to hit the coast at Sollum; the first we saw of it was Tobruk so we skirted the balloons and carried on.

It was a lovely morning with about 3/10ths cloud all the way and good visibility. I wasn't feeling too well; my chin was covered with desert sores and hot little pimples which just weep all the time, and itch like mad. Johnny didn't want to fly so I carried on all the way. Johnny's navigator did all the oil pumping, 2 gallons to port and 2½ gallons to starboard engine per hour; that is 180 pumps to port and 225 pumps to starboard every hour, a *lot* of work.

We curved round Sollum and later Mersa Matruh, while I took snapshots of each. Landed at Helio in perfect ease at 2.45.

February 10th: Woken with tea at 7.00 in Wellington House, the penthouse suite of Cairo's only skyscraper run by Arthur Howard for aircrew officers, and got up straightaway, breakfast, loaded with Brian Drury's dinner jacket (which he had lent to Arthur for his playing of *Private Lives*) I trammed to Gazira. Arrived at Bay's pension at 8.45 when she had just woken. She wanted no breakfast, so we taxied to the Naafi at the Kasr-el-Nil barracks to buy our bar stocks.

In no time at all we had bought four cases of beer, (8 piastres a bottle) four bottles of gin, four of whisky, two lime and one orange. Cost: £19.98½ pts, leaving 1½ pts change from the £20 I carried from the bar for this purpose. (With 97.5 pts to the pound, it was almost like 2½ pence change, 36 years later.)

With only so few places in which to eat, drink, or be merry, Cairo was to me Piccadilly and Bond Street all rolled into one; at almost any hour of day – but not night – one would meet old friends. So it was that we met 'Nipper' Joyce (now flight lieutenant since he took over A Flight in 73 Squadron, and the night flying training flight. Also with him a Canadian Kittyhawk pilot, Flight Lieutenant Smith, one of the pre-war instructors.

We all hopped off to Groppi's and there Nipper and I talked hard for about an hour and a half. He is on his way to the OTU that Baker is at, and very annoyed about it, much preferring to continue his night fighting, but on Beaus in future, he hopes.

February 11th: Feeling very tired when I got up; spottiness worse than ever. A nasty blind boil on my right wrist is making my whole arm ache. (Met Commander Scot Hansen yesterday, he goes home via the USA tomorrow lucky devil. Bay advises me to go home after a tour on Wimpys if I come through. Bless her; who am I to open such doors?)

I paid Hassan for my stay at Wellington House and got out to Helio by Metro at 8.45. Rang up the servicing flight to get 'N' ready, and build up some brake pressure – there is a leak somewhere. I borrowed a truck from the MT section and dashed around trying to find my seat-type parachute; it was not to be found anywhere so I collected the beer etc from the mess and went up to the watch tower.

There I found only five of our ground crew staff; nine still to come. Two chaps there had been posted to 37 Squadron so I took them along with us. We took off at 10.45 although the starboard engine simply stopped when the port magneto was switched off; I wanted to get back so off we went. The watch office had advised against the trip. Sandstorms over the Western Desert, with rain and low cloud over Libya. I used my silk handkerchief as a rough guide and it was very helpful.

We met the coast at Mersa Matruh and went along it in gradually decreasing visibility to Sollum. For the previous hour I had been down to 500 feet over the sea watching the coast. When we got to Sollum at 13.30 – rather late I thought – I climbed to 5,000 feet and set course for Benghazi or rather slightly south. The visibility improved and we cruised at 155 mph losing height gently. The country was completely different from that which I had seen on the way to Cairo so I just held on and trusted my compass. By 2.30 I was down to 1,000 feet skimming the hill tops under low cloud and in endless rain, praying for the coastline to appear. At 3.00 I saw what I thought was Benina and on the coast could just see Benghazi twenty miles to the north. *Hooray*, what a relief: sped down the road and landed at 3.45.

February 12th: Woke up feeling wretched again, full of gippy tummy. Tubby and I struck our tent, but after last night's and yesterday's heavy rain-fall, take-off was impossible. Four of B Flight's machines got bogged down to the axles. The mess had been partly struck and we sat around in the sunshine drinking beer and wondering if we will eventually get off.

Was it that beer (made with dried onion skins to give it its colour, crude ethyl alcohol for the legal requirement and aspirins to make you say *Maaleesh* to anything of less than urgent importance)? Whatever it was, we abandoned hope of leaving and put up the mess again. Tubby had been given the Mk III so I will fly with him, he having agreed to snake down the road so that I can take some snapshots from the bomb aimer's panel.

We sat about the mess all day, reading and feeling utterly bored. It rained again in torrents all evening. No telephone, no electric lights, and no wireless, so we sat around the fire telling stories which proved to be a most humorous evening. Nobody drinking, no one wanted to somehow.

McFellow, a flight lieutenant observer from Wing, nicknamed 'Hank', is a broad Devonian and he has a host of dialect stories which he tells so well. The CO's were good but on the smutty side. A number of people had nancy-boy stories which I had never heard; possibly because that aspect of life is so utterly foreign to the RAF I found them the funniest of them all.

February 13th: A wizard morning. Hardly any breeze, 3/10ths cloud, of cumulus and brilliant sunshine. Tubby and I slept in McNamara's tent last night, he had gone to LG224 to pick up a plane coming out of service on Thursday, five days off yet. Some of us had slight hopes of going today but last night's rain has made everywhere a bog. One of 37 Squadron's aircraft went out to the drome to take off and one wheel went right in; you can rest your elbow in the wing tip. The runways here have to be scraped with a road-making grader, and once the firm crust is removed, the subsoil just becomes a sponge, and just about as soft.

February 15th: No rain last night, a moderately clear sky and a good drying wind so maybe we'll get off tomorrow. McInnes of 40 Squadron lent me his copy of the *The Last Enemy*. This time I thoroughly enjoyed it. Unfortunately Hillary was killed on active service some weeks ago, I understand; he would surely have made a good writer.

The ration lorry went into town today with the mail; I had written an airgraph letter home, a letter each to the Photographic Reconnaissance Unit and 178 Squadron, thanking them for the films. Nipper told me that Davis was killed about three weeks ago. I'm sorry for his wife, she is an enchanting girl, and I'm told, one of the best-looking WRNS of Port Said.

We broached the last case of beer this morning – there was nothing else to do. The ration lorry came back with a young lamb, £2-worth of extra messing. It broke loose and took two hours to catch, even using a truck to chase it.

February 16th: Up early, around 7.30, and packed. 40 Squadron robbed all our transport and cracked off at about 10.00 (our chaps were probably still asleep and didn't hear them go) – taking nothing with them to help *us*; one up to them perhaps? We eventually packed our kit along with that of Doc and Dave, our intelligence lad, who incidentally knows Jack Firth very well (Firth Stainless Steel and Newquay ITW) I must write to him. We got to the aircraft by 11.00 and waited, and waited still more, for the ground-crew to arrive.

I didn't worry, for I was lying in the grass reading a book, bathed in sunshine and thoroughly enjoying myself when a lorry came along and gave us our ground-crew. The tents stowed very well into the two outer bomb-bays and the inside was chockful of kit bags and mail bags full of personal stuff. One fellow had a German mail bag, made out of double strands of string, woven Aertex fashion, a truly handsome piece of work and virtually everlasting.

While we were running-up the engines two machines got bogged while taxying out. We took off without difficulty – rather nose-heavy – at 1.20 I lay on the escape hatch reading. We orbited Marble Arch while I took two snapshots. At 2.45 I took over and we

(*Left*) Wash Day at 70 Squadron, January 1943. (*Right*) Jo Lunt and myself censoring letters, April 1943.

(*Left*) Bath, Mk I (ex-40 gallon oil drum). (*Right*) Bath, Mk II, compliments of bombed house at Tripoli. Tubby Fieldhouse in ardent occupation.

flew along the seashore past a lifeboat and a dirty great floating mine. Took a snapshot of – I think – Sirte. At 4.00 we hit Misurata; quite a well-planned town, it looks.

The land is very flat, grey-brown where cultivated, palm trees round the little square fields (dates for the house, or market?) and curious little blockhouse estates. The houses built in pairs along the road with just so much farm land between them. The aerodrome lies about 25 miles south-west, and has been made by grading camel-thorn type desert in the last ten days. The camp is pitched in a slight hollow; probably with a stream running through it when it rains! (They're bright, these bomber boys, or are they being artful?)

We had tea in the airmen's mess, minus any *tea*, so Tubby and I invited Doc and Dave to our tent *for* tea. Mac arrived yesterday from Cairo; first time he's been stuck without his kit, poor chap.

February 17th: Got up at about 8.30. Breakfast of four sausages and tea in the airmen's mess. Water is hard to get here; it's 25 miles each way to our only source. Our 450 gallon Bowser is the only one on the camp. I scrounged some water from it and quickly boiled it on a petrol fire in some old tin I had cut up yesterday, and soon we were all washed and shaved.

Yesterday Liberators attacked Palermo in daylight and shot down four fighters. We now have four Mk IIIs and all the old Mk 1Cs will go to 37 Squadron. If ops are on, it will be Palermo for us also, taking 5,000 lbs of bombs and 650 gallons of gravy.

The hierarchy have decided that in future we will operate as two wings, on alternate nights. 70 and 40 Squadrons will be 231 Wing and 37 and 462 (I believe) 237 Wing. The others were 'on' tonight, but bad weather cancelled it. Tubby and I went into Misurata for extra messing but could find nothing. Mud walls and a well in every little patch of half an acre or so. Not much of a town; a village in size but the buildings are large and town-like.

February 20th: No wind this morning but a very thick fog in its place. Visibility about 50 yards. I tried to get hold of the dual machine, but no aircraft were available; may be able to get one this afternoon. Maximum effort is called for tonight; the three Wimpy Squadrons, 70, 40 and 37, plus 12 Halifaxes of 462 Squadron, 54 aircraft all told.

No kite for me this afternoon either, so hoping to get airborne tomorrow. The fog cleared by 11.30 and everyone went up on air test. The rear party arrived from Magrun at about 4.30 and we put up another EPI for the mess.

Briefing was at 7.45 and take-off 9.15. The weather was not reported to be too good, low cloud mostly, but I went to bed. At about 1.15 I heard an aircraft circling overhead and looking out of the tent saw its navigation lights on, and only a hundred feet above the deck. The moon was full tonight and I thought he was just having fun and games – waking everybody up – when I heard his engines cut, and then very shortly afterwards the horrible noise of a crashing aircraft. I waited, but no fire ensued so quickly donned battle dress, flying boots and Irvin to go out and see what had happened. Dave told me that the whole Balbo had been recalled. The cloud was very low here and visibility bad, despite the full moon above. The crew of the pranged kite were all okay – just a belly landing, petrol ran out, and they had no power for the hydraulics.

Tubby was the next back; he was over Sicily when recalled so he dropped his four 500-pounders and came back. After that, chaos reigned. Aircraft in all directions and heights from 0 feet to 1,500. Collisions looked inevitable. Two of the Halifaxes landed here, three of 37 Squadron's landed at Malta – one of theirs is missing altogether – Lawson landed at Misurata West, and hit a parked Hurricane. Sergeant Cross burst a tyre on the Halifax drome and twisted the fuselage. What a night!

February 22nd: A beautiful morning, no wind and no cloud. B Flight took the dual machine this morning so we'll take it tomorrow. I collected my films from the section and cut them up for the negative album. We prepared the mess for the *Hello Happiness* ENSA party and at 2.00 went along to the end of the gully in which we are camped to build their stage in this natural amphitheatre; we thoroughly enjoyed the show. At 3.00 they came to the mess for tea, then dashed off to give another show at 4.00. Nothing like as blue as *You're Welcome* and on the whole a better show.

Ops on tonight, full strength and the weather looks better. Lawson went over to Malta, flying the AOC who is querying the Met forecasts; they have proved very bad all the time we have been operating over Sicily. No mail for me today.

The ops went off very well, Tubby starting two fires with his stick of nine, 500-pounders and four rodded 250s. Jock Smith followed him in and confirmed them. 40 Squadron lost one machine; thirteen landed at Malta, mostly pretty shot-up. One of ours is there, plus five of 37 Squadron and various others from the other squadrons participating.

Jack Marsh came back from Tripoli with a barrel of Chianti; it's very young and rather acid but creates a marvellous feeling of well-being, as experienced perhaps after three pints of bitter?

February 23rd: The dual machine is unserviceable again this morning. Tubby and Mac fast asleep so I didn't wake them till 10.15. Put our watches back one hour, being so far west now, so it is 9.15! Nonetheless, I missed my breakfast, so somebody missed some sleep.

Went up the flights but there was nothing doing so went over to see the prang we suffered on the runway last night. His tyre burst on take-off and he tried to land again, naturally swinging and crabbing when going very fast. Firstly the port wheel leg collapsed, then the tail wheel hit a bump and the whole aircraft snapped at the astro dome hatch, a complete write-off. A pressure build-up blew all the engine instruments pipes and the bump – presumably – released the dinghy too.

One of 40 Squadron's kites is definitely missing. It seems that the flak last night was always ahead, and those who dived in at 250 mph caught it. Lawson went down to Marble Arch and collected a Wimpy Mk X, with Hercules engines giving 1,650 hp instead of 1,400 in the Mk IIIs. At 1,700 rpm and maximum weak cruising mixture i.e. about Minus $\frac{1}{2}$-lb boost, he got 180 mph at 2,000 feet. Crossley did this too, collecting one from Castel Benito (Tripoli West). Lawson put on 2,400 rpm plus 4 lbs boost, straight and level, and the speed leapt up to 250 mph, very nice.

We'll be doing daylights, I hope, soon on them when we get them. Jerry has captured a pass from the Yanks. British reinforcements arrived and stemmed it. The boys are off to crump them tonight; everyone delighted at going on 'battle stooges'.

Dick Milburn left in a DUK Harrow for MA (direct to UK) very drunk on Chianti. It's excellent stuff for making you very sleepy.

We now have electric light in the mess and darts are played very hard. We had the lamb for lunch and dinner, beautifully tender. No mail today.

February 24th: A beautiful morning with nothing to do. No wind and perhaps ½/10th of cloud. The dual may be available tomorrow. Sergeant Frazer is on his last op tonight, then he'll be used as an instructor for a while before going on 'rest'.

Tubby woke me when he came in at 5.30. Jock Smith is the only one to have claimed that he found the wadi (a gully in a cliff face or mountain range, usually a dried-up river bed). The country was evidently featureless and covered with haze and low cloud. They succeeded in keeping Jerry awake and thinking, for some time anyway, and that was half the objective. (Thinking back to our days with 73 Squadron, just before the El Alamein attack, these bomber boys were called upon to do just that: make the Jerry sand-happy, just as our troops were flak-happy through lack of sleep and punch-drunk from the noise all around. It was so effective that our ground troops found the Jerry perfectly content to lift his arm and give up, which he did in his thousands.)

Another battle stooge tonight, maximum effort. Crossley went away to collect another Mk X if he can find it. Five of them have arrived in the Middle East.

Joe Lush went up to the mail tent on his way to the barber's tent (we now have one of our very own!) in the hope of getting his seven letters a day – his usual average. He got some, and collected four for me.

Chianti flowing like water in the mess. It gives one a hilarious stage of merriment to begin with, but after that, it simply takes all the strength from one's knees; wonderful stuff.

Tubby and I had a hot bath this afternoon, and jolly good it was too. I feel like a new born babe, having sloughed so many skins; there are many more to come off yet. We'll pour off the clear water from the top and use it again. The water is so hard that all the dirt and soap curdles and coagulates, settling to the bottom.

The bath took me about two hours to make, we had to split a 40-gallon drum from top to bottom – like paunching a rabbit – and cutting the sides clear of top and bottom to 90 degrees either side of the split. These sides are now folded outwards, to make arm rests, and the top end, made hollow by dint of many dents with a sledge hammer, wherein one's back may rest. (Lump hammer and bolster chisel have left their bloody marks, but it's worth it.)

The water supply comes from two more 40-gallon drums, one each for hot and cold, mounted on sand filled petrol tins with a petrol fire under the hot one.

The evaporation rate here is so high that water too hot to bathe in it too cold after some twenty minutes, despite its being kept 'warm' by another three or four bathers after the first.

February 25th: The ops last night were to have been an all-night show; Slater and Crossley got off and the third aircraft burst a tyre on take-off. She swung round on the runway, the leg collapsed, puncturing the wing tank and she caught fire. They all had about ten minutes in which to get out and get away from it all, and all others congregating towards the runway for their getaway scattered in all directions; then she blew up, bombs and all.

Sergeant Frazer burst a tyre while taxying, and yesterday A's tyres were so cut and about to burst even while standing at dispersal. 37 Squadron were due to do some night flying but found – on the daily inspection – that their tyres were too badly cut. They lost one machine on ops last night. The very brittle limestone in the sand here has very sharp edges; once splintered by the grader blade, its effect could be lethal.

We moved today to another drome about five miles east. Evidently the name of the one we were on is Gardabia East. We left after lunch. I went by road so as to look after our kit. Tubby and MacNamara went by air. By 2.00 we had bundled everything into the lorry and trundled off into the blue.

On arrival we pitched our tent with the help of the two Johnstones, and dug a pit for our bath through the stone-flakey clay, which was dry for the top eight inches, down to the crumbling limestone. We put up our EPI for the mess and had M & V, biscuits and tea as usual. We sat in the dark round the wireless when suddenly Tubby was told he was operating. Mac took a tin of M & V to our tent and cooked up a meal in Jock Smith's tent, but I didn't want any. The target was the aerodrome at Gabes again.

Went to bed at 10.00 there was a late take-off. This drome is known as Gardabia West, and the field on which Squadron 462 and 104 are based is known as Gardabia Main.

February 26th: Woke up at 8.30 this morning, that extra hour makes the whole world seem warmer when one gets up (wearing bush shirt and shorts; and battle-dress in the evening).

Breakfast of two half slices of bacon and an egg-cup portion of beans. (I always wonder 'where do the half bacon-slices go?) Tea, biscuits and margarine. Water is short, so only a half cup of tea.

The Gabes aerodrome last night was found okay but no aircraft on it. One of 104 Squadron had a 4,000-pounder on board and dropped it slap on the barracks at Gabes. 37 Squadron had the illuminating job, with parachute flares, and ordered to fire red Very cartridges once the target was sighted. Tubby jettisoned his load on the target area of the town; all returned safely.

The blitz is now supposed to be *on*, though nothing doing all day. Tubby and I went over to Gardabia East and collected our sand-filled petrol tins to rebuild our bathroom. Jock went over to collect an aircraft, while I went over later to see the remains of the blow-up. The hole in the ground is about 3′ 6″ deep and 16′ long; there is nothing left of the aircraft itself. Ops are on tonight, last night's was on Gabes; the army should take it tomorrow.

Still no sign of aircraft there so they bombed the town again; it was an early take-off, and all kites were back by 11.30.

Food still very short, two 1-cm slices of Bully and desiccated cabbage (which I cannot eat) together with three spring onions, and biscuits and cheese. It probably is fully nourishing, but the quantity provided no roughage and even Enos doesn't seem to help. We're all very liverish and touchy.

Thirty-seven Squadron pinched two of our Mk Xs; they are to be re-equipped with Mk IIIs also ...

The SAAF wing of Bostons and Baltimores are continually flying around practising their tight formations; they're quite good even now. They'll be needed shortly. The distance between the landing grounds north of the Jerry is only 200 miles from those south of the line, all of which are now in our hands.

Seen in *London Opinion*:

Sing a song of Spitfires, racing through the air,
Four and twenty squadrons flying ev'ry where.
When the Hun comes over, Ev'ry Spitfire spits;
Now isn't that a dainty way to mess up Messerschmitts?

March 1st: A cold morning again, but less cloud, about 3/10ths, base 3,000 feet. I asked Lawson again if I could fly and so here I am, as second dickie to a Pilot Officer Alderman, (quite clueful but nothing spectacular). Took off at 10.30 on an air test. Without a load, these Mk IIIs fairly hurtle along with the forward thrust, just like a Miles Master II when you go through the gate.

The 37 Squadron kite which was lost over Gabes the other night force-landed just inside our lines. We are off on a maximum effort to Palermo tonight, take-off at 9.30. We all rather hoped for a daylight take-off since the weather is somewhat doubtful and it had to be well-nigh perfect for a maximum effort over the target. A Flight are putting on seven machines, B Flight, five.

Briefing was at 8.15 and we did take off at 9.30, just like clockwork. Intercom was a bit scratchy at times, but not bad. At about 10.00, we were over 5/10ths cloud flying at 5,000 feet doing 150 mph indicated with a load of nine 500-pounders and four 250s plus 650 gallons of petrol. It *is* an overload, no matter how much the CO knocks my block off for telling him so. He actually threatened me with a court martial for 'spreading alarm and despondency' among the men. Luckily I had not spread it to anyone but him, in the hope that he would do something about it.

When we started to lose so many aircraft with burst tyres on take-off, and almost equally on landing, I checked the various handbooks for the Mk I, III and X's etc with the Flight Sergeant *and found that three grades of tyres were available*, or meant to be, rather like 4-ply and 6-ply on cars. Lighter grades were for empty aircraft, such as for training purposes, and others for differing loads or landing ground conditions and we were using the *wrong ones*, full stop! Knowing that I knew the situation, and he probably hadn't a clue anyway, I think he did try to do something about it after that skirmish.

He calmed immediately after the outburst, once reassured by me, but I pointed out that maximum load was 34,000 lbs, and no more, *please*!

By 10.30 the clouds were just odd negligible patches and at 10.40 we sighted the four searchlights of Malta. At 11.35 we passed over Gozo Island. Valletta and the whole of the main island were brilliantly lighted, and there was an aircraft circling with its navigation lights on.

Palermo was one big firework display. We went up to 14,500 feet but no flares appeared by the blitz period opening; we learned later that the two illuminating aircraft were from 40 Squadron, and both had had to land at Malta on their way to the target. At 12.20, all the guns stopped firing and the lights went out; most odd. But, at 12.30, daylight was resumed, or so it seemed. Everything opened up at us, the searchlights, about twenty of them, with six or seven masters illuminated a smoke screen which came from about five or six big generators from the NNW side of the harbour. At the same time, a large dummy fire was lighted about eight miles north of the town. No one had been to bomb as yet, so we knew that for a dummy fire, it was very impressive.

Blitz time was 12.40, and everyone was waiting for the flares which never came, except for one lad who went in, and everything from God's earth seemed to be thrown at him. The searchlights are becoming quite clued up and were on him in one big cone. They held him for about 50 seconds, a very long time. At 12.55, the second blitz period, everyone but us went in and did some quite good work.

'A' was a bit jumpy it seemed to me, and always turned away from the target, but we cut across the bottom of the town and bombed the railways there – not much cop. About four heavies and three searchlights paid us a call but we were moving just a little bit faster than they thought. The thermometer read minus 15 degrees C up there and we were glad to get down; ground level temp was plus 9 degrees C. It was quite a bit warmer in Palermo when we had all finished with it.

George flew us home and by 3.10 we were in the circuit. One kite pranged on a shot-up undercart just as we followed him in so we had to go round again from about 50 feet, but at 3.40 we were down. We were just climbing into the lorry to take us to de-briefing when someone landed and ran smack into the pranged kite just off the runway. Nobody was hurt.

I had egg, bacon and porridge for breakfast (reversed order I think it was) and went sleepily to bed just as the dawn overcame the starlight in the east.

March 3rd: Woke up at 9.10 this morning, too late for breakfast. I'm on tonight, as second dickie to Alderman again, for the double op; briefing 3.30, tea at 4.00, and take-off at 5.30. That means being over our target from 7.30 to 8.30, then having returned, refuelled and re-bombed the aircraft, we return to the target and stay over it from three to four. That'll keep them awake, we hope.

Last night, nobody seemed to find the target (a bunch of troops said to be five miles north-east of Mareth) a convoy was said to have halted there. Tonight we take 18 rodded 250-pounders and 750 gallons of petrol.

Just after our tea-cum-supper of bully fritters, potatoes (canned) and fresh carrots – which quite a few people are eating raw – we waited outside the tent for the lorry to take us out to our aircraft and the CO told us that the first op was scrubbed. Nonetheless, we went out and taxied them to their marshalling point at the flarepath. Quite an impressive sight, fifteen of ours on one side and ten from 37 Squadron on the other, almost wing-tip to wing-tip. We'll have 'tea' at 11.00, then take off at 1 a.m. Last night's ops were a flop, few saw anything to bomb and somebody pranged one of our forward landing grounds, just inside our lines.

March 4th: I went to bed at barely 9.00 last night – there is often the chance that the op will be scrubbed – and Tubby woke me at 10.00 to tell me that there was a meal waiting for us. It was excellent. Tinned ham – which is always broken and rather like minced ham – and we had about half a tin each on fried bread. We now get a few loaves every day, which is very nearly white, and last night it was *almost* white, the nearest yet.

We were picked up and taken to 'A' – our machines for the trip – at 12.40 and started up. Unfortunately 37 Squadron were to take off at the same time and the queueing was rather a hectic mêlée. Everything went well, from beacon to beacon and eventually at 3.00 we were over the little town of Mareth and, at 3.03, over our target.

The army put lights on for us so that we could set our proper courses, from an X in the north and an N in the south; very useful. No illumination had arrived from the appointed aircraft, so it was just everyone for himself. The light from the parachute flares lit up several aircraft and it was my job to mention if any were near. We saw about ten during the hour. A Macchi 200 or 202 fighter went by very close about 150 yards away in the opposite direction. I could see the pilot looking at us, just as I saw him. Our cockpit lighting was rather more brilliant than I would have chosen but I was not the pilot. We must have looked like a greenhouse with its lights on! He was passing to starboard and I suggested a quick turn that way, in the hope of catching him within range with the forward guns; a forlorn hope. Had he decided to do the same manoeuvre, our forward guns could have achieved something, but he was gone – much to everyone's relief.

The town was ringed by six searchlights, three pairs in fact and we bombed one pair, scoring only a near miss. The main target was the town itself, but Crossley had forgotten to tell us this so we went on hunting for lorries and so on. Nothing to be seen, but knowing that the town was full of Jerries we bombed that, with three double runs, making six in all with three bombs released on each run and had a very good time. Quite a bit of light flak making colourful patterns of green, blue, grey-white and red. Perhaps they carry some code, just as we have our 'colours for the day' for identification purposes using Very cartridges. No wonder the Jerry flak (the 40mm stuff) is called 'Dingleberries', they deserve such a pretty name, lethal as they sometimes can be.

At five past four I took over and we came back. Managed to urge her up to 160 mph (1,600 rpm, zero boost and weak mixture) and landed in light-hazed darkness at five to six. Breakfast and to bed. The sun was just heralding a beautiful day, no cloud or wind, just hot sunshine.

March 5th: Unfortunately ops were scrubbed last night just as I went into briefing, but all being well, we'll go tonight. Our photographs were not too good, though Lawson got some very good ones of the town.

There seems to be some argument at Group Headquarters as to who will control us. Presumably we came to help the army in which case we come under Western Desert Command and do battle stooges which everyone likes. If Middle East gets us, it means long sea stooges to Palermo every night. As the defences there will shortly come under the Germans, it means we will probably lose many aircraft and Middle East does not like that; it's their choice, not ours and they know the likely consequences of flying over the Med.

Weather duff over Palermo tonight so if no battle stooge, we will be stood-down. It is a lovely day again, with spring-like puffs of white cloud, each with its own little pink bottom (reflection from the red sand of the desert below). I've seen only one bird here, there are very few around, though in the twilight and early dawn one hears them.

Log books returned from the CO's office, so mine is made up. Time quickly mounts up on these Twins; in only three pages I've clocked over 100 hours.

No ops by teatime, but we marshalled the aircraft just in case. Three Spits came practising line-astern chasing over the drome. They were shocking: Nos 2 and 3 never cut corners and were left miles behind. Surely the OTUs can do better than that?

The wireless gives hardly any news of air warfare in southern Tunisia these days, and seeing plus *hearing* all the various squadrons both here and at Castel Benito (Tripoli West) it seems that we're pretty well back and well away from aerial opposition while building-up our strength.

Ida Haendel gave a marvellous performance of Beethoven's concerto for violin on the BBC Scottish.

March 6th: The wind rose yesterday afternoon and lasted all night, bringing rain with it in quite sharp storms. Two of our aircraft were due to return from Malta today, but weather over the Med still too dicey.

Horrible galey morning. Both of 'V's' turrets are unserviceable, so no ops for us tonight, and I doubt if there will be for anyone.

Cigarette shortage becoming acute, most of us having finished our ration of Indian 'V's' by now. No more till Tuesday, three days hence.

At 5.45, everyone told 'ops on', tea at 6.00, briefing 6.30; then at 6.50, at the end of the briefing, the phone rang and 'ops are off'.

The AOC says that the army have pushed east and got to 50 miles south of Sousse; Eighth Army still on the same line. At briefing we were told that all army convoys on our side of the line will use full headlights, except during air raids on them, in which case the Bofors guns will fire red-coloured incendiaries. Marvellous co-operation. The other night searchlights on our side swung their beams directly into line with the target for us. The lines are so close that only very accurate bombing is safe for the army.

Quite a party in the mess, Williamson made a complete fool of himself by driving the flight pick-up into it, nearly killing Inky and the barman. Long Johnny started well by swallowing two lighted cigarettes – but finished early! Tubby and I both left at 11.00, made tea and boiled eggs in our tent.

March 7th: A quiet morning again, no mail. Spits, Hurries, Bostons and Baltimores diving all around us. What are they trying to say? 'OK, boys, you've done your stint, now let us show you how it should be done. Daylight bravery, that's the thing.' It makes me, as one of *them* and not one of *these* feel very small. If no one else knows, God does, that my colleagues here have done their bit, if no more, and most of them have done a hell of a lot more than that. A three-hour trip back from the target area, possibly more like four hours, not knowing how your oil supply will last, or your engines, will they get you home, if not both, will just one be enough?

Who is going to look for you throughout the length and breadth of the Med when your wireless is duff and there is no hope whatever of sending a May Day signal?

March 8th: It's my job to be the 'Orderly Dog' today, which does not entail much. Everyone lends a hand censoring the airmen's mail and there are few, if any, complaints in their mess. The cookhouse is doing very well, by getting five eggs for a pint mug of rice. We rarely eat rice in the mess but now we get an egg every morning for breakfast. The chief horror these days is desiccated potatoes, which look like slabs of hoof and horn glue. When broken, the edge is sharp, hard, brown and shiney, *exactly* like glue. Even when soaked for 24 hours and then cooked, the end product is like leather; sole or upper? No one can distinguish.

Dave gave us a very interesting lecture on Escape. Evidently the Arabs in these parts are very pro-German and anti-Italian, therefore one has to avoid them here. Today is warm and sunny again with no wind, it makes the place very relaxing. Ops are doubtful, owing to weather, but if we do go, it will probably be Palermo again.

Yes, it was Palermo. Took off at 9.00 into thick haze. Passed Malta at 10.30 (somebody jettisoned his flares and landed there, plus three of 40 Squadron who should have illuminated the target for us). There was a little low cloud and over Sicily itself only thin patches of mist from 10,000 feet to 16,000.

Someone had illuminated the town for us over the south, and we did a grand run towards the north, over the docks and the shipping in the harbour. At the critical moment, one of those sheets of mist blinded us from our target like someone pulling a sheet under us, so we decided to have another run at it; the opposition was only light.

This time, on the reciprocal course, we dropped our bombs but had not altered our height so although the bombs went safely on their way, our photo-flash bomb went off just when we had again passed over the same sheet of mist. To get a good photograph we would have been far better to go below it. One or two searchlights took a short look at us, but passed on; hardly any flak. We were the second in to land, at 3.05. I flew her back, or rather George did, but he got rather tired and eventually packed-up altogether. He started to wander, then dropped the nose twice rather alarmingly so I put him to bed for a rest.

March 9th: Last night's op was very pleasing, but a good photograph would have made it the more so. Woke at 12.00, having got to bed at 5.00. A 30 mph wind blew steadily all day.

Four of our chaps landed at Malta, probably short of petrol. We very nearly were. I suppose we landed with half an hour's worth to spare. Dickie Day had been flying for an hour on his gravity tanks, so he would have only twenty minutes left.

The GC is on his way up to Algeria and the CO is now to take over the wing. Lawson is being sent on rest in about ten days' time, and for the last four nights has been holding large drinking singsongs in the mess.

Wing Commander Newman is to take over, ex-flight commander of 104 Squadron. He's coming along some time tomorrow. Two very quick Air Mail Letter Cards arrived today, both dated 24th February only twelve days ago. I was just writing my replies in the mess when a sand-storm blew up, almost a *Khamsin* but more of a whirlwind. Its track passed straight over the mess and so the whole thing just took off; a very good thing that it did for had it dragged, as well it might have done, it would have collapsed onto the kitchen fire and the whole lot gone up in smoke. After about three minutes, we could see each other again, the desert was white with papers. All the airmen's mail about to be censored in the mess just *went* (though at least half of it was collected later).

Having put the thing up again basically, we were still collecting papers when I saw another storm coming on the same track as before. I yelled to everyone to hold on to the guy ropes on the windward side and there we stuck, for all we were worth. Visibility just closed down to a very dark red three feet, but after no more than two minutes it was over.

By the help of our electric light, we got the whole thing sorted and settled but it took us two and half hours since it blew down. By that time we were eating bacon, bully, ham mash and tea, eventually to bed at 10.00. The Sergeants' and airmen's mess and several ridge tents had all suffered the same fate.

March 12th: We never got off last night, the wireless was NBG (no bloody good) and we were not getting sufficient revs from either engine. New rev counters were fitted during the afternoon and both connected so that they read backwards!

A trailer cinema arrived and gave us a showing of *Midnight* with Don Ameche and Claudette Colbert; very good. Got back to the mess by 9.50 and found a meal waiting for us, fried tinned ham on fried bread.

It was a case of bad luck last night that three of our aircraft did not get off for various reasons. There is a convoy out to sea going east, just about due north of us now, and we were told to steer well clear because Jerry had already attacked it once, and was sending in further waves of bombers. We did not want to get anywhere near those trigger-happy naval types. We could see the heavy and light flashes going off a long way away to the north, so I expect that convoy was having it pretty heavily.

The attack on Palermo was not very good, low cloud at 7,000 feet, so most people just bombed on the searchlights. A very dull wireless programme, so went to bed at 10.00. A wizard night, crystal clear right down to the horizon, I have never seen so many stars all at once.

March 13th: Lawson told me this morning that I can be a captain any time I like; only a crew is missing! I took 'J' up on air test, used only 2½-lbs boost which is ample. I wanted to find the Spits' drome and have a look at the Bostons but the oil pressure dropped on the port engine to 30 psi and on these sleeve valve Hercules engines (reputedly bad for this sort of thing) you need to maintain a minimum of 70 psi and that for only five minutes, so I brought her back, and to my delighted surprise made a perfect three-pointer.

The MkIc arrived with all the bar stocks. Lawson had been over to Castel Benito to contact a certain Captain Bun who was brought up from the Delta on a MkIII the other day, which pleased him a lot. He happens to be the head of the Naafi at Tripoli so we are well in there now. Lawson came back laden with Johnny Walker red label, two cases of beer, chocolate and so on, a magnificent haul. Quite a party in the mess.

March 15th: A dirty wet night, but this morning was fair enough, until 10.00 when the wind sprang up as usual to 15-20 mph, but now it is back to the north. A rumour went around that Lawson would go up with me in a Mk III tonight to see if I were OK: then at teatime, I asked Pilley – now assistant flight commander – if this was so. 'Oh, Lawson doesn't think that'll be necessary, he's got a crew for you now' ... so there I am, I suppose, but *when*: for crying out loud?

Spits and Kittyhawks have been recalled due to bad weather; our ops too were cancelled. We came under 'Western Desert' at midnight last night, so from now on – Western Desert Targets! HOORAY!

CHAPTER FOUR

Farewell to the Hazardous Med

March 17th 1943: New brooms everywhere, it seems. The new flight commander brought a Mk X and crew from the UK, ex-training command, a very likable lad. The crew is to go to Ken Larby.

A pleasant day, hardly any cloud, a few sand devils and quite a spot of wind. Ops are probable tonight. Alderman detailed to take 'A' but the Doc stopped him because of a cold and nobody wants sinus trouble aggravated by dust. Lawson says he'll take his place, with me as second dickie, doing the take-off and landing.

I went out to give 'A' her daily inspection and found one of the bomb door jacks leaking, but by 1.20 had it repaired. Took various types with me on air test, a Sergeant Hughes, as navigator (a super Australian); Lenk, a very jumpy type – some of the gunners were firing short bursts into the sand testing their guns, and he nearly jumped out of his skin every time. Pilling as rear gunner and Wilson at the front.

We flew off and up to 2,000 feet, found a suitable bit of desert and literally shot it up. Guns all okay, put in George and he's okay, flying a bit tail heavy and left wing low, but she'll do, having 60-lbs pressure indicated. It was getting late so came back and landed leaving the ground crews and armourers to load the eighteen 250s we'll be taking, on our desert stooge.

Lunch, and at 1.30 a mess meeting. Mac told me that Lawson will not be allowed off duty at the drome so I wonder if he'll let me go alone? I now have a crew, all but first and second WOP/AGs (wireless operator air gunners). Ops were scrubbed at 6.30 so I dashed out and dispersed about six of the aircraft (even if I can't fly them, they are fun to play with on the ground).

I tested the Mauser and found it firing a bit low at 100 yards. The butt jumps very high and bruises my cheek-bone, but hardly any backward kicks, so I cut away enough of the stock to stop it hitting my cheekbone in future.

Micky Mount came over with some of his chaps and we talked for some time. He's very happy to be the CO of 104 Squadron. He tells me that John Selby has been awarded the DSO which I think is far more appropriate than the DFC – Lawson says, 'now an issue like the Vs and chocolate ration.'

Pilley is to take A Flight, and tonight if ops are on. Evidence tells us that the Eighth Army has decided to wait a bit.

The nights are now beautifully clear, with about half a moon. Alderman still has a nasty cold but when he goes on ops again he will act as captain, while I do the take-off, bombing-run and the landing; then next time I go myself.

Now I have a complete crew; Chubb, a Canadian as rear gunner – docile and not easily flapped; Quartermain, as front gunner – bright and very alert; Frierson, an Aussie, as my wireless operator-air gunner (the sort you could ask to fly the plane if necessary. I reckon he could cope with anything) and Parry, our navigator-bomb aimer. It should be recorded somewhere – and probably has already – that these navigators have to have far greater perceptive powers than any 'bus driver' (such it is that the pilot is frequently and accurately called) and Arthur Parry was no exception. He could make us laugh – and frequently did – when something, or anything or even *everything* went wrong, and there is an awful lot which can, with an aeroplane under war operations. Arthur was our umbrella whose shield we valued more than has ever been expressed.

The larks are making beautiful noises outside, all day long. In a broadcast last night a blackbird's song was used and it sounded so rich after the rather reedy piping of these little birds.

It rained quite hard at 5.00 having been spitting all day. Everyone got busy throwing sand over the tents as a form of camouflage. (These orders come along every few months, but never to much effect; the sand and dust sticks just as long as the tents are wet.) Wrote to John Selby on his DSO.

The AOC gave us a lecture: of the 50 tank shoot-up, the attack is now on. 73 Squadron is now at El Assa; our target, same as before. Prisoners tell us that Rommel is far from fit, covered with desert sores. If this attack of his fails, it will be farewell to Africa for him, and it did fail.

Ops were scrubbed fourteen minutes before take-off. 37

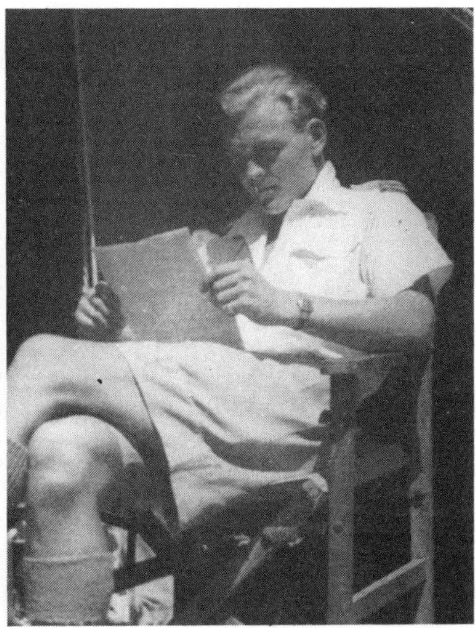

(*Left*) John Selby (standing on right), ex-Flight Commander of 73 Squadron after his DSO award. (*Right*) Our lifeline – mail from home.

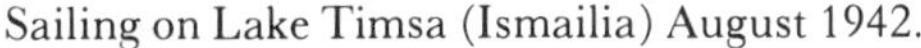

Sailing on Lake Timsa (Ismailia) August 1942.

Squadron, who had gone off an hour before, were recalled. (10/10ths cloud over target; impossible.)

I'm sorry for the Eighth Army; we won't be too popular if we don't help to smash their attackers. Quite a party in the mess to say farewell to Lawson, now off to 205 Group. Everyone was sorry to see him go, Micky Mount came over and various types from Wing including Tamahill from 178. He told me that B. Champaigne was shot-down south of Naples about six weeks ago. It's truly amazing the way only the best seem to go that way, in line with the age-old adage, 'Only the best, die young'.

A very dull day, thunderstorms, sheets of rain, ops scrubbed at lunchtime.

I was writing a letter home when the CO sat down next to me in readiness for dinner. In the course of conversation it appeared that he is John Stanton's brother-in-law, John being perhaps my closest college friend at Cambridge while reading agriculture together in 1939. Our CO's exploits had been made known to me many times in John's letters to me during the first year of war. John is now '2nd Battalion, Royal Tank Regiment, Persia and Iraq Forces'; sounds very cushy to me. Newman had just written a letter to him so pulled it out of the box and opened it to put in a few lines about me.

He also mentioned that Ivan Strutt was illuminating the night he was shot down; he flew straight and level all the time and was bound to get it. Nonetheless, there is quite a chance he got out.

March 19th: A bright sunny morning, steady 35 mph wind, then came a gale warning. All aircraft had to be picketed, i.e. clamped to the ground with the 4-foot long cork-screws with eye rings at their tops to attach the ropes to wing-tips. Quite a job even using a crow-bar, to screw the things into the ground to a worthwhile depth when the subsoil is limestone rock!

We rang the MT section and they brought two 3-tonner lorries which we tied to the mess tent guy ropes. Now I think it should stand anything from the northerly quarter.

I decided to take 'A' up on air test; nobody else wanted to test theirs but she hasn't flown for three days and that makes her sulky, as they all are, if so treated. She went like a bird and I quite felt that she did it in response for my feeling for her. We talk to the trees, and we flatter the flowers, because in our humble way we can thank

God for such gifts to us by so doing. Kick a 'kite' and see what happens. You'll probably get dunked in the drink, if not drowned there. If it's man-made, then since man is God-made, so is man's making God's making, and we must not forget it.

Flight Sergeant Carter from NZ came along as second dickie. Rather too keen for my liking, always fiddling with the gills – for the air cooling, and oil radiator flaps which control the air flow through them also. They are at the fingertips of the pilot anyway, and if he wants assistance, he can ask for it.

We went over to the Boston drome, most of them have gone and only the main body of Baltimores are left. Coming in to land, while I was on the cross-wind leg, the dual 'Y' taxied just onto the runway, slightly blocking my line of approach. Then as I turned in for the final approach he taxied further and was obviously on the point of taking off. I decided to land immediately beside him to teach him a lesson. Happily enough his first pilot, Jock Smith saw me coming and opened his throttles and cleared my path. A very nice trip of 35 minutes.

More rain and thunderstorms. Ops okay; they took-off at 9.00. Target quite clear below 4,000 feet cloud base. Two of B Flight are missing. Jack Marsh thought he saw one kite burning on the ground. Unfortunately every machine was a black silhouette against the moonlit cloud. It rained steadily all night. Most of them landed at Castel Benito, and others at Gardabia Main, but there, as here, they bogged in soft clay mud.

March 20th: More rain this morning; the desert is rapidly become much greener. Everything rather damp and cold. Wrote to John Stanton in Iraq.

Thirteen of ours got off last night; but one is still missing. Only one returned here, four landed on Gardabia Main and the rest at Castel Benito. It was a stand-down, obviously; seeing our state of preparedness at 9 a.m., then at 11.30 ops were reported to be on! At 12.00, the news came through that the order was for *double ops* sorties. The chaps saw a lot of stuff in the wadis last night so there's lots to bomb.

12.30: ops back to single sortie now, no longer a double one by the two wings. All the aircraft from Gardabia main went to Castel Benito at 3.00. They are to operate from there and land there, so tonight there are only sixteen of us in the mess. Someone saw what looked like a machine hit the deck with its bombs on, just our side of the lines. No sign of Johnny tonight!

The battle started this morning. The new A Flight commander, Squadron Leader Tinny, told me after dinner that I can take 'A' or 'C' tomorrow on a double sortie from here. A beautiful night (full moon tomorrow) very little cloud, just some huge cumulus jobs hanging over the coast up to 14,000 feet.

March 21st: A fine morning which later became overcast. The north wind which gave us such a wizard night has swung to the south and the sky is very grey with stratus at about 5,000 feet. I took 'B' up on air test, and the trimming gear is still u/s; all the wires are too stretched to be of any use and will have to be replaced; the turnbuckles are up to the limit of their threads.

Met my WOP/AG and my Canadian rear gunner Chubb – who tells me he won £50 last night at poker in the sergeants' mess.

I shall have Mackay as my front gunner instead of Quartermain. He and I were at Newquay together in B Flight before we ever saw an aeroplane. He duffed his pilot's course, so opted for air gunner – brave lad!

After lunch, we went out and cleaned the guns etc, and marshalled the aircraft with the rest. The chaps operating from Castel Benito last night said that there was no opposition at all. The night before last, people saw quite a lot of transport and tanks hidden in the wadis, but last night it had nearly all gone.

Briefing went off at 8.00 and at 9.30 I was about to start up when Dave came along telling us not to bomb anything east of 9.53 ... What the hell did that mean? The army is advancing we know. This held us up a bit and being anxious to get off on time (9.30) I dashed over to the Chance Light on the flarepath and we got off at 9.34 in fact. I had wondered what a fully laden aircraft was like to get off, but she came off like a seagull soaring up a cliff face, smoothly and with a steady air speed of 135 mph. Flaps up, I turned left onto the beacon, and away we went.

March 22nd: There were about 3/10ths cloud at 2,000 feet for the first hundred miles; we never saw any of the beacons but crossed the coast at about 10.45 above a thin layer of stratus. The moon was full and everything was brilliantly clear. Gradually as we neared the island the cloud was mounting up and my ears became deaf to the engines. Flying over and between those huge clouds seemed like something quite unearthly; no doubt the moonlight had something to do with it.

I put up the revs to 2,100 from 1,900, and climbed gently to 8,000 feet. Turned left handed at the north-western corner of the island, in over the 'V' marker, heading west-south-west; quite a lot of artillery firing from our lines, little yellow darts of light and others, great red spurts. A pretty sight for us, but what of the other end?

When west of Mareth we turned north and most regrettably found ourselves slap over one of those silent batteries of heavy stuff and five searchlights, RDF's I think, i.e. guided by Radio Direction Finders. We were weaving all the time yet when they switched on, they were on us and we were held in their grip. Then the hard work started, skidding down and out and up again so that all the bursts went up well above us and behind, and soon they left us alone. A lot of light stuff in the form of Dingleberries came up to greet us over Mareth.

A parachute flare to the north-east attracted our attention. We went to have a look and found a hutted camp already illuminated for us by a Halifax, plainly visible 2,000 feet above us. We went down to 6,000 feet and dropped a flare, then made a good run-up and dropped six of our eighteen 250-pounders. The camp was beside the road running up to Gabes and our little effort must have given someone a headache. The object of the raid was to weaken the enemy's morale, mostly through lack of sleep.

We hunted roads, tracks and wadis and eventually left at 12.40, making for the coast. (10.30 to 12.00 was all the time given us to stay but it didn't matter staying a bit longer.) A single-engined fighter (an Me109) came along to see if we were awake. We were, and when I turned smartly onto him he peeled off down hill in quite a hurry.

At 1.00 we crossed the coast accompanied by bursting shells from the shore batteries, which gave us a useful pinpoint on their positions for future use. And so back to base, at a good 170 mph, minus ½ lb boost, 1,800 revs.

As we passed over Castel Benito, the Watch Officer kindly gave us a 'green' with his Aldis lamp. I winked at them with the navigation lights and passed on. Then we were kept waiting for three quarters of an hour on our circuit, and landed – not bad at all – at 3.25. Breakfast, and slept all day.

March 23rd: Yesterday was grand, lying in bed; it rained very gently all day, no wind and everything peacefully quiet.

A Flight took-off at 7.00 and B at 8.00 on a double op from Castel Benito, starting and finishing from here. Frazer, Bebbington and Rakow got their commissions yesterday. A great shock hit us when we learned that the Bebbington and Tinny, the new A Flight commander, were blown up while crossing the coast by very accurate flak from one battery and four searchlights, using a number of 88-mm guns. (If they were the ones we reported why did they not hit us, for one question, and why did the others fly within their range for another?)

Reports indicate that their bursts were dead accurate and it was probably they who caught Johnny the other night. The weather was perfect for both sides, evidently, attackers and defenders. Even the second sortie found no cloud at all visible anywhere.

I shall be taking 'M' tonight. I've never flown her and there's no time or real need for an air test so we hope for the best. I'm taking Sergeant Greenshields as front gunner; it's his last op before going on rest.

The new flight commander, a Squadron Leader Barber, recently of training command like Tinny, but from Canada, arrived before lunch from 37 Squadron. Quick work! I went out to the aircraft while the fitters and riggers tinkered with it, slow running of the port engine was bad, popping-back. The starboard engine won't run below 1,000 rpm. The port engine then caught fire after one of its 'backfires' and gave us a clue as to where the leak was in the induction manifold. I put this right, put the guns in and came back. I took my helmet to be tested and they say that the mike is earthing somewhere, so was given a reconditioned one.

Doc, Frazer, Tubby and Jock Smith are going on leave to Cairo tomorrow, ostensibly for 48 hours, but they are to bring back two other machines and I expect they'll be there more like a week. They are taking £100 for bar stocks.

Went to marshal the aircraft on the runway at 4.00 but it was not made serviceable until 4.50, so I missed tea. Briefing at 7.15. Just getting into the lorry to go out to the kites when Western Desert rang and told us they only want a reduced effort so the GC scrubbed us and left 37 Squadron to do it, since theirs was scrubbed last night.

Newman's brother is with the Eighth Army and says that he and his chaps get a great filip seeing and hearing us on the 24-hour bombing process, day bombing by Mitchells, Marauders, Bostons etc followed by us at night.

March 24th: Last night was one of the most perfect since the moon came up. It was full two nights ago, yet there is not even a shadow in its top; it's still perfectly round – most odd – and not a cloud anywhere. The news is excellent. On Monday, two days ago, the Eighth Army went in, 5,000 yards wide and 1,500 deep. The Royal Engineers built a road over a deep wadi which was part of the Jerry defence and the tanks and guns went through.

They pushed on in the north-east, round Medenine and another division has come round the right flank of the line, and straight west as far as El Hamma, fifteen miles west of Gabes which gives Jerry just fifteen miles to run through, should he decide to do so. The Yanks have done almost the same, driving east from their western positions as far as Macknassy (25 miles west of the coast) and are now branching north-east to Sfax. East to the coast, and south-east to El Hamma. In the north Jerry is still making little gains here and there but is usually sent back.

I'm on tonight, taking 'M', with Mackay who has asked to be my front gunner, so I hope to please him.

The news at 5.00 was rather a set-back. For the past thirty-six hours Churchill says that it is Jerry who is doing the attacking. They have taken back the bridgehead we had made but the NZs are still okay west of El Hamma. We were briefed at 11.30 and the target was a bombing square, twelve miles by twelve, south of El Hamma and east of the hills just including the road running north to south.

Since Crossley came *out* so easily north of Gabes the other night we decided to go *in* there. At 3,000 feet the air temperature here is 12 degrees C, yet north of the Djerba island it was up to 20. This fact did not delay us, but others did. On inspection of the kite we found that someone had very neatly cut a 4-inch piece out of our IFF aerial, the vital tool which tells our troops on the deck as to whether we are Friend or Foe (identification). We called-up the duty electrician on the TR9 (Telephone Transmitter, Radio Mk 9) and he came out. The CO and Crossley also very interested; it was obviously deliberate.

We started up on time and would have been second off. (In

order, we would have been about eighth, but those due to start-up at 12.45 were late.) On our way out to the flarepath I smelt a lot of burning rubber; I waited till the rest of the crew complained in case it was just my imagination, but it wasn't. I had had enough sabotage for one night so I switched off everything. Jumping out and sniffing around, as we all did, we could only find that one of the cockpit heating pipes had got rather hot. It took no time to dope her up and trundle off to the flarepath and we were away.

The port cylinder head temperature soared up to 275 degrees, while the maximum permitted in the air is 270, and that for a short while only. We were only up to 500 feet but the only thing to do was to throttle back. At 1,900 rpm the temperature dropped to 250, with using 2 lbs boost. Very slowly we got up to 3,000 feet and stayed there all the way out to Zuara. I put the revs up to 2,100 and reduced speed to 140 mph but even so the temperature went up again to 260. It was not pleasant, especially as the outside temperature went up as we went north.

We crossed the coast at 8,000 feet, watching about two of the Gabes heavy guns firing over themselves and well to the left of us. Went straight along the salt marsh and when light tracer came up from a white patch, we knew it to be El Hamma aerodrome. There we turned south and followed the road south along the hills. A lorry was burning well, and with flares we spotted about three or four lorries in each of the numerous wadis to the west of the road and some of the hollows to the east.

We arrived at 3.35 a.m. and stayed till about 4.00. Our intercom telephone cut on us just as we crossed the coast so all our bombing had to be done by the aid of vicious pointings and nudgings. (Our time over target should have been 3.00 to 3.40 but everyone was rather late, owing to headwinds.) We stooged north-east and waited till the El Hamma flak came up – the haze and moon hid the marsh from any distance – but the flak gave us its very useful pinpoint at which to turn right, and so home.

A beautiful sunrise, deep blue turning to duck-egg then red underneath to yellow and eventually sunshine itself. Landed at 6.15 and slept nearly all day.

March 26th: Saw two house-martins this morning, having a silent hurried feed. In a few days I hope they'll be squealing excitedly over some quiet English stream.

Several, in fact almost everyone, was shot up the night before last; two had to be pranged. Pilley lost a lot of fabric and a lot of people came back full of holes. One of B Flight had a tyre shot through, but made a wizard landing on the one good one. Unfortunately my aeroplane ('C', and one of the best) had her hydraulics shot away and was one of those which had to be pranged.

More gales today, as yesterday. Luckily the pulverised clay made very thick mud when the rains came and on most of the tracks it had been pressed and dried till it's like concrete.

March 27th: A bad haze all day with a half a gale blowing steadily from a depression to the south of Tunis, said to be fading out, but bone dry and bringing a lot of dust with it. Every night we get inversions with the ground temperature around 12 degrees C. and that at 7,000 feet up to 20,000, then suddenly as you climb a little higher it drops to plus 2. Ken Larby was climbing over the target area last night, sweating profusely, when suddenly the aircraft came into the colder air and climbed like fun, shooting up another 1,000 feet!

Last night the haze was so bad that nobody found the target. 37 Squadron did though, and Ben Bolt, a very popular SAAF major is missing after it.

Had a very full day on 'M' during the daily inspection with the crew, mostly on repairing the intercom and TR9. Waited till 12.00 to do an air test, but the crews going off for lunch postponed it till 2.00. Eventually we got off at 2.45. George absolutely u/s. (All the auto-pilots are gradually going that way on the squadron.) Chubb used his guns in the rear turret and when we landed the armourers were waiting to bomb-up. I was hoping to do the illumination but the target was a road one, between Gabes and Sousse so it's everyone for himself.

Went into the flight tent to sign the DCO only to find that 'M' had to be swung for correct compass action. That meant that all the bombs had to come off again (if it were my job, I would at least tell the left hand what the right hand is doing!). We swung the aircraft to correct the compass with the tractor on the tail wheel, and then put the bombs back on again. Marshalled her at 6.15 and came back to dinner. Ops were scrubbed at 8.00, after all the rush to get her ready before dark. (A little bird told me that much of our 'tyre problem' was due to leaving aircraft fully loaded overnight and through the heat of the following morning, but if Groups Ops cannot tell the army if the weather will be OK or NBG, who can?)

Ops were to have been a battle stooge, take-off at 2.00 and landing well in daylight, about 7.30. Brought 'M' back early this morning and now sharing 'D' with Flight Sergeant Brown – funny how the colours always seem to stick together.

March 28th: In the mess last night, everyone was feeling a bit deflated after the effort of the day, and the negative effort tonight. The subject turned to that of names, why was Tommy christened a Thomas? Did his father doubt his wife, for instance, or did the wife doubt the milkman's competence in taking all necessary precautions – all these Music Hall jokes had to be aired.

At just about 5.00 the wind turned from south to east and then stopped! To the west, just grey-brown murk. Visibility over the target is said to be three miles; no moon, so we'll have to take the sea route, yet we have no flame floats, and therefore no way of calculating our drifts. It'll be difficult to find the drome on our way back. If this haze persists to any great height, there will be no stars for astro-navigation, so here's hoping that the wireless holds good for us. We should be able to get some loop bearings, but no one is keen to go, mostly because of the inversion which has put the temperature up to 20 degrees C even at 6,000 feet.

Luckily someone is marshalling the aircraft for me – being Orderly Officer I have other things to do – though at the moment we are due to take off down wind!

5.30: a line squall just passed Tripoli, heading east and is due here between 8.00 and 8.30. Briefing put off till 11.30; east wind getting up, low cloud forming, and getting very dark. A very filthy night, hot gusts of wind with rain suddenly rushing in from any direction. Eventually we were briefed for take-off at 2 a.m. Chubb's reflector gun sight went u/s at the last minute but Mackay came out when called over the TR9 and had it right in no time.

March 29th: Taxied out and would have been first off had the wind not changed round 180 degrees, thereby putting me at the wrong end of the line, and someone nipped out in front of me.

We got off very well at 1.50 and climbed straight up to 4,500 feet. Almost immediately we were hit by a very heavy rainstorm and water came pouring in in streams. For a solid three-quarters of an hour I had to fight with the aeroplane to keep her the right way up and on course. The Met forecast winds were utterly wrong and we went too far north but the cloud finished about fifty miles beyond Tripoli; the haze was very thick.

We went miles north-west of Djerba island and had to cut due south to the target. I knew where we were far better than the navigator and I got rather annoyed at having to follow his courses. At 4.10 went in to the north of the target area – which was about a ten mile length of road going south as far as the railway junction north of Gabes. We got some heavy flak sent up at us in the north, so went south to the junction. There was no major illumination laid on but others from 70 Squadron were already on target and everyone helped themselves.

There were aircraft everywhere and heavy flak poked up a continuous umbrella. We made four runs and started two fires in a cultivated area – covered transport we thought – and claimed a beautiful fire as a 'probable' on an ammunition train in the junction. There were bombs dropping all the time and it was difficult to know which was whose. The flak seemed pretty close all the time, even when we went down to 4,000 feet and it still threw the aircraft about in vicious jerks, being unpleasantly audible.

Later – I hear – the guns packed-up at 4.45, just fifteen minutes after our time to leave the area! Some Albacores arrived and with two sticks of flares they turned night into day, by all accounts. Excellent. A very pleasant return trip, no bad weather and landed at 6.40. Dawn broke at 5 a.m. to the dot, at 3,000 feet.

March 30th: Ops tonight take them to Sfax aerodrome, quite hot I expect. Squadron Leader Barber is 'on'. A lovely feeling of relief not being 'on' myself, and knowing it as from 9.00 in the morning. There is so much to do when one is operating; then when ops are scrubbed it all has to be done again on the morrow. Daily inspection, bombing-up, air test occasionally, seeing that the turrets are clean, guns o.k.; this takes all morning and a bit of the afternoon; hanging round the flight tent to get the latest gen of wind, and runway to use, marshalling the aircraft, briefing and getting out to the kites before take-off, all in a rush.

March 31st: Trying to find a reason – or perhaps a reasonable answer – to the perpetual questions from our Commonwealth cousins (from Canada, Australia, New Zealand, South Africa etc.) 'Why do you English always think and know – or think you know – so much about the weather, it's the main subject of any conversation with you and if not that, certainly the opening gambit among new arrivals?' How can I tell my colleagues that when scanning the skies, we lift up our eyes to Heaven, or at least the hills, 'whence cometh my strength'? It gives us – the English at least, a chance to thank the Almighty for our bountiful island, and pray that we may be allowed to return there soon, in full health and vigour if it so pleases Him.

Every other day is bliss, and the others pure Hell (if the weather can be said to play *any* part in *that* place). Today again is a summer's day, small clouds drifting about, and high stratus; the mare's tails of a front coming our way, are streaming from the north-west.

I'm taking 'V' to Sfax tonight, a moderate target, and what guns there are are said to be very accurate. 'V' is a lovely aeroplane, unfortunately she has only three ops to go before being due back in the Delta for engine changes. Jock Smith and Tubby came back today; Smith's posting is through so off he goes on 'D' tomorrow. Brown will take his crew along. I, or maybe Ken Larby, will take 'V' when she's ready. By rights of more ops per crew, I should take her down, but we shall settle that later.

'Wadi' Lawson came in today from Castel Benito. He tells me that at the moment they have 250 pranged Kittyhawks; ten come in every day and they can rebuild four a day to send off again. The place looks like Heliopolis used to look, smothered with wings and fuselages everywhere. The War-Hawks, fitted with Rolls-Royce Packard engines, never give much trouble, but the Allison engines, well, that's very different.

Marshalled 'V' at 4.00 and by my position I ought to be first off. At 5.00, Bob Lewis came back from Tripoli with a piano, apart from all the beer! For the RAF Jubilee concert we are holding tomorrow, the camp musicians got together round the piano and we had a great time. Corporal Turner plays a banjo beautifully; he even looks – as well as sings – exactly like George Formby; he'll be about the star of the show.

Ops were scrubbed, which helped the party preparations to go even better but I still had to disperse my 'V'. Had fun using the Aldis lamp out of the roof hatch as a headlamp, very effective.

April 1st: A windy morning with small cumulus clouds coming in; I expect the main front will hit us late tomorrow. We worked hard all morning getting the keys of the piano not to stick down when used. The lead weights were heavily corroded and stuck against each other. (Instead of the more usual round weights counter-sunk into the base of the keys, these were rectangular, running the full width of each key, so fouling the next in line.)

Ops were scrubbed at lunch time and three brand-new Hercules Mk IIIs arrived. Barber, Larby and I dashed out to them and brought them back to A Flight's dispersal and we are having their letters painted onto them immediately so that B Flight cannot snaffle them. Quite a lot to do getting things organised for the party tonight.

Captain Bun of the Naafi in Tripoli was brought over and he told us of the rumour that Rommel is pleading for an armistice. He is going to buy it one way or another. Will they kill him or do we have to do it?

At 5.00 I shaved and put on a blue shirt and tie, and the party started at 6.00, or should have done. The AOC arrived late – about 7.00 – and the concert had to be put off till 7.30. Eventually we sat down to dinner, fresh mutton etc, quite good, and set off for the show at 7.45.

It went down very well and the CO introduced the AOC who gave us a pep talk. The army seem to be mighty pleased with the job our chaps are doing, bombing that which officially was the wrong target! When the last Albacores left he said the fires covered at least a mile square. (More thanks to the army than to us for telling us where they wanted the bombs to land; all we had to do was to plant them. At least that's my way of looking at it.)

April 2nd: A gorgeous morning again, and I took 'V' on air test. Beat-up some camel thorn for Chubb and Mac to have some shooting from about 50 feet, something they have never done before, and very much enjoyed. The guns were pretty duff and stoppages didn't help matters. We came back a bit higher so that I could see if George was awake, but he wasn't. He kept dozing off after staying in gear for about three minutes; after that, the air pressure dropped to 30 psi and he let us slide into a very disconcerting dive, so we put him to bed again. Made a peach of a landing and brought her in.

It's a very nice aeroplane but the engines are definitely clapped-out. I shall probably take her down to the Delta after two more ops. Ken Larby now shares 'V' with me, and, as he's not taking her tonight (because I will), he has been given one of the new Mk IIIs, lucky devil.

The news is precisely the same as for the last two days, namely that the Eighth Army is just north of Quadreff, ten miles north of Gabes. It makes one think that the rumour may be right.

Again ops were scrubbed at about 1.30. Complete stand-down. Wadi Lawson came into the mess at lunch time and told me that he was reporting to the AOC that I have been flying without an automatic pilot, or second dickie. Newman doesn't think it necessary to have them, but Lawson does, for any trip likely to take over six hours, and I think maybe he's right. (One got a little tired of being regarded as one of the 'Whizz-kids' or 'Brylcream Boys'.) In other words being a fighter pilot one is supposed to be capable of anything! How little do they know! One does have to be pretty awake to do a good landing, or cope with a great variety of emergencies – with a bomb hangup for instance – and sitting in one position for 5½ hours is quite a lot.

The reason for bringing this up now, it seems, is that our targets might again be northerly, Sardinia, or Sicily, that sort of thing and some of those trips can be rather wearying, not to say hazardous in the extreme.

Went into Misurata with Newman, and we had hot showers at the Iti barracks there. The water is naturally hot from the sulphur springs, rather like Bath in Somerset – also thanks to the Romans.

Quite a party in the mess, John Elder and a type from 37 Squadron really going to town on the piano, four-handed all the time and taking turns in playing the melody while calling the harmonies to the bass by way of chord symbols.

April 4th: A dull wet morning. 'V' undergoing her 40 hour inspection. Got hold of the George Basher (a sad misnomer for this expert in aerodynamics) and we ran up the starboard engine which drives the air compressor and in no time at all found that the rudder clutch was slipping out. I left him to play with it and came back to the mess to play with the piano. We lose it tomorrow. Sad! John Elder taught me to play 'Baphoon', which was new to me, a delightful and simple piece, which sounds most effective.

Went out to 'V' again after lunch, ran-up the starboard engine again, plugged in George and he worked very well, maintaining 50 psi and so on. Back to the mess for 'Stand-by for stand down'. Ops scrubbed at 2.30 anyway.

Jock Smith, Kitson and Dennison leave for the Delta at sunrise tomorrow; I'm sorry to see them go. Tubby had told Wing what they can do with the Ops Officer job they offered him, as I so advised. I know that he'd be sick to death of it after a few weeks, though it must have considerable appeal at this moment.

Nearly one hundred Fortresses attacked Naples the other night, from some phenomenal height no doubt, and with their secret bomb sight obtained excellent results. We are now obviously only good for desert stooges, I suppose, for which it is cheaper for us to operate on anyway.

Took 'V' up on air test again, and proved to myself finally that she really is a lovely aeroplane. Such delicacy of touch and response, never a judder or a shake. Even George flew her like a bird. Newman asked me to play in a cricket match, but it was too late when I got back, but I went across to watch. It was a lovely afternoon, the cloud gradually disappeared and the larks sang on high above us, just like an English summer's day.

CHAPTER FIVE

Bombs, Dust and Victory

April 6th 1943: A wizard morning, hardly any wind and not a cloud in the sky. MacKay, Frierson and Chubb went into town for a bath as I had recommended them. Went out to 'V' to do a general DI and found the port wheel unbolted so they are probably changing the tyre as I had hoped. The walls appear to be very perished.

Went out again at a quarter to three and found a fitter and a rigger, both new to me, who had just come over from Castel Benito. The rigger had just made up a wheel to take out to 'V' when the crew of 'J' – my old ground crew pair for 'V' – claimed it as theirs, so my chaps had to start all over again and make up another! I felt a bit sick for them, but they had their orders and it was not for me to intervene.

The 'second phase' is to start today we hear, so it's maximum effort. Briefing is at a quarter to six and we take off at 7.15, so we ought to be back and in bed by 2.30 a.m. *At last*, I've got myself a pilot-type – or better known as a seat-type – parachute, on which I can sit, complete with dinghy, instead of having to grab one off its hooks on the side walls if ever I have to take to a brolly. Now I feel really at home.

I changed from shorts and shirt into battle-dress, had tea and marshalled the aircraft. Being so late my position was rather poor but after briefing I found that we and the other nine machines nearest to the Chance light were to start up first, so all was well. As soon as the engines were running, Frierson told me that the aerial was not getting any current. We called for the duty mechanic, and by the time I was ready, all was o.k.

We took off at 7.14 and climbed straight to 3,000 feet. It was getting quite dark and the new moon was just above the haze horizon. Plonked in George and he worked marvellously; did all my turns for me, with just a twiddle of my fingers. You pull the 'Turn lever' back into its notch, hold the control switch to On for as many seconds as needed and 'Bob's your uncle'. We went out dead on track, with no need to drop any incendiaries to check our drift since we got those from bearings from the beacons which were working for a change, and our position from loop bearings.

We crossed the coast and the moon (having set by then) left us his illuminated Venus to light our way. She was so bright that she made a silver streak across the water towards us. At 9.15 we spied Kneice Island and went north to Mahares which we could not see from the coast, so waited for our 'Time over Target', which was 9.30. One flare was dropped dead on time which made us think that the Albacores were looking for a place to illuminate for us; we stooged up and down the road but no illumination came. At 10.05, we went from south-west to north-east and dropped four flares along the road; three lorries, miles apart and stationary were all we saw. Only about four other flares were dropped and we seemed to be doing all the work. There was a closely wooded patch beside the road and we bombed it in the hope of finding some hidden transport, but no joy.

Then we dropped our other two flares, but nothing was to be seen. We dropped our third stick of bombs along the road to Mahares (nearly into the town in fact) and took our photograph at the same time. Turned over Mahares and bombed that which looked like a parking square, just on the west side of the town. No fires. By now it was 11.25 so we turned for home.

George brought us back at 165 mph, minus $\frac{1}{2}$ lb boost and 1,800 revs. Got a 'green' straightaway and came in. Turned into the final approach at 500 feet slap on the green of the glide-path indicator and it changed to yellow, almost at once. I was always taught that your engine – or engines – are an aid to judgement, *not* a substitute, so as a general practice, particularly with these floating kites called Wimpys, I glide to a three-point landing as part of the fun. On this occasion I did just that, seeing the yellow, shut the engines to nothing, put on full flap and even at something like 100 feet over the Chance light we still had runway to spare.

The Group Captain came to interrogation, I think to apologise. We landed *down* wind in a 15-20 mph air stream. He had seen eight aircraft overshoot and go round again; we were the third to land.

Three photos from the whole squadron, and we got two of them. The second was from somebody else's flash, which opportunely went off at the right time for us. The only danger was the other machines which we passed only too close and too often.

Medium effort tonight, maximum tomorrow, and then I shall be *on.* The army is going full blast northwards.

One of B Flight's aircraft's engines cut, on fire on take-off, as we heard later. He dropped his nine 500-pounders (which were rodded but not fused), at 300 feet and none of them went off, so he belly-landed safely. Tonight, one of B Flight's circuits and bumps aircraft, a Mk III, pranged also, after both engines cut. Practically, every prang and the last two kites lost, were theirs!

April 9th: The news yesterday was that the Yanks have linked up with the Eighth Army, and a great offensive drive by the US Ninth Army has begun.

A hard gale blowing the whole day, just a sea breeze on a large scale, which accounts for our landing down wind on the land breeze at 12.30 the other night. Sand and dust blowing up all the time, making our air test impossible. One big gust of wind caught the mess at 12.30 and we thought it would come down but it held surprisingly well.

Did my DI on 'V'. The compass seems to rattle about a lot so told the instrument section to have a look at it, and also the oxygen control valve is leaking.

Reading through the intelligence reports I saw that 127 Spitfires are already on Cyprus, and every now and then bag a Ju88. If our position is – as rumoured – that from now on we stay out for a second tour here, I'll work on getting myself posted to them so when the front begins, I'll be well placed for the offensive in that corner.

Wood came into the mess at 9.30 with the latest gen. The NZs have gone north, after coming in from the west and last night were thirty miles nor-nor-west of Sfax. The Eighth Army had knocked out a two-division tank attack further south near the coast, and sent Jerry scooting north. The day before, fighter bombers and light bombers had destroyed 130 MT and tanks, plus 200 others damaged.

April 11th: At 3.10 the news came through of an early take-off so we didn't bother to marshal the aircraft. Briefing was held up towards the end until photographs of the target arrived. Taken this afternoon and delivered to us by 5.00; nice work by somebody. The

Myself with Pilot Officer MacNamara, soon after we both joined 70 Squadron to fly Wellingtons.

'V for Victory', 70 Squadron, April 1943. My first wholly-crewed kite. *Standing, l to r*: Tubby Chubb (rear gunner, Canada), Junior Frierson (wireless operator, Australia), Snowy (myself, England), Arthur Parry (navigator, England) Mac Mackay (front gunner, Scotland); *ground crew*, Paddy Harris (rigger, Ireland), Clem Clements (fitter, England).

aerodrome which is our target is said to have 60 aircraft on it and the whole area is covered with craters. Obviously pattern-bombing by Baltimores and so on.

We took off at 6.40, five minutes before time actually but we were second off. It was rather lovely chasing the sunset, flying at 5,000 feet we had a perfect haze horizon. Slowly this haze and darkness closed-in from behind and engulfed us.

We had nearly half a moon, and turning right over Zuara soon arrived at Djerba Island. We crossed straight over the finger north of the town, and as it grew really dark, the moon's light seemed to be more penetrating and we crossed Kerkenna islands as if by day. Sergeant Harris (NZ) was flying then (he brought a plane and crew out from England and came as my second dickie for experience).

Eventually at 9.20 we arrived at the target area – just off the coast. I took over here and with the moon over the land we could read the coast-line comfortably, and the salt lakes.

We had rather fun 'probing the defences', weaving amply and just over the sea we got all the guns to fire at us and soon picked a spot at which to go in. Just north of Sousse, the coast runs north and south. The landing-ground of St Marie is a mile or so inland, north of the salt lake and some eight miles north of Sousse. Almost equidistant from each other were the groups of guns, possibly a mile or so apart, A, B, C, and D. There were four light and two heavies at A, one heavy on its own at B, four light at C and four heavies at D, just south of the lake. A big fire was burning in Sousse, which we thought was probably Jerry destroying stores.

Our time over target was 10.15 to 10.45 and we went in at 10.10. While spotting our entry point, at 9.50 actually, a Wimpy got four direct hits from a battery just south of the target, burst into flames and broke up as it went down. Not a pretty sight, and it gave Harris more experience than he probably hoped to see. We stooged around and dropped a flare, but its parachute streamed and it spun straight in. We turned and tried again; couldn't see much but a long graded strip which we took to be a runway and dropped three bombs on it at 45 degrees. A beautiful stick, the first and last on the edge, and the middle one slap in the centre. It sent up a huge cloud of dust, so we dropped our flash bomb and hoped to get a picture, but the hatch had vibrated back halfway across the camera.

The second stick went onto the eastern edge of the western extension of the landing ground and the third on the buildings between the two LGs. All the aircraft had been removed; they usually are once our recce kite has been over, but all our bombs went home and must have done some good damage.

By now it was 10.55 so we turned for home. We made four exposures on the camera, turning it by hand and possibly got a snap shot – thanks to three other flash bombs which someone had provided, but all ours were fogged. George brought us along very steadily at 165 mph, minus 1 lb boost and 1800 revs with weak mixture. We had gone in at 9,000 feet and bombed at 6,000 to 5,000. Over Kerkenna and Djerba islands I flashed ...-, ...-, ...-, repeatedly on the downward identification light just for fun. On the wireless we heard the 'news', and got some good dance music all the way home.

The wing tanks were finally empty and the engines cut just after Castel Benito. I had gone up to 4,000 feet just as a precaution but was down to 3,200 before the nacelle tanks gave us the juice we needed. We got four 'Reds' due to others on the circuit, but at last landed. A peach, because the ground is like a billiards table. I was the most astonished of the crew; they were delighted. Switched off with 20 gallons of gravy left, i.e. about 12 minutes fuel, after 7 hours 10 minutes flying time.

April 12th: At briefing I met Arthur Parry and Chubb; they had heard of 'B' being scrubbed but nothing of our new mount 'X'. Parry took notes on a piece of paper and Chubb rushed off to collect Mac and Frierson. We dashed out in the flight commander's truck and eventually got there – B Flight seem to be miles away from the rest of us. There were no two volt accumulators for the intercom, so I sent the fitter running for them from the spares truck by the Chance light. I had marshalled her after bombing-up and we all went off in fine style. No overtaking in the line!

April 13th: We were off at 7.50. Very hazy and the moon not much use. We went out at 5,000 feet above a little low stratus and under 6/10th cumulus. All the beacons were out at Castel Benito, and we soon realised why. The guns at Tripoli were firing like mad. A convoy was being unloaded in the harbour and they were being attacked. I learned later that our Beaufighters got one torpedo bomber.

After Djerba I handed over to Dickie and half sat in the front turret. Eventually about an hour before ETA (Estimated Time of Arrival) we left all the cloud behind us. The guns were firing at Hammamet point, which was clearly visible towards the moon in the west. I took over and weaved up and down the coast, slowly climbing to 7,000 feet. There appeared to be only one gun firing about a mile south of our landing ground target, but Jerry is using those beastly flashless guns that are hardly fair, we feel, so there may well be others of which we know not!

At 11.08 I ran in over the coast, watching only the position of the gun I had seen firing. It fired immediately and I gently turned away from it when suddenly a huge explosion lit up the sky off my port wing, about 1,000 feet above. A great display of Very cartridges rose fan-shaped higher still, and seemed to hang poised in the shape of a multi-coloured umbrella canopy. Despite the enormity of the explosion the Wimpy appeared to be in one piece, but alight from stem to stern so that the geodetic frame was silhouetted against the flaming interior, all fabric having gone. It then became a flaming comet, slowly trailing into the deck, where it left a huge V of burning petrol and aluminium on the northern edge of the drome.

We dropped our first stick along the southern boundary at 10.10, 'first blitz'. Flared it and turned west for the second blitz, dropping our 12-hour delay bombs onto it. Flew 'straight and level' for a horrible length of time until our photo-flash bomb went off, and then home. Tried to economise on juice this trip and after an uneventful journey home landed with 100 gallons in the wing tanks, and the nacelles full!

We were the fourth kite in to land. A quick interrogation, breakfast and to bed at 4.00. Cockerels were crowing in the Senussi camps and the larks singing on high. Rather lovely these peaceful sounds so far from, yet so near to, the barbaric noises of war.

I forgot to mention that the Jerry night-fighters were up last night. Chandelier flares were dropped over us and a Me109 – as clear as daylight – passed head-on about 50 feet away and 15 feet above our starboard wing. We saw each other for just that split second, but time stood still and I got a stationary picture of him just off our bows before he flashed by. I turned onto his tail but he had gone.

I woke up again at 8.30, and at 9.30 decided that I could not sleep again so got up. Went over to B Flight office and wrote up the engine log of 'X'. I was very pleased with the petrol consumption, having gone out at minus ½ lb boost and 1,900 rpm on weak mixture, and returned at minus 1½ lbs boost, 1,750 rpm with weak mixture.

Barber met me shortly after and we whistled off with Spurdens and Shafto to Castel Benito to pinch two Mk Xs which had been seen there yesterday. We were off by 11.35 and I took several snapshots of the take-off and camp, and of CB when we arrived at 12.30. Tripoli harbour had about 25 ships in, and two sunk in the middle. The Mk Xs had gone off to India so we mooched about and came back at 2.45.

'Spud' Tate, Shafto and I took turns in flying. I took more snapshots of Homs but when we turned to take some of Leptis Magna, Barber reminded us that we had to be home early. I took over, brought her back and landed. We learned the sad news that we lost four officers in the blow-up last night; Jack March, Holloway (of Netherhall Gardens), Baxter and John Elder. That aerodrome – Korbia – has several satellites and there is a reduced effort onto them tonight.

Jerry now has only eight landing grounds left to him so we are systematically destroying them. His fighters still use Pantellaria Island too much for our liking. The Me109 probably came from there. Pantellaria and Menzel Temime are on our black list, though we do nothing about them. For God's sake, why not? (Possibly because no one has reported any losses due to night-fighters, as yet!)

The Eighth Army is now battering its way through Enfidaville, about thirty miles north of Sousse. The people of the town welcomed them with flowers and bouquets!

April 16th: Very busy day again. Only fifteen aircraft required each night now – conserving strength? So we are on tonight. 37 Squadron took it last night with 40 Squadron, and each one lost a kite; night fighters from Pantellaria suspected. I tried to get 'B' ready but on run-up she burst a hydraulic pipe so the tank will have to come out again. A new Mk X arrived at lunch-time and we decided that I should take her in 'B''s place.

Looking her over, I disliked her from the very first for I felt that we had been 'done'. She was very old; type 1C windows even, above the wing, and she was plastered all over with bits and bobs, inside and out; I have to work the TR9 from the control column and so on. By 3.10 we had got all the overload tanks out of her, plus the paper wrappings from many items of stores, the crew's orange peel and so much rubbish, and we took her up on test. The captain says he had nothing but trouble with her all the way out; or so I learned later. She behaved very well and has a good AP; she does vibrate rather a lot.

Landed at 3.45 to hear the briefing was at 4.30. Only one gun working in the turrets so the armourers worked like fiends to clear the duff 4B (tracer) ammo and charge the guns. I dashed off, had a biscuit and a cup of tea, changed and rushed down to briefing. All went well and I was about to start up at 5.45 when the CO drove up telling me that I was only the 'spare aircraft and crew'. Knowing something of the serviceability record I decided to taxi out and wait. All but 'H' went off so we flew in its place ... 'Sorry "H", whoever you are.'

These Mk Xs certainly have a good take-off but throughout the trip I found her slower per pound of boost and revs per minutes than the Mk III. We went out in a very dull haze at 3,000 feet. No beauteous sunset to watch, just overcast greyness. The moon soon helped us along and we timed it beautifully going out at about 143 mph all the way. Turned at Zuara across to Djerba and Kneice Islands then went due north to the target. We came up west of the 4,000 feet mountain, turned right over the 'race-course' and ran in just on 9.50, (our first blitz period) going north-east, and dropped the stick along a curving line of aircraft bays of the drome.

The flares were further east and so the moon did our illuminating – the flares only made a rather disconcerting pool of light in the haze. The delayed action bombs straddled one bay and the two high explosives landed one on each side of a bay, and Frierson was overjoyed. The whole thing simply disrupted and flew up towards us, powered by much more than the explosive we dropped onto it.

We were at 3,800 feet, then we climbed away in various turns when someone was hit and caught fire. He flew on, straight and level. Three, possibly four, were seen to bale out by one of our crew, but slowly it dived in a curve to vertical into the north side of the drome. It was one of 462 Squadron; they have only four serviceable Halifaxes now, and have been given Wellington Mk 1cs to operate on; it was one of these.

Then turning south, we headed back in again, and seeing about eight bays, north-west to south-east, swung slightly east and let them go; it was beautiful! I turned hard left to see them go in. From the third bomb a fire burst-out in about four lumps, the second of these going up in blue and white explosions. Our job over, we turned for home. Fifteen minutes south I was thinking of putting George in charge, there being no more jinking required so far south of the lines, when suddenly from a wadi a big green bubble appeared and spluttered ... then it reached us. Green tracer shells came pouring over the port wing – I must have put her on her side quicker than that, having spied the ominous bubble – and Chubb said he could have caught the stuff as it appeared to flow over the tail. I next saw this stream over the starboard wing as it soared over the top of us while we were flying on our side. Just like Very cartridges with flames about ten inches long and five inches wide. It gave us quite a surprise, coming as it must have done from our own lines, but we were soon on our way home. Flying, as we were at 3,000 feet at the time, we must have been a perfect silhouette against the high white ceiling of stratus cloud, with the moon above that.

Frierson found some good music on the wireless. Carol Gibbons, Geraldo? We shall never know. Parry took our spirits to ecstatic heights, by playing the part of a night club cabaret compère, as if we were at the Café de Paris (before destroyed by bombing) or maybe even now the Savoy? He was hilarious, describing the celebrities and 'guest' with great wit and imagination ... telling one little boy ... 'Don't wipe your lollipop on that gentleman's suit, you'll get it all covered with fluff!'

April 18th: Lots of silly rumours have been heard about our recent losses being due to the six-hour delay pistols fitted (and possibly being energised) when screwed into the bombs, therefore blowing up the kite six hours later. In other words, there are no 'flashless guns' knocking us out of the sky, just our own cargoes! Today the bombs were fused this afternoon so if the rumour is true, the whole line of marshalled aircraft will blow up.

April 19th: Tubby came over this evening, very glad to see him. Last night was the first out of six consecutive nights that the Group has *not* lost a machine. One theory is an aerial acoustic mine which can be sent up time and again till it sends someone elsewhere! There was no trouble with the delayed action pistols so perhaps the bad rumourmongers are convinced.

April 20th: A really wizard day, tremendously hot and the whole time one has that cool feeling from continuous evaporation. 37 Squadron went to two landing grounds last night, just east of those on the southern shore of the Gulf of Tunis, one flight doing each target. 'V' is to have a scrounged VSG pump fitted, (now returned with her reconditioned engines) and I shall air test her this afternoon. We learned at lunch time that take-off is due at 12.30. It's good to learn the times in the morning, then there's no rush.

'B' (our new Mk X unflown by Spud or me on Ops) has now been ordered for Malta. She is to be fitted for torpedo dropping and the boys on that job deserve the highest-powered kites they can get.

No 462 Squadron had a hell of a burn-up this morning, when one of the bombs went off while bombing up the kite. A Halifax carries a lot of petrol.

April 21st: When that Halifax blew up yesterday – incidentally killing fourteen people – a sergeant walking with an airman beside him about 100 yards away lost his voice for three days. Turning to speak to the airman he found himself talking to a headless trunk, with blood spurting skywards from its severed neck. A bomb splinter had carried the airman's head clean away, in that fraction of a second before the blast put them both flat on the deck.

When I heard the bang, I jumped; a thing I've never done before, but seeing those three kites going down in flames on successive ops only affects me long afterwards; and then only while on the ground with nothing to do.

April 22nd: A morning of hard work, cleaning-up 'V'. Oil spots had collected the dust, the de-icing grease had melted, as it always does out here, and left sandy streamers down the rudder and over the wings. There happened to be a few extra riggers hanging about so we all got busy with bits of shirt and petrol in incendiary containers. It took all morning, but now, patched-up with black dope over the usual red patches she looks almost as new.

The hyraulic oil was leaking from the power feed pipes on both windscreen wipers, so these we blanked-off. It was very hot, working or not, and we would have given pounds for a few mugs of ale.

(We have had a lot of trouble getting even water. Our lorry takes the Jerricans into town – the Bowser has broken-down, and apparently our Jerricans are always confiscated! Who is running this war anyway? Obviously not us.)

Perhaps it is this lack of baths, showers, or even a decent wash, let alone a bathe in the sea that reminds me of Father's favourite bathroom ditty ...

Water is the finest thing that man to man may bring,
But who am I that I should ask the best of any thing?
Let princes revel in the brook, and peers with the pump make free,
while whisky, wine or even ale is good enough for me!

Listening to the Yank news in the mess, we heard that they made a daylight raid on Bremen – unescorted! They claim to have shot down 95 of the attacking fighter aircraft numbering 160! The rest of the news was lost due to wholesale laughter for everyone there knew full well that no observer in the air could count 160 fighters coming in at various times. They lost 16 Fortresses anyway, which was sad enough. (One fighter for one bomber would be a good dividend for the Jerry, so why not 16 fighters downed, with 16 Fortresses lost? That's more likely to be the true picture.)

Secret wireless in Warsaw reports 35,000 Jews are being or have been executed by 'order'. The streets echo with the shots and screams of the men, women and children being mown down in compounds.

April 25th: A beautiful morning, and why not? It's Easter Sunday, not a cloud in the sky, and for some unknown reason a *cool* fresh breeze from the east.

We got 'V' serviceable again and I took her up for five minutes to test the starboard feathering gear and the flaps under the new VSG pump; all okay.

Some larks have built a nest very close to 'V's' dispersal point, in the roots of a camel thorn. It is very spherical, about 3½ inches in diameter. Yesterday there were two eggs; today, there are three! The 'Victory Triplets' the crew call them as our 'V' is always V for *Victory*, not the orthodox 'Victor.'

Somebody told me that Jerry has only 30,000 troops left in Tunisia so we'll not be expected to operate for five days, when the evacuation of his troops is expected; we keep eight aircraft standing by, just in case.

'V' is really looking first-class now. We have new fabric between the front turret and the fuselage, black paint everywhere, and she looks almost new. Clements lent me a file – almost more of a rasp – with which I carved grooves in the soft celluloid covering of the control column 'spectacles'. For one thing the shining surface reflected too much light from the instruments (I always turn off the lights, leaving the painted luminosity to do the work) and secondly if my hands are wet with perspiration, I don't have to grip the thing so hard, thanks to the corrugations now imposed.

The Eighth Army is now reported to be within thirty-six miles of Tunis, and the First Army, only twenty-four miles. The whole front is only 120 miles long; looks like time to start airing our blue uniforms?

April 26th: Another very hot day, we did our daily inspection on the kite and there's a leak on the constant speed unit in a pipe or a washer.

There are rumours of another offensive somewhere in the Med. We shall shortly be doing double ops from Ben Gardane; probably the day after tomorrow the fun will begin. According to the 'news' we are knocking out 40 to 70 tanks every battle.

Two cases of typhus in 462 Squadron. The disease is carried by fleas so all our tents have to be treated with dusting powder. Had a marvellous sleep all afternoon, a thing I rarely do but my head-ache is as bad as ever, Aspirins don't help. Went out to 'V' again after tea and they have done a wonderful job but it was getting too late so we decided to run it up tomorrow.

Darts are lately becoming a rage, and the whole mess took part in a match – at cricket! Joe Lush, as slap-happy as ever, was knocking down wickets like nine-pins. Everybody now takes delight in going round the bend every evening – must be the Chianti?

April 28th: A very hot day again, and no wind. I went straight out to 'V' to find that Clements had run the engines and both were dry as bones. Thank Heaven for that!

The air gunners report to their section half an hour after we do so

I intended giving her a quick flip and straight down again but as Clements went off to tell the duty pilot of my intention, Barber drew up in his truck and out jumped Frierson, Chubb and Mac so we all went off together.

The props feathered perfectly and she flew very comfortably on one engine. Tested the rear turret south of here, but the guns would not fire on automatic; individually and hand-operated they fire well. I came straight back and landed for there was nothing for me to do, but I managed to get a syringe for Harris, our rigger. He had been told that there were none in the stores, but knowing that they always keep two for emergencies I got one of them. It was nearly 12.00 so I helped them cover up, then took them back to lunch.

I met MacKay and Chubb back at the flight tent after we had cleared our tents – they reek of moth-balls now – with the flight pick-up and an armourer corporal. He couldn't get the guns to fire either, even though I had run the engines to provide the servo power. The guns in the front turret are okay according to inspection, but also won't fire!

These forward guns are much more important to us now than those at the rear since we are most unlikely to meet night-fighter opposition doing battle stooges. But, if we do find transport convoys etc after one of our rodded bombing raids, the idea is to get down to deck level and straff them off the road. Engines bone dry after air test, so all leaks now rectified.

A captured Savoia Macchetti 79 landed after tea, looks rather like an overgrown Anson. Exceedingly light controls – on the ground anyway.

April 30th: A very hot dusty day again, south-east wind of about 25 mph. We eventually got the front guns to fire and found that the link shutes are jamming the belts. The rear turret is serviceable, all but for the Palmer firing gear on the left hand guns. Ops were *on* again, but were scrubbed at lunch-time as usual.

I had a marvellous sleep till 4.00 after lunch, but had a horrible dream of having taken off on ops quite automatically then at about 500 feet realised that I was losing height. Eased back on the stick and watched the air speed indicator and found that I couldn't see it properly. Switched on the dashboard lights, but no light came. Tried to call the crew on the intercom but no joy. The horizon was very hazy and I could hardly see, then I began to feel that this is what happened when chaps prang for no obvious reason just after take-off.

I could hear Doc's voice saying, 'What bad luck, wonder what happened?' and then other recognisable voices said the same thing while I was frantically trying to read the instruments. Felt more and more sleepy, banged on the door to attract Frier's attention, but again no joy. At last I just could not stay awake any longer, collapsed over the stick and thankfully woke up. (Probably the cheese of the welsh rarebit we had for lunch).

Barber told me that Mac had left the covers off his turret so I raked him out and helped him to fit them. We are not likely to be raided by bombers at night, but reflexion off the perspex even from the moonlight can be seen a long way. Furthermore both guns and turrets would be rendered useless very quickly if the sand is allowed to settle in the many available resting places. (If the turret cannot be turned back to front, there would be no chance for the rear gunner to bale out of a burning kite.)

CHAPTER SIX

Which Way from Here?

May 4th 1943: The weather a great deal better today. The wind is steady from the north, and cool at that. I felt particularly brassed off so didn't do much. I did the DI of the kite and left the armourers to carry on working on the turrets.

Sixteen aircraft required for tonight, so I'll take 'V'; she'll like that. It's a strange feeling of anticipation one feels when ops have for so long been cancelled. You begin to wonder what the opposition will be like and so on, but it all went smoothly.

It was a fairly late take-off, briefing at 8.45. We went down to find 37 Squadron still being briefed and we got in at 9.15 when the AOC gave us a short message ... 'The end is beginning.' A few all-night jobs to soften him up, then a few maximum efforts and it will all be over, and we – poor Bs – carry on bombing strategically rather than tactically, which means Sicily every night from the new drome at the holy city of Kairouan. The jobs ought to be fairly regular and simple, even with Pantellaria and its night-fighters in the way.

We took off at 10.15 into the darkest night I have known here. I lived that horrid dream again. All the instruments 'stuck' in position – correct, but were they stuck? One just hangs on and puts one's trust in the one and only.

We went out at 3,000 feet and soon were flying over low cloud that hid everything, and the stars above were clear; no longer hazy. I had a flight sergeant second dickie who had been sick and had never flown a Mk III or used a George. He was extraordinarily competent and took to it like a duck to water.

We were completely lost, kept crossing the coast at the wrong sort of angles, and when we should not have been anywhere near the coast! The ground haze was very thick and one could see the ground only directly beneath us.

We took bearings off various radio beacons which put us all over

Africa in position, so we just had to carry on on dead reckoning. The cloud blanketed all visual beacons. We flew over a huge convoy with lights ablaze about twenty miles south of the line. The cloud dispersed to patches and later, to nil.

I flew on northwards and came to the salt-lakes just south of Menzel Temime. Not a shot fired at us so turned south and soon the Army letters, TEL & K made of paraffin flares – about 100 yards apart – were lit; at least the T and the E were. These were to be lit in the centre of each of the four corps, about eight miles behind our lines.

Turned over the 'E' and some clot from America fired at us: four well placed shots close under the tail. We were climbing up to 10,000 feet so it didn't worry us unduly, 'unless there are more to come?' said someone. On ETA we dropped a flare and below us was the target area, a wadi and roads. Then the intercom went dead and all the fun and games began.

The second dickie had to hurdle the main spar to tell Frierson when to drop the flares, and get the photo-flash bomb started. Every now and then I felt four to six sharp 'cracks' buffet the aircraft but could not see any guns firing or flashes in the air. Most people find these flashless guns most worrying, but for myself, not seeing anything, they don't worry me.

The haze was very thick and the flares – about four altogether – made the world a ball of hazy light in which one felt like a solitary black spot to anyone on the deck. We probably were. At 10,000 feet there were 7/10ths stratus of about 50 feet thickness. It was a lovely blanket to play in, like a porpoise, but it was wasting time. We came down to 8,000 feet and, as we had been in the target area for about half an hour already, (looking for a suitable target while hoping to get the intercom repaired) we decided to bomb and get home before the gravy ran out.

So, by forewarning Parry of the run-up to the target (no intercom so I couldn't talk to him), I opened the bomb doors, which brings on the light on his panel, and flew straight and level across the wadi and road. Down went the stick of nine 250-pounders (rodded). Beautiful to watch, tearing up the wadi and the road. I turned left-handed and suddenly the photo-flash went off so Parry turned the camera film over by hand (the machine was u/s). Then we lined up on the road this time and down went the other nine. I peeled off, rather steeply I'm afraid. It terrified the crew for a second, but, not having any intercom to warn them, at least they could not swear back – not until we got back on the ground that was, by which time all was forgiven!) I just wanted to see how they had landed because Parry could not give me the usual guidance of 'left, left, steady at that' etc. We got round in time to see them plod, every one of them like great fiery footsteps along the road up the wadi. More luck than judgement, but never mind; the job was done.

Starting for home, we had to guess the position of the letter 'E', (position and distance being quite critical). We all agreed which way to go before taking it, but the capacious cockpit can hold a remarkable number of types who wish to argue their viewpoint into bared ears (all at my expense! Or was it?). We flew slap over the Red Beacon at Fauconnerie, dead on track – for which I thanked them. Still no cloud when we went over the centre of Kneice Island. It really was a 'piece of cake' – pity was, we didn't have any with us, and it's a long way to Groppi's from here!

Shortly after passing Djerba Island the cloud covered everything, so we turned for home on ETA. At 4.04 the first light of dawn showed. We were doing 160 mph so I opened up a bit to push her along at 165. The stratus at 1,000 foot was a beautiful greeny-blue satin-like quilt with a symmetrical pattern in it, and one felt with tremendous compulsion that one must *touch* it, to ascertain that it really was as soft and gentle, and uniform as it appeared.

The mountains around Castel Benito protruded and were closely shrouded with mist, so that they appeared snow-covered. Very high up was an enormous V of mackerel sky, quite twenty miles long in each leg, with a red-coloured belly given to it by the invisible rising sun. I hoped it was for the chaps on the ground who would surely see it, after all they've been through, *Victory* must be theirs.

As we came near to the drome we called for a QPM (bearing onto drome) as cloud was at 500 feet and obscured all sight of land. It was just after 5.00 and quite light so we flew rolling and sliding and porpoising about with everyone in the 'office' to enjoy the fun through this quilt of exquisite early morning nature. It was rather fun doing the circuit from 200 feet. The camp was hard to recognise from such an unusual height, but we came straight in and landed at 5.50. Quickly interrogated and to bed.

The flies made sleep impossible and at 10.00 I roused myself, a most reluctant but necessary effort, to string up my Mosi-net, and so slept till 12.00.

The op last night for us was good; only 7 out of 16 kites found the target, two photographs were taken, and one was mine, a good one. After lunch I took it down to Intelligence and pin-pointed it on their map.

Maximum effort tonight but Ted is taking 'V'. The AOC tells us that two fresh divisions of armour have gone up to the front, and the whole ring closes at 4.00 tomorrow morning. They expect to be in Tunis within thirty-six hours from then. So that's that. A long awaited airgraph letter from A; wrote a letter in reply.

May 6th: Coming back to yesterday morning, I was amazed to see the colour coming back into the desert. After the hot dry southerly winds the desert was *yellow*, as one would expect perhaps, but this northerly wind, damp from the sea and heavy dews again brought the cultivated earth to a rich brown, and a new green to the half-ripened crops. As I went to bed last night, the earth smelt sweet, of fresh hay almost.

This morning the wind is in the south again, as yet quite cool but hot gusts foretell the future. The translation of *Khamsin* is 'a fifty day wind' so the odd days from the north are just a God-send.

'Bobby' Shafto force-landed at Fauconnerie and Slater flew over La Goulette and had his hydraulics shot away. They were diverted to Castel Benito and came back here at between seven and eight. Weather much better last night, all the beacons were visible and the 'A' signal in its proper place.

A letter from Cookie, Bay's very dear Canadian Navy friend, just off on his way home on leave. No gen on the target at tea-time, though take-off was to be at 7.15. In case it was postponed, we marshalled just in case.

Briefing at 5.45, after a rapid half-eaten tea supper. Still no target was given us, so waited on 'readiness' in the mess. At 9.30, we were noddingly thinking of bed, because we *have* to leave the target before 4.00, when at 9.35 came the 'Scramble': two roads, very restricted, from Pont du Fars to Tunis.

Off the deck at 11.15, very dark, no stars and thick haze. No low cloud so all the beacons were plainly visible. After Gabes we went up to 8,000 feet and it was terribly hot, 24 degrees C in the cockpit. The plane felt as if it were flying in a vacuum; horribly bumpy, with the air speed indicator going from 80 to 200 mph for no reason other than air pockets; that's very rare at this height.

Later we ran into a heavy rainstorm and all the artillery flashes went invisible, but the 'T' and the 'E' paraffin flares were plain to be seen. It was very tiring flying in such haze, high cloud obliterating the stars, and so with no horizon all jinking had to be done on instruments, which made my eyes weep with pain and strain.

We set course from the 'T' and dropped three flares. The third went off, the first two being failures. Took a good look and then set course for the 'E'. Dropped a flare over our spot and it lit; showing us that we were just where we were the first time! The maps look so different from the real thing and it takes time to make absolutely sure you're in the right place. We dropped two sticks, a five and a seven of 250-pounders, of NI rodded, very nicely over the roads and wadis just about five miles north of Pont du Fars. Our photo-flash went off about ten seconds early so our photo did not come out. Owing to four flare failures, we were left with five bombs and no flares! We wandered to and fro over the area, went a bit too far north looking towards Tunis and were *hotly* received.

Eventually at 2.30 (our time to leave the target area) we thought of going home but so few people had dropped flares as yet. We thought we would wait a little longer in the hope of getting rid of our remainder profitably. Almost as we decided to hang on for a bit, B Flight turned up and with the help of their flares we were able to drop our remainders on a useful 'Y' junction of a road. And so home, after a pleasant trip of 6 hours 25 minutes.

Last night the armies were twelve miles from Tunis, and nine from Bizerta. According to the timetable, they should be in Tunis by 4.00.

And they made it! News at 5.00 told us of fighting in the outskirts. 9.00: the docks taken; 10.00: Tunis and Bizerta have fallen!

2,500 sorties: a record for aircraft over the Tunis area yesterday. The squadron record was that 346 tons of bombs were dropped onto the Jerry positions last month.

'Z' of B Flight returned early with engine trouble. He circuited the drome then left to jettison his bombs in the desert. He returned on the 90 degree leg and went round again, dived, climbed again and dived into the deck and blew up with his 'hang-up bombs'; that at 10.55.

May 8th: BBC confirmed that Tunis and Bizerta fell, at 10.40 last night.

The weather over the target was much better last night and

nearly everyone got there. The rear gunner got away from that prang last night; he was thrown about 60 yards and landed with a cut on one leg, grazed hands and face. No such luck for the others.

Harris also had to come back, with a bad oil leak. The GC had left instructions for returning aircraft to jettison only half of their bombs; bloody stupid for anyone flying and hoping to land with only one and a half or only one engine. That's why the crew were blown up last night when they pranged.

Harris's wireless operator applied the Nelson Touch and they dropped *all* their bombs. 'K', another B Flight kite, is missing. Three new crews and aircraft arrived, all to go to B Flight.

Stand-down was rung through at 9.30. Mac landed here after being re-fuelled at Castel Benito. He went up to 16,000 feet over an occlusion, then had to jettison his bombs because his distributor got stuck, but all this took place over the target area, he tells me.

Our photographs of last night did come out after all but the flash being so close behind the aircraft fogged the first half of the film. It plainly shows the roads and railway near Seprienne.

May 9th: Up early this morning and saw the Doc about getting my X-ray seen to. He says okay if Barber agrees and this he did without any ado. (Doc thinks that the accumulation of dust and congenital catarrh is causing some blockage of my sinuses and a chronic infection there may be the reason for the outburst of boils in a less well fortified area, such as the bone of my head!)

Maybe this is my chance to get back on Spits, east or west, north or south, I am not in a fit state to care much. In any event things are going to move fast now – including the squadron no doubt – and there is no knowing how long the medics will want to keep me as their guinea pig. I hurriedly packed all my tent kit as well as my bag. The Group advance party was leaving today and I might be separated for weeks.

I dashed over to Wing and collected some money, then a quick lunch, and we set off at 1.15. The driver said he knew the track so we headed south-west for two hours and this worried me a bit. I asked him if he really knew it and he admitted that he was lost! We went on for a little and came across a track heading north-east which, to my mind, was a more correct heading. We took it and found ourselves going over a disused but heavily mined Jerry airfield; 'L for Leather' over that one!

Found ourselves looking at a fort, Bir Dufan, which we had passed an hour before, so this time we took a track heading north west, very little used. After about ten miles it turned west into the hills so we took a caravan route north which was very good going till we got to within twenty miles of the coast. At that point the track which had only carried camels and donkeys ran through steep wadis, and loose gravel river beds. That 3-tonner did things most tanks would not tackle. Eventually after four hours we got onto the coast road, only about twenty miles west of Misurata, but it had been interesting.

I saw a heron-like bird, brown with 2-inch bands of black, white and black again at the wing tips. Span abut 2′ 9″. Then, on a mud wall about twenty feet away, a true Blue Bird, exactly like the stuffed one Bay was given after her performance in Maeterlinck's *Blue Bird* fairy tale. In flight it's rather like a magpie, pale blue all over except for the last three inches of wings on which the trailing edges were royal blue completely.

Camels tread the corn here to thresh out the grain, which the Arabs *pull*, and do not cut. Two donkeys tied together pull the head of the camel round over the 10-foot diameter area of piled corn, or two camels tied head to tail, prodded by a boy.

Cornering too fast in our lorry we suffered a prang, not too serious, just a burst tyre but we arrived in Tripoli by 9 p.m. What a marvellous place, this Whadden Casino. It was German army headquarters until so few weeks ago. The Whadden gazelle is the house mascot; its image is engraved on all the glass and cutlery, and embroidered on the table and bed linen.

I had been frozen riding in the back of the lorry wearing only shirt and shorts; to arrive at the warm hotel, to wash in a porcelain basin, to have high ceilings above me, walls to echo the noise of voices, clean neat waiters, glass and crockery – in lieu of chipped enamel mugs – a piano and violin being played in the musicians' gallery ... almost too much for the tired and weary, but how enervating? What could be better for the beginning of a holiday, no matter how short-lived?

And so to bed, after a glorious dinner of service rations imaginatively camouflaged, with an ice cream for pudding. My waiter speaks no English, but the Chianti must have helped my French; at least he understood my meanings. That *bed*, so clean and springy; I had quite forgotten.

May 10th: Woke much too early, but so excited I couldn't sleep. The sun bathed the harbour – in full view from my bedroom window – and everything on earth with a warm smiling of peace. (Rudely interrupted by a Jerry Recce kite, coming to have a look-see just as I was getting up. Quite an accurate barrage went up at him but there are only five ships in dock so I doubt if we'll get a raid.)

Flies were flying in squares, just as they do at home, just below the ceiling, paying me no attention what so ever; how different from the blood-sucking Gypos!

Down to breakfast at 8.30, the fountains in the shallow fish pool, spraying cool mist into the room through the open french windows. A delicious breakfast, and after it a professional shampoo and shave. I didn't know that hair could ever be so soft to touch. It felt as if I hadn't any hair at all when combing it through afterwards.

May 11th: Taken round to No 24 MRS by ambulance of 210 Group sick quarters. 'Yes, Flight Lieutenant Barber will see you.' The name rang a bell and suddenly through his office door bounded Doc, (ex-222 Squadron at North Weald) apparently overjoyed to see me; he must have been practising his peacetime bedside manner, I thought, for the days not too far off for any of us, we hoped.

The X-ray apparatus was occupied for the moment so we talked hard over tea and cigarettes. Bob Seed went out to Malta, did a tour and got his DFC and has now gone home. Sandy has gone to an OTU as an instructor, Feathers is lecturing in the USA, the lucky b ... Dickie Milne is now a POW, and Wenty Beaumont also, which was a Godsend for him. He was said to be drinking himself to death, thinking that it 'looked good' and was too young to know better. He was shot down by Van Houten – his Number 2 – who was over-enthusiastic in a tail-chase shoot-up of a flak ship off the Dutch coast. Ironically, Beaumont made a perfect belly landing on the beach which lies immediately alongside the drome which was Van Houten's elementary flying training school! V.H. himself bought it a few days later from a FW190.

Eventually had my X-ray photograph taken with a little portable job and all it showed was solid bone – what else did they expect? After careful scrutiny it was established that I *do* have frontal sinuses, but they happen to be pea-sized, not the walnut-sized cavity one usually expects. This means, so I was told, that the slightest congestion, let alone infection, would cause pain through pressure points etc.

The ENT (Ear, nose and throat) type there, a squadron leader, suffers similarly he tells me, and between them they agreed that my treatment should comprise inhalations and 'plugs'. 'Come back in a week'.

Willie arrived on a week's leave, so off to see *Pardon my Sarong* again, well worth it.

A whole party of '70 types' arrived on their way back from Fauconnerie; Spud, Inky, Ted, Barber, Slater, Sweetman, Crossley etc, so it was more of a squadron party than a holiday. We all went up to the Pongos' club after dinner where an Iti quartet played marvellously. On the way back to our 'pub' one of our party – walking alone at that moment – was approached by some army type who made a most improper suggestion. At the same moment as he was told to push off, he was *pushed*, with a hefty right hook to his jaw!

Arriving back, Doc Barber was there, having been invited by his CO. We talked some more of the members still around, including 'Cyril' Fletcher, a marvellous dry wit, if ever there was one. He went down with peritonitis and was put into the hospital at Torquay, where he was buried for hours, after it was bombed. Nothing would shake him, and as they dragged him out, all he would say was that 'I take a rather dim view of all this, don't you agree?' Later, he had a row with his CO, so got posted to an OTU; he should be flight commander by now.

May 12th: A mild flap this morning from the army, evidently one of their chaps had his jaw broken last night, did anyone know anything about it?

We got away at 10.30, a lovely drive with the fields full of well-spaced olive, mixed with apricot trees, and vivid green vines or ripening corn between the rows. About nine out of twelve bridges had been blown, but all the river beds were dry and detours were not too difficult, though the going was very rough. We stopped at Homs and had a wizard bathe in the clear but very cold sea. Lunch of bread and cheese and tea, then on again at 2 pm.

By 3.45 we had run out of anything which could be called a road, and all the way till 6.00 we toiled along at 7 to 10 mph over the rocky track. My shirt, gripping the canvas seat cover rather than me, gently scoured all the skin off my back, due to the very soft springing, making us bounce like peas on a drum; I'm very sore.

Very cold by the time we got back to base so I changed into battle dress. A lovely letter from 'Spy', giving lots of news. Bill Gill is now a flight commander with DFC, nearly all the types I know have finished up with them, Robin Johnston is okay; he got a ground job in England. John Selby is now the CO of a Hurri Squadron in North Africa somewhere.

Jerry is now surrounded in Cap Bon. All bombing ceased at 12.00 yesterday, so that lets us off the hook in that direction anyway. The latest rumour from the photo section is that AOC Gayford is in India, preparing the way for our arrival. Another is that we are off to Gibraltar for six weeks to re-form; the latter is most unlikely I think.

Seven minutes to 10 p.m. 'All organised resistance in North Africa has ceased; 150,000 prisoners taken!

May 14th: Flew to Castel Benito today for treatment at the hospital in Tripoli, taking a whole load of sergeant aircrew, who desperately need a bit of leave as we all do. Landing at CB, I noticed a 73 Squadron Hurricane there with its unique flash along the fuselage. As far as I know, *all* other squadrons have to use code letters, but 73 is unique!

No, I could not borrow it, it was there for an engine change or something equally drastic; I just long to fly off and visit them wherever they are, feeling confident that my job with 70 – fun though it was – has come to a full stop and I could be of more use elsewhere.

*

The investigation into my headache problem dragged on with further X-rays and treatment; nothing did any good for long. It culminated in having 2 cc of absolute alcohol injected into the supra orbital nerve – in the hope – or so I believed – of putting it to sleep for ever.

Within an hour of my jab, my eye simply shut like a prize fighter's, blue and yellow then finally black, which made a highly humorous appearance for all of us, but it still didn't stop the pain!

By this time it was June 2nd already and the general opinion was that I should see the ENT specialist back in the Delta or in the UK; that last *would* be nice.

It wasn't quite that simple because I was beginning to erupt with boils and abscesses in a most horrid manner, though feeling almost normal in myself. Finally, when I was carried out of the hospital on a stretcher, it was to a hospital ship in the harbour!

I remember somebody saying 'take him below' and in like vein remember asking myself 'below what?' I could not feel lower than I am now, disinterested, disenchanted, and after all the pills to 'clean my system' as they called it, damn near disembowelled. The thought suddenly struck me with that word in mind, I must be in the '*bowels* of the ship!' Never did I think to find myself so low that I was to be found in the bowels of anything, least of all a ship!

So be it, I thought, and wondered for whom I might pray with any consequence, as I lay in such clean sheets, listening to the throb of the generator engines. My Angel arrived, as unexpectedly as always. My usual greeting of 'Hullo Angel' was acknowledged with her single blink in that amorphous smile of hers, so I tried again. 'Hi Gorgeous' I said – which must have been something I had learned from the Bob Hope films, *two* blinks this time, so it must have done something. 'What now?' was my question – we always have to communicate telepathically, so that was no problem to her.

Nobody stopped me getting out of bed, so out I slipped, and gave thanks. I felt a lot better for doing so – she had indicated that I would anyway – and once in bed again, I slept.

It so happened that alternate ships went either east, to Egypt, or west, to Gibraltar and the UK so it was quite a toss-up as to which would carry us on our 'rest cure'. Needless to say I was rather beyond caring, but I didn't relish the idea of being torpedoed which ever way I went.

At Port Said those of us on stretchers had a perilous journey down the gang-plank; heaven knows how anyone survives if they cannot hang on with both hands, but I suppose they strap you in. From there it was a hospital train down the Suez canal, to the 23rd Scottish Hospital, about half way to Ismailia.

More days went by until it was discovered that I had scarlet fever, so all the fun of the general ward was lost to me and I was carted off into solitary confinement of the isolation ward. Much the brightest part of every day – twice a day in fact – was the visit to me by a beauteous little Palestinian ATS girl who came to bathe me. She was very shy, but those hands did more good than all the medicaments.

All my personal clobber had to be taken away and fumigated so once the temperature and paralysis of various limbs had gone, I was shipped to a hospital in Cairo which was much more fun. My stay there really only amounted to clearing my whole system so that the boils and abscesses were eliminated, and life was back to normal by mid-July.

On the 6th, in fact, I was given a job by HQME as the Briefing Officer at Azzizia, the spot where the 'Singles' were ferried across the Med' in convoy with a Boston or Beaufighter to escort them. It took another week nearly to get a plane going to 205 group and at 1.30 on July 12th, we set off, loaded with air freight, mostly welfare stuff. We dropped in to a drome just beyond Fuka for a cuppa, then straight on to Benina.

July 13th: Having stayed the night, we set off at 9.30 and landed at Castel Benito for lunch, only to find that the transit mess was shut from 11.00 till 2.00, just when anyone might be expected to drop in! The station mess is forbidden to transit passengers, but we managed to get a cup of tea at the AQU and set off at 12.00 (11.00 that far west) and found the weather much clearer, even from Djerba Island one could just see the far coast from 5,000 feet.

To say farewell to my 70 Squadron friends, I dropped in on them for the night. The area is smothered with about twelve landing grounds, which is quite a feat of engineering for the ground is not all that level. We were down by 2.00 but found that nearly everyone had gone swimming. Black brought the flight pick-up to bring me in and I dumped my gear in Mac's tent. This site is glorious, in mud-walled fields of vines, olive, fig, even apple and pear trees on a slight slope overlooking the drome. It's terribly hot but beautifully quiet.

Lots of little long-tailed thrushes fly fitfully everywhere, and little brown owls scoot from place to place as if lost.

The ground growth had been luxuriant with flowers, all now tinder-dry, very dangerous in case of fire. The mess is pleasantly open and cool; cold water from large *chattis* – unglazed pots which allow seepage of the water so that evaporation cools the contents.

Grass mats, a bricked entrance and bar stand, so sophisticated, it looks like a film set.

July 18th: Woken at 5.30 with the help of the guard, finished my packing, and at 6 a.m., had a wizard breakfast of two fried eggs with bacon and fried bread. Our driver came up at 6.30 and having been offered a cuppa, he told us that he had not had breakfast, so we did the best we could for him and he was most grateful.

Trying to make our get-away without disturbing anyone was difficult, for our driver's pick-up truck would not start. I took the Adj's and pushed him along to get him going, then we raced over to Group to collect the others to go with us and transferred all our gear into their 3-tonner, and off we went.

There was little corn as such, but the deep loam proudly supported great stands of olives and rows of vines. We got to Sfax at 11.00, had a cup of coffee at a cafe, run by the first Frenchwoman I had met, and bought some plums, and peaches from her. The country became more of a switchback from here on, till about ten miles from Gabes where it become a dead flat plain. We called at the DID and I drew three days' rations for the seven of us, and had lunch in a little railway station – where no trains had run for months, and may never run again.

The Station Master was Corsican, who told me in French, 'When the Germans were here, I am Italian; now that you are here, I am French. When you go, I go; back to Corsica!'

We spent the night in Gabes.

July 19th: Set off at 6.30, stopping for breakfast at 7 a.m. Made quite good time in the morning, 45 mph much of the time. Dropped one passenger off at Ben Gardane (No 6 Squadron) and pressed on, for it was getting late. A quick lunch and off again to Mareth, over very dull flat desert. There were only few houses left, and none had doors nor windows, all blasted to barren emptiness by shells and bombs.

From there for twenty miles we followed a horrid desert track and arrived at Zuara at 3.00, where we dropped off more passengers and got into Tripoli at 6.00, which was quite a relief.

Seven hospital ships here (shades of such a distant past), and 22 empty merchantmen outside, but 28 others in the harbour itself.

Made my way to the local RAF HQ and got the details of the

briefing job, sending off Spits to Malta and Sicily from Sorman. Squadron Leader Turner (SAAF) says he wants me to be a staff pilot with them, the briefing job will only take a month or so. Nothing in the Officers' shop, and no Palmolive at the Naafi.

July 21st: Left at 8.15 and dawdled off to Sorman at a steady 30 mph in a 15-cwt truck arriving at 9.45. Found the briefing tent, then went along to the cook-house, and got tea for my driver, his mate, and myself.

The aircraft we sent from Sorman must have been in the hundreds, if not thousands. Day after day, with many prangs, several burn-ups, (either on take-off or landing) but nobody was hurt as I recall, despite the horrific way in which great big things like Beaufighters were cart-wheeled across the drome on occasion – a high-level stall on landing, readily caused a wing to drop, an undercarriage leg to break, and the whole kite went rolling along sideways, shrinking visibly at every revolution until just the vital piece of pilot-bearing nose came to rest unharmed.

CHAPTER SEVEN

Battle Training for Sprogs

That job done, I reckoned I would have a change of scene, even if I had to fight for it. Getting back to the Delta took some time and being a ferry-pilot was not my idea of 'fighting' a war; that job had been done by girls in the UK since the onset, so why not here and now?

Badgering various tour-expired friends, now sitting behind desks in HQME in the flesh-pot of Cairo itself I was able to 'forget' that I had ever flown 'Twins' and was posted to a Hurricane OTU just outside Ismailia. It suited me well since I could hitch-hike into Cairo or Ismailia as duties permitted and keep in touch with my sister and most of her ENSA friends and colleagues; just that which I thought was the *idea* of 'Resting' – as the stage profession so aptly call a period off work – out of the limelight.

Our job as instructors was to teach the sprogs battle tactics and formation flying such as they had never done before, on operational aircraft. Our quarters were superb, fully peacetime Air Force standard; even the baths were of Victorian proportions and were vast, one could *float* in them with ease, and great comfort. Due to the wartime increase in personnel numbers, it is true that we did have to double up in our bedrooms.

For close formation flying, my room-mate was a perfect instructor; he never flapped or moved at anything. Regrettably, I fear that this was his undoing, to the ultimate!

As instructors, we had to encourage our pupils to have faith in their machines to start with, and develop their skill to such an extent that they – and many others – could have faith in that too!

I am quite sure that we did not rub this in too much, but left it to the individual to do his best (when flying as an instructor between *two* such sprogs). To a novice at the game who was flying at your level, but 30 feet away, one would call him over the RT as Red One or Red Two, be he to the right or left of you – you being Red Leader for the sake of your followers and ground control.

Telling Red One or Red Two to come closer was a frightening experience, but one simply had to do it. On such occasions, if I called Red One to do just that, Red Two immediately followed suit to such an extent that had I not pulled back on the stick I would have become the meat in a triple aeroplane sandwich. Many times, I simply had to pull up, for dear life! Close though my followers came to killing each other, even when I had lifted out of 'Orange', no harm ever came to them.

On the day I shall never forget, my room-mate had just *one* rather slow pupil, so he took him up to try to teach him to formate properly on his own. The command 'come closer' causes a double effect: firstly, it ensures that your pupil lowers the wing which is nearest towards you which initiates his turn in that direction without the use of rudder. The pupil, seeing that his wing is on the point of colliding with his instructor, lifts it with his aileron, but – almost instinctively – presses on his rudder pedal to keep his plane close to the leader, which it does most effectively by 'skidding sideways'.

Secondly, the fact that the pupil's wing-tip has now blotted out his sight of the instructor means nothing to him – he thinks – provided that he can *rudder* his way out of trouble. Result? He goes on skidding into his instructor's machine, willy-nilly. On this occasion, the pupil had enough appreciation of sideways drift to drop his wing – to see where he was going, alas, too late. At that moment, his propeller shattered his instructor's wing tip, as his own wing tip penetrated the cockpit of his instructor's plane, and broke off.

The pupil had no prop' and did the best thing possible, he rolled over, opened his sliding hood and baled out. My room-mate was trapped. Half a yard of wing tip had axed its way through his fuselage over his knees and locked him there, not even able to lift himself from his seat, let alone bale out. His wing tip and aileron control gone for ever, he simply spun into the deck, the Sinai desert, over which we did all such aerobatic practice.

The pupil, landing from some 3,000 feet about one minute later, kindly pulled the body from the wreck, and finding the flies worrying it as fast as he got there, smothered it with sand to stop them. Another pupil, practising his aerobatics in the same area, but somewhat higher, happened to see the accident and went down to have a look. With his gaze fixed – one can but presume – on the parachuted pupil waving from the ground to his colleague, pulled round in a steep turn, stalled and spun into the deck from about 200 feet.

Three aircraft and two useful pilots lost. Dear God, what a waste in the name of freedom, or is it? Who are we to judge? 'I am a jealous God,' saith the Lord, 'Justice (vengeance) belongs to me.' My room felt a lot emptier for some weeks after that.

Maybe there was a lull in the flow of SFTS (Service flying training school) pilots coming up from South Africa, though my diary makes no note of it. Nevertheless, having phoned the CO of the Spitfire OTU at Abu Sueir – a bit closer to Cairo in fact – I was granted a three weeks' stay there. Such bliss, I could hardly believe it.

If only the 'ground types' would respect their charges more; a thousand years ago it would have been charg*ers* whose well-being was in their hands. The reason for this mental outburst was because I was given a Spitfire which could hardly walk, let alone fly. Controls were slack, engine rough, and far too much smoke from the exhaust ports so after the initial run-up I switched off. 'Sorry chaps, I think this one has a bit of a cold, she coughs and splutters too, and no one should fly like that. See if you can make her better.'

The next one they gave me had just come out from her 40-hour inspection, and she was beautiful. Took her up to 8,000 feet, and closed the throttle while pulling the nose into the blue, and blue above. I thought she would never stop. Finally the speed did fall off, and a squeeze on the rudder pedal, and down she came in the smoothest of all stall-turns, never a judder or a flick of any sort. I don't know why, but the childhood jingle ran through my head, 'That's what little Spitfires are made of'.

I was happy to participate in helping to teach the novo Spit pilots their 'turnabouts, and crossover turns' in the hope that as a result they would be less likely to catch a packet later, but my time was up after such a glorious holiday because I was told that I was posted to Ballah (a dried salt lake on the western shore of the Suez canal) to train air gunners. That meant flying those heavenly toys called Harvards, for cine-film gunnery only, and Lysanders, for target towing and the real thing!

6th December 1943: At 11.00 I took off a 'Lysie'. Very odd aircraft, but the easiest yet to land. They rather tend to climb to the right and dive to the left, due to the torque on climb and lack of it in the dive. The prop pitch you change from fine for take-off or landing into coarse pitch by pulling a knob on the dash-board. It brings the rpm back from 2,400 to 1,800 completely on its own; wonders will never cease!

Most of these aircraft have flown only some 300 hours, and their engines only 35 hours. Very smooth. To land, I made a Spitfire approach, cutting the engine and wound back the trim wheel, an enormous thing which takes nearly a minute to run from one extreme to the other, altering the angle of attack of the whole 'cantilever' tail plane. The position of the nose doesn't seem to alter much on the horizon, but I feel the tail lowering itself a little, and so gently. As the full effect of the trimmer took control, the airspeed dropped slowly from 120 to 90, and the aircraft did likewise, i.e. it sank slowly towards the ground. It was marvellous, the machine seemed to stand still, while the *runway* swung round.

At about 50 feet, I had got the trim wheel fully back and with a slight pressure backwards on the stick – very little movement there at any time, and she was down, rumbling along on all three and nothing felt before that rumble of the wheels. I promptly thought this too good to be true, so with bags of runway left, took straight off again, hardly realising how long it takes to wind the trim forward again into the take-off position. Anyway, we made it!

For that which I like to think of as 'hawking it', that is flying as slowly as possible while spying-out the ground beneath, the Lysander is my absolute *pet.* On a hot day, flying into Heliopolis, one could raise one's hat (metaphorically) to the Kite hawks flying alongside, as those gracious birds helped Cairo to provide the sewage disposal system which the city itself entirely lacked; or so it seemed to us.

On arrival, with the beggars pleading for alms, one felt sorry for them and I did for fully two years. The *felaheen*, or tenant farmers of the Delta, were being bled white, if not by their landlords then by the water-bailiffs who threatened to cut the vitally needed water supply to their meadows of Alfalfa which feeds the race horses of the rich. The levies, if not blackmail, seemed to increase all the time, and the struggling farmers had a very rough time of it.

Sad perhaps, but after two years had passed, the sun had got

(*right*)
'Tropical' (gabardine) uniform, Cairo, May 1944.

Back on Spits. Sorman, September 1943.

under our skin and we were as willing as the rest to lie down, under the noonday sun – or at least in shade from it – and say *Maaleesh* (it does not matter). The more philosophical ones would quote the proverb '*Fila buchra mish mish*' which translated means 'Tomorrow, when the apricots ripen', which they never do, any more than 'When our ship comes in' at home.

It came to pass that the parasol structure of the Lysander suffered from metal fatigue, which few, if any of us had heard about previously. The daily inspection had revealed that some of the six bolts holding the tailplane in place had sheared at various times, but the one and only main plane structure was now in doubt.

Many of us today will know well the square tubular sections used in office furniture and other structures. So it was with the supporting struts of the Lysie mainplane, except that these were of aluminium. Some eight in all connected wing to fuselage and for ease of manufacture, they were made in two halves, joined halfway along their length by smaller sections of square tubing fitted inside and riveted solidly in place.

After so many hours – and nobody knew just how many – the flexing of the wing in all its gyrations was a bit too much for the slender inner sleeve connectors. We received an urgent signal from the Air Ministry grounding all Lysanders forthwith. It took some five days for the reason for this signal to be made known to us. 'If the rear pair of parasol struts part company at their joint by one quarter of an inch or more while loaded at 2 G (as in a Rate 2 turn which involves the aircraft in twice its natural weight, being borne by the mainplane) the aircraft is unsafe to fly and the inner members of the struts must be replaced, see Service Modification No' ... etc.

It so happened that I was flight commander at the time and immediately contacted our Flight Sergeant Rigger with the signal in hand. With a glint in his eyes as could only have come from someone used to 'string-bag' aircraft like the Fury and all the Hawker variants and other riggers' dreams – or nightmares – straightaway he said, 'Shall we try it, sir?' and so we did.

Flight records showed us the one with the most flying hours and I took her up to 3,000 feet – the Flight Sergeant hadn't flown with a brolly to sit on since the war began – and did the requisite rate 2 turn. OK, there was the suspected $\frac{1}{4}$-inch gap, so tried a Rate 3, and it opened to $\frac{3}{8}$-inch plus a $\frac{1}{8}$-inch gap on the more forward pair of struts, but we blessed the designer for giving us at least 110% safety. On landing we checked the tailplane bolts, and found that of the six employed, three had sheared.

I was very sad indeed having to 'drop' the Lysie, just like that; but no one was allowed to fly them from then on. Only a test flight could prove the parasol structure – or so we were told, and no meant *no*. By this time already many stories had come out of Europe about the wonderful job these Lysies had done by flying in our 'life-line' participants, and as often as not flying out our aircrews and agents. There seemed to be nothing to replace this wonderful machine and it brought more than a sigh to many of us whose friends in Europe had found such relief in their very being.

For me, it seemed that yet another job had burned itself out, after four months, so where do I go from here? I went to make a nuisance of myself again at RAF HQME and by now, with two stripes on my epaulettes my request may have carried some more weight. So many of the office boys were very new pilot officers, with very white knees.

Somebody had kindly put me down for the Junior Commanders' Course, presumably as somewhere to pigeon-hole me for a while. (I think I must have expressed my terror at being attacked by trainee pilots flying Harvards firing their camera guns at me, while I had to simulate a gently weaving bomber; feeling instinctively as one does, that one day one of those types will get so camera-happy that he'll chop off your tail before he breaks away; a colleague in a Spitfire from North Weald had done just that to a camera crew in an Anson).

So, I'm off to a 'House Boat on the Nile', what could sound more like a holiday resort than that, in these days of war? Off I went to Wellington House to await my attendance on the course itself.

Feeling well-lectured, and somewhat the wiser, I said goodbye to the boys by a hand-wave and taxied into town. Straightway to Abassia and informed that Micky had been down with malaria, but was now up and about again. Arranged to meet him tomorrow. Back into Wellington House, I was surprised to see the number 106756 above my own, (106656) on the list of residents. I met the fellow after tea, he was commissioned in July '41, going straight from OTU onto Beaufighters on a RP squadron. They have suffered no losses in the squadron as yet, and after only three months on his first tour of ops, sports his DFC ribbon; he must have done some remarkably 'distinguished flying' in that short time.

Heaven only knows where we go from here but after a 'jab' of 3 cc of bubonic plague vaccine, I lie on my bed feeling very hot and miserable, (probably half-delirious at least) and try to write this diary with a splitting head-ache.

We've sweet all work, and much less pay, so
What can we do but sit here all day?
We'd ask for a posting, but what would we hear?
'Sorry old boy, not a hope till next year'
So we sit here and think, get jabbed in the pink
So we can't even *sit* any longer, so it's *stood*
On the spot 'till you feel like a clot, whence
No one however keen may wander.
At six o'clock dead, with expressions of lead,
We crawl to the bar for a beer;
With a lump in our throats, we live with one hope,
To see England, so far, yet so near.

May 1st 1944: While still cool I went to Malika Farida Square, our local Petticoat Lane and tried to get some gabardine, but still without luck. Someone had suggested the Committee of Adjustment, the place to which all service clothes were sent by relatives of the deceased if unwanted elsewhere. They found me a very reasonable Canadian suit, very light cloth, and tight across the chest so at least I have blue, if not buff.

En route, all I possessed other than binocular case essentials had been nicked from my truck at traffic lights. So I had to go shopping. Coffee at Groppi's, mooched around the shops still trying to replace so much in the way of lost clothing such as shirts (for uniform and mufti) pyjamas and socks etc. To the sporting club for tea by the pool with two from the JC Course who are still stuck here like me. A very lovely girl was sitting talking to a Yugoslav I had met at Ismailia. When the opportunity presented itself, I asked him her name; she is one Diana Dawson, of the ENSA brigade. She is the first person I have ever seen with truly violet-coloured eyes; very large, and beautifully mounted against a sea of auburn hair which really shone, it was so clean; very rare in this filthy city.

Having learned that Noel Howlett was producing her in a

(*Left*) An oasis in the Sinai desert from 2,000 feet. (*Right*) 'Marble Arch' from 500 feet.

En route for Malta and Italy, June 1944. DC3s, Dakotas, at Marble Arch, 7 a.m.

performance of *Ladies in Waiting* at the Ezlukir Theatre I went round to listen to the rehearsal. Met Pat Mahoney also, now with the Fol de Rols. Evidently they played *Ladies in Waiting* for three weeks in Ismailia, where the nightdress scene brought yells from the troops. Poor devils, no wonder they rush out and catch a dose after being so aroused. (One thing at least, we learned at the JC course, is that a 'Full House' is both syphilis and gonorrhoea.)

*

For the rest of that month I helped out a bit with the Harvards at Ballah but felt more than ever that I was wasting time. By early June the sparrows were busily feeding their newly hatched young under the eaves of the shower house but I decided to move back to Cairo, despite the expense and try to shove things along a bit.

June 4th: Saw a bird I've not seen here before, though I imagine I have seen one like it on the South Downs near Eastbourne. Rather like a skylark in size and buff-coloured, with a huge red, black-tipped fan tail, which it raises black-bird fashion in jerks, as it fans out. Packed my one and only bag but there's no plane tomorrow, so I'll have to go by train.

June 5th: Finished packing last minute oddments by 7.45, had breakfast and into Ismailia on the mail van by 9.00 train. Very hot and sandy, I arrived at Wellington House in time for lunch. Got a room for myself and then had a long lazy bath while sipping iced Stella beer, one of my favourite afternoon pastimes. Cairo seems emptier than ever; one or two divisions here on rest, it seems. The troops wander around in groups, obviously new to the place.

June 6th: Called at HQME at 10.00, still no news or movement. At 10.20 the news came through that we had landed on a 100 mile front from Le Havre to the west of the Cherbourg peninsula. Overwhelming paratroops dropped far inland. We were all very bucked. Oddly enough these landed at 6.30 to 8.00 in broad daylight yet with complete surprise, even though the landing had been held up for 24 hours by weather. Security must be getting better.

Four thousand naval craft were used and many thousands of

smaller boats, with 11,000 first line aircraft ready for anything.

Went to see *Are Husbands Necessary?* not a bad film but much more exciting was the King's speech which was relayed through the cinema's loud-speaker system; excellent. Made us rather homesick. At the first chord of our National anthem, everyone stood bolt upright, even the wogs!

June 15th: Medical check-up. Evidently I am A1B what ever that means, 'with a bit to spare'. Off to HQME to get my release from 203. B. was very friendly, his greeting was 'Well, White, bind now or for ever hold your peace'. He got quite a shock when I replied to his question of 'Last Squadron?' '70 Sir' but he appreciated my fighter feelings and phoned the department to put me down for a Spitfire Squadron.

CHAPTER EIGHT

Back on Spits at Last

June 19th 1944: We took off en route at 2.20 a.m. on the dot. I wearing shirt and shorts and greatcoat, which I found to be *the* combination for all-purpose travel, since one is at maximum coolness and ample warmth, and the shirt and shorts are washed very easily on arrival. Didn't like the night take-off and flying at all; the air was a globe of haze and a big inversion gave us a very bumpy passage.

The aluminium side-panel seats got harder and harder but I slept a little. At long last the dawn arrived, oh so slowly at 5 a.m. and I felt a bit happier. Came out south of Benghazi over such familiar country and landed at the border of Egypt and Cyrenaica ('Marble Arch' built by Mussolini) for breakfast. Not very good and a filthy mess. Some people just seem to enjoy living like pigs, and expect their fellows to follow.

At 9.00 we bade good-riddance to Africa for good and all, and droned across to Malta, such a tiny island. Funny little quarries riddle the place, probably only 50 yards across, but the stone cut vertically downwards. There is a lot of re-building going-on now.

A cup of tea at the Naafi and off again at 1.00. Held up by two partisans (Yugoslav) girls who were late. They looked like pictures of all Russian women. I hear that when they were collected in Yugoslavia they rushed the plane like cannibals, armed with knives, and their shirts full of hand grenades. They looked horribly tough.

We flew straight to the south-eastern tip of Sicily, then left it to port, disappearing in the haze, with 4,000 feet of Etna – snow-capped – rising out into our vision. We followed the coast-line of Italy rigidly till we swung off across the bay towards the 'heel'. There were heavenly little villages in the rising hills, snuggling into the green, green trees, by little streams. Fishing villages, as if in a world of their very own, with about forty little boats up on the hard.

Red-tiled roofs – how funny, I'd forgotten how lovely an eaved roof can be.

The cloud got pretty thick up the heel and we sank into Bari under 10/10ths cloud and pretty cold. Very glad to be on dry land again at 4.00 when we were due to catch a plane to Naples at 4.30. It was cancelled because the weather over the mountains was too thick for our safety. Nice to be thought about as a person for a change.

June 20th: Our early call for 5.30 misfired. We woke at 6.00 but missed our bus to the transit camp. The door was locked and we had to squeeze through a missing window pane. My cigarette case dropped out of my top pocket onto a grating below the window, bounced, and sprung open only to land as an inverted V on one of the few grating bars, quite a piece of luck for it would have been lost irretrievably otherwise.

We got a lift along the very magnificent front (the harbour being very like Tripoli), passed the docks to the main road. Another lift to the camp entrance and another to the booking office. Told to come back at 7.15 so went up to the Yank canteen for breakfast. All meals there cost two pence halfpenny, and are typically American we were told. Breakfast comprised a cereal bowl half filled with maple syrup in which floated a slice of fried bread, larded with marmalade and topped with two slices of fried bacon. I couldn't face that but the coffee was excellent.

Airborne by 7.45 and flew over the richest looking corn country I had ever seen. That which had been a bog i.e. the whole of the Foggia plain, had been drained by Mussolini and now massive combines in echelon gobbled up hundreds of hectares a day, and every inch of it was beautifully farmed. We passed over largish towns frequently appearing far too large to be supported by even the most prosperous farming country.

At Foggia we turned left-handed into the pass through the mountains sometimes only a few hundred feet over the peaceful red-roofed houses. Again I was struck by the snug feeling engendered by the pitched roof, after so long looking down onto flat ones. Cloud built up around the peaks and we climbed to about 6,000 feet flying between their tips when suddenly we were over the sea again and flying down the coast which is lined with villas and expensive gardens.

Almost immediately we were over the bay of Naples, with little Capri lying to the left and rising vertically from the deep, blue water. We landed at the airport which lies in the suburbs just behind the town, in cloud and drizzle at 9 a.m. Coffee and sandwiches at the 'Tuppenny hapenny' bar and were collected at 10.00 for the No 3 transit base; a commandeered hotel overlooking the bay, so tranquil. Actually it is in the village of Portici, I learned, about eight miles south of Naples, with Vesuvius rising steeply behind us.

This afternoon I took the bull by the horns and hitch-hiked to the barracks at Caserta, truly the biggest building I have ever seen. Versailles is like a doll's house in comparison. It is eight floors high, all offices, tiled floors throughout and electric lifts every so often along the corridors. There are vast washrooms with sixty basins in each, four lines of fifteen each. At last I got to the Personnel staff office. A sympathetic hearing was given me and I should get to a squadron before too long, maybe a month!

June 21st: After breakfast I hitched straight into town and found the officers' shop and managed to get a trench coat after a bit of a wangle, also two blue shirts and pair of Lotus shoes (excellent, but only brown ones available). I walked around the town for an hour and a half, getting to know the landmarks readily enough. 60% of the shops are open and 90% of these are shoe shops! There are delicately worked straw hats, bags and baskets, and numerous outlets for the inlaid wooden boxes. Horse-drawn traffic predominates, a light cart with one horse, and a heavy one having two extra horses one on either side harnessed to the shafts. Cabs are the Russian Drotski type.

Infantry landing craft streamed across the bay like gaggles of ducks all day; we flew over twenty-six of them in one line yesterday. I went into town at 3.00 and had a wizard bath in the underground toilet house near the opera house, plus haircut and shampoo. Back to dinner and then to see *This Happy Breed* at the local cinema, which has been taken over by the RAF.

June 30th: Having spent an interesting day in the currently excavated Pompeii, I returned to HQ in search of a job. Spent the morning waiting to see the squadron leader type at Personnel, then told to come back at 2.00. Anyway I've got myself down for 92 or 145 Squadron, in 244 Wing; though it will be another ten days before the move. Decided to toddle off to the rest camp at Sorrento, about forty miles down the coast, close to the famous Amalfi, such a gorgeous spot. The last word in comfort I am told.

The weather is now as hot as Egypt, and wet like Alexandria. The flies which used to fly in squares under the ceiling have turned Egyptian and stick to you like lice.

July 1st: After breakfast, feeling liverish and bad tempered I went up to the Adjutant and handed him a pass to get me to the rest camp at Sorrento. After such a crop of boils I still feel poisoned and in need of toning-up before the expected onslaught ensues. Just yesterday they issued orders to say that no one may leave the camp until 4 p.m. After a haggle with the CO I got my way. Packed my bags and had lunch; bags into store – with just a towel and bathing trunks plus one change of clothes – and hitched into Sorrento. A Yankee Colonel took me all the way!

It was an exciting drive through the little townships clinging literally to the cliff face and the coast road winds along it, up and down with bends round and in and out of crags every few yards.

I arrived at 4.00, feeling rather dirty to find that water is practically unobtainable; *no baths*! At least I was able to have a good wash and change into clean clothes, then I went down to tea. Excellent little cakes made from custard powder and cornflakes – and I loathe custard other than that from eggs.

Dicky Day is here, and Tubby Fieldhouse, so they'll beat me home at last. (Having suffered Tubby's snoring to the extent that I woke him many times for fear of his choking to death, I am delighted that he has survived asphyxiation so long.)

Wing Commander Webb – of the Junior Commanders' course – arrived and I hailed him; only to see that he had caught a packet. A cannon shell had exploded six inches from his face which lost him his right eye. We had tea together and mooched around the lovely garden, looking 200 feet vertically to the sea below.

July 2nd: Having woken every morning since I arrived in Europe (what a joy to be here at all) at around 6.00, I was surprised to find myself called at 8.00. I asked for some tea, and ten minutes later along came *breakfast*! Porridge, fried egg and bacon, tea, bread and *butter* and marmalade.

A Pole shares my room and expressed his gratitude at being able to talk to someone other than a Pole who knows something of the way the Russians and Germans are emptying Poland. He said that he likes to talk politics, but he doesn't when he finds that nearly everyone knows nothing, or is not interested in anything but *self*, and the end of the war for *self*.

Sunday, July 9th: After a week of breathing air scented with bougainvilia, hydrangeas and clematis, not to mention night-scented tobacco blooms galore, I was ready for anything.

Holiday over; now for it, Hooray!

Went straight up to 'Movements' and they confirmed my posting to the Desert Air Force at Sinello, so I'm on my way at last. Went down to see Major Guest about a Jeep, but they are now in the midst of a move themselves. He said that the vehicle Reserve Park was practically empty and that he would not recommend one and kindly suggested that I contact a Major Dawson on the west coast, if and when I got there. Sandwiches and lemon squash at the ready, we 'entrained' about 4.00 p.m. for the East coast. The guard's van carried a Tommy, complete with Primus stove etc, so we gave him our tea, sugar and canned milk and ordered tea for all of us.

We set off at 5.00 at a snail's pace and stopped every ten minutes so at 7.00 we had another brew-up and at 8.00 got into Caserta. (Thinking of Cassata, no doubt, some bright spark shouted, 'Wot, no ice cream?') We have covered the 30 kms in 3 hours, i.e. about 8 mph. Didn't bother with another brew at 9.00 since we were due at Benevento and scheduled for a meal there. Our engine was the smokiest I had ever seen and laboured up even the gentlest gradients.

July 10th: By 3 a.m. having passed Benevento and Cervasa, the train had got us to Foggia, where it dropped five box cars, and ours among them. Since we would be forwarded to Vasto, we had to drag all our kit out again and wait for our train which was due to leave at 6.24. At the other end of the platform I found a lighted brazier and soon we had a good pot of tea and some spam and biscuit sandwiches for everyone.

By 4.30 it was getting lighter and I found a tap in front of the station so was able to have good wash and teeth scrub; then sat wrapped in a blanket on my kit polishing my very dirty shoes to keep warm. The storms were getting closer, and dust was borne down on us from the battered town and station buildings by a rather bitter wind.

Having seen no movement by 6.30 I asked the RTO Sergeant why our train had not pulled in. He rather shocked me by saying that he had told a few sergeants to get into one of the box cars at 5.00 which had been shunted away to the marshalling yards and had gone! Feeling a bit narked I had to ask him why he had not found me as the officer in command, explaining that none of us had been together before on the whole trip and he was the only one to know who belonged with any one group.

That sergeant must have had one hell of a job, day after day, night after night. There were about 60 of us going in all sorts of directions out of Foggia and it must have been impossible for the one RTO to find and move everyone in the right directions. Seeing one bunch of our chaps, he told them where to go, and they obeyed by climbing aboard. The next train was due out at 9.15 so the five of us left remaining, all officers, walked to the Yankee transit camp mess and had – or at least were offered – another typical breakfast. Half a glass of grapefruit juice, a soup plate of raisins floating in maple syrup plus about 15 cc of spam served with a marmalade pancake. I was not alone in opting for the coffee only.

At 9.00 we clambered aboard with as many stray sergeants as I had collected. This time we had a steamer again, which proved useful. After half an hour of shunting we moved off and I slept until 11.00, being woken by a violent jolt of the train being stopped; the engine needed a drink.

Our car was second from the engine so I took our sugar-tin teapot to the driver and showed him our dry tea-and-sugar mix. He understood quickly enough and having filled the tin with water from the canvas water pipe, he placed it onto his coal shovel, opened the fire-box door and *Presto, Magnifico*, another fine brew was made in about three minutes, which helped the cheese and biscuits go down.

At 1 p.m. another stop, so I dashed up to the driver for some hot water for us all. Readily provided so we all had a good wash and shave. By 2.30 we were at Termoli. Quite a long pause here so off to the local officers' club on the beach for tea. Fish sandwiches, and far too much delicious bread, margarine and sauces.

We pulled out of Termoli at 4.00 from which I had telephoned for transport to meet us at Vasto. With the 15 sergeants who had caught the 6.34 from Foggia, we sat and lay on our baggage for the 1 hour 15 minutes trip to Vasto. There, after only ten minutes, we all clambered aboard a 3-tonner lorry. The rail line had followed the coast from Termoli and even on the sand dunes, vines were planted and growing well. All the corn had been cut, and much of it carted. The climb up the hill from Vasto Station was pretty hair-raising on the unmade road, but after 30 minutes we arrived on the camp at Sinello, which itself has been 'planted' in the middle of about four cornfields with orange trees dotted about. After dinner – and a pint of pineapple juice (they won't tell us where they got it) – went straight to bed.

July 11th: Awoke into a glorious sunny morning at 8.00. It's so invigorating to stand and wash and shave in warm morning sunshine again. A quick breakfast and over to the orderly room to book in. Several of the chaps here remember me from Sorman days, and it was a happy welcome that they gave me. The CO is Bill Hay, now a Squadron Leader; he remembered me and seemed glad that I was on my way up to the Wing; he has put me down for 244 Wing.

At 10.15 we met the flight commander, a Canadian named Bracken. While we were still standing outside the CO's trailer he said, 'Well, I want the first six in the air by 11.00.' We thought this to be very short notice but by going straight back to collect helmet, gloves and overalls, and read the order book we *were* airborne by 11.00!

Nearly all the Spits here are clipped-wing Mk VCs. I felt gloriously happy as I sat there wondering which tit was which, after so many years, or so it seemed.

I started up and went off straight away; we all did, so I had to do the same. All the other types have come straight from OTU as pupils or instructors. Take-off was a bit ropey but I soon felt at home. Up to 5,500 feet, scattered strato cumulus cloud at 5,000 feet giving a wonderful horizon and something to play in as I cruised south to view the country. I picked up a Yankee Mustang who thought I wasn't looking when he 'attacked', but I was and was under *his* tail before he could have got a bead on me.

I spent a glorious hour playing about and looking at the picturesque little villages built in individual style on sharp-edged ridges of the hills. Then I made a peach of a landing slap in the middle of the runway. Bracken came up and congratulated me. One of the riggers standing by said 'kind words from him really mean something'!

Back to my lunch and up again at 2.30, this time with Ken Mills as my leader. His job in life is making sausages it seems, somewhere in the north country. My machine only gave 8½ lbs boost flat out, and I had to use 7 to his 3½. Formation was good, and damn near perfect, *far* better than I had hoped. Stern chases and successive slow rolls in line astern formation brought back all the old thrills and the joy of absolute discipline commanding every muscle to play it cool.

After a few cross-over turns we came in and landed; still pleased with it but my speed was a little high so I upped the tail and 'wheeled' her a bit further along the runway.

After tea we walked the odd two miles and had a heavenly swim, sans clothes, from a pebble beach. The beer came in tonight, 3½ bottles per man; they haven't had any for nearly a month. Four of us sat in the cool evening outside my tent lounging and talking. A kindly South African was passing and offered to take a picture of us with my camera. Heavy cloud forming up, looks like rain. Turned in at 9.45.

July 12th: No toast for breakfast so I went over to the armoury and made a toaster from a 16 gauge sheet iron, size 2 foot x 1 foot. I punched holes every inch or so apart in one half of the sheet, and folded it at the half way mark to make it one foot square. Placed over the fire, the lower, plain half gets red hot and the bread sitting on the torn crowns of punched metal, toasts in no time at all. Riveted a simple handle onto one side and gave it to the cooks with my compliments: 'Please use it!'

July 13th: Awoke at 8.00 and after breakfast straight down to the flight. Mackay led off the first section at 9.15 and I took a No 2 position in the second section. We climbed fast – more lying than sitting in the cockpit – up to 5,000 feet over just odd patches of cloud and levelled off. I tightened my seat straps to the ultimate, which always makes me feel welded to my steed.

Thinking back to those first Hurricane flying days at Montrose I recall that feeling of sitting *on* it rather than *in* it. Like someone on a penny-farthing bicycle one always had an uncanny feeling of being top heavy, no doubt enhanced by the very light aileron control and the kite's tendency to roll over if your hand followed your head as you turned to look left or right; rather too self-willed, I always thought them, but not so the redoubtable Spitfire.

We practised our turns to port and starboard, turnabouts and then line astern chases; grand fun. The wind was due west and, the runway being on a hillside, any strength in the wind tended to add disturbing turbulence close to the ground. The lower end of the landing strip was shrouded with trees and these sheltered your touch-down area well. We landed Nos 1 to 6 in pretty close line astern and it rather shook Bracken who told us not to do it again. Down by 10.45 and then lay reading till an early lunch at 12.00.

The wind held at a good 35 mph all afternoon. Saw two formations of 23 Fortresses and Liberators coming back at 11.00; the non-painted ones shone like stars at 8,000 feet. Only four of us took off at 1.00; Mac led one section and I the other. We really got the turns buttoned up and got them pretty fast. Doing a line astern slow roll up to the left my No 2 got left miles behind which could have meant curtains for both of us a few miles north of here. Landed at 2.15 and spent the afternoon sun bathing on the beach.

By evening the wind had died away so sat outside the tent enjoying the sun and perfect quiet. Raided the kitchen for bread and margarine to make Bovril sandwiches. The sunsets here tell the same story as at home, or perhaps I should say foretell. Red means Rain, peach means a peach of a day to come while yellow means wind. According to the blend you are given it usually works; last night I forecast patches of cloud, no rain and a strong wind, and so it was.

July 14th: Woken at 5.30 by the cook, who said it was 6.00! It was a pleasant quiet morning, so I took my time over dressing. Tea at 6.00 and down to the flight by 6.30. Told the lads what I intended to do and we were off by 7.00. They formed up well and when I had ascertained the boost pressure obtained by the slowest of them I really made them work. It was great fun and they all pulled together well. A short line astern chase with steep turns, steep aileron turns and up to see how quickly they could re-form into battle formation.

They were pretty good, though they needed a little boosting and a bit of encouragement, and some of them were very throttle-shy.

Our Desert-filtered Vs were flown away, and we were left with our most welcome Mk VIIIs (no camouflage needed). Sinello, Italy.

Up to echelon starboard and mock dive-bombed a farm house from 8,500 feet down to 3,000; up again into battle formation, echelon port, and 'bombed' a bridge. Battle formation all the way home, into a 'box' over the drome, up into echelon starboard, going into wind, throttles closed into a 360 degree gliding approach turn to a well spaced landing. Bracken pleased all round.

Back to breakfast, washed, and with camera walked up to the parachute section to have a new canvas bowl made for my wash-basin; though only gone at the seams, the canvas is stiff with congealed soap and a lighter construction would be welcome. Took some photographs of the mountains over the river and the river-mouth, and coast looking north west.

Back to the flight at 10.30 and off again, this time not leading a section. All went well but the leader was fool enough to stern-chase below 3,000 feet and slow rolls thrown in! Back for lunch, then spent the afternoon reading *Rogue Male* till 2.30, and spent the rest of the afternoon sunbathing and swimming at our beach.

July 15th: Awoke very early after a very cold night, Ken Mills led us off but since the starboard rudder pedal was useless on my kite I changed over the flight commander's Mk 8. He was not very pleased but my case was too strong for him to argue against. We joined up at 9.15 and went air-to-ground shooting on one of the rivers. Machine guns firing a bit low, but the cannon was spot-on.

It was grand fun going down to about 20 feet, which was very much against the rules, and screaming up again. There was not much time for formation flying but we came back over the drome 'well tucked-in'. These clipped wing Spits are *odd* for close formation. They look like, and *feel* like a solo instrumentalist who has to do his bit before a vast antagonistic audience and get home unscathed. Rollability, Squashability, Lawn-mowability ... and you have it all, and never a high speed stall; it's marvellous! But, for our war, where? Obviously not for training *ab initio* pilots, I am sure, for it lacks that warning the standard wing shape gives you when too dangerously close to your leader.

When the standard eliptical wing is flown with its tip pointing at the leader's fuselage roundel, and as close as feels comfortable, the pilot will find that the 'down-flow' from his leader's wing gives his wing tip a lift which has to be counteracted; if not, then he loses sight of his leader's roundel under his own wing tip.

I was not prepared to take risks, such as chopping off my leader's wing tip with my prop (that has been done once too often for my liking). For thousands of years – millions probably – aquatic birds have learned to use their leader's 'lift' by flying in echelon. Witness any flock of geese, swans, duck etc. Feeling very much a new-boy again, I steered clear enough.

I did a peach of an approach and touched down on the 'pot holes' i.e. that patch of rough ground between the trees before the runway proper. So, I lifted the tail, and 'buzzed her' onto the flat. Everyone behind me, having followed me in, had shut their throttles. Result? They bounced badly and Bracken scrubbed the 3.00 trip, in order to have all undercarriages checked for strain and distortion. Much as I am sorry and expressed it, I thought my followers were pilots?

July 16th: Up at 6.30 after a solid night's sleep, shaved and washed in the early morning sunshine. Yesterday's papers were in the mess – a rare occurrence – so I read these to keep abreast of things in general while awaiting breakfast. I now buy eggs at 6d apiece (2½p or 30p per dozen) to help a very dull breakfast ... remembering those days in the desert when our unwanted rice ration provided us with all the eggs we needed exemplifies my thoughts about the cooks here, and not helping themselves or us. (They probably never had to live in the desert, so who am I to blame them?)

We took off at 9.00 and went into battle formation very smartly. We climbed north, as if to an imaginary 'bomb line'. Did turn-abouts across the sun, then quickly into open echelon starboard, 'bombed' a bridge then up again to echelon port, and down again. Line astern chase with slow rolls left and right. The pupils still break away as if to do some separate aerobatic rather than following closely. They'll learn: I pray to God they'll learn, or else? (Perhaps I ought to ask them to think of their own particular futures on which their present prowess and acumen may rest? ... I'll do that if nothing else.)

My pride and joy at the moment – unsurpassed by Mac or Ken as yet – because they use line astern to come in to land – is to fly in close battle formation up to and just over the drome heading north at 500 feet. Change radio telephone over to channel C (to include ground control with the formation) and quote 'Echelon starboard and turning to port' ... 'Permission to land?' Given the green light.

Now heading south, pull up to 1,000 feet to lose speed while everyone spaces himself from his neighbour for his turning glide approach and all of us are on the deck within three minutes of approaching the drome. It just might save precious pints if not gallons of fuel for some of us in the future.

Early lunch at 12.00 and Ken led off at 1.00. Lots of line astern chases and one dive bomb attack, left rather late. Landed down and slightly across wind; nearly overshot the runway and practically lost the pitot head off my port wing tip as she keeled over dangerously close to the earth while I had to brake and swing her hard to starboard. Down for a swim in those cool, cool waters.

About 60 Spit Mk 8s and 9s have arrived here; it's to be a pool, we understand, though Hay says we may not fly them, nor ferry them to squadrons should the need arise. What a pity.

July 17th: Called at 6.00, into a clear, still, and bright morning so went down to the flight. Not a soul about anywhere but the pilots arrived at ten to seven. I found one of the ground staff from C flight and asked him why the aircraft had not been inspected and approved for flying? I was told that it was not only *pilots* who took alternate late and early morning duties, but ground staff too! It did not answer my question but I felt that in my place I had better let 'sleeping dogs lie'; not that I regarded any of our precious ground staff as dogs!

Perhaps it was because Bracken was away attending a court martial and a more junior flight lieutenant had taken over without many (if any we wondered) clues, so I scrubbed the trip and slept all morning.

It really is a perfect holiday spot, hot and ultra relaxing. Bracken came back at lunch-time and re-arranged the programme. I had led too many sorties (so I was told) so he gave the lead to one Cummings, one of three ex-instructors we have with us. The formation flying with turn-abouts and cross-over turns and so on are now almost second nature. I was given 'A3' to fly, a very old Mk V which flies like a bird but is so worn-out that she nearly 'pinks' going up hill.

With careful flying and hard work she can be made to keep up with the formation, nearly. Came back really tucked in close. I find it very hot, flying these Spits. I think they are cooler than Hurries, but not as much ventilation gets through. We went valley-chasing at nought feet. Grand fun, but not to be recommended when you can't see your way up, or out. I couldn't fly out upwards, due to low cloud, and, being 'hignorant' of the topography of that area, enjoyed the added thrill of steep turning at ground level and thanking God that there were no hedges in the way.

The mobile cinema arrived and gave us *Desert Victory* and *Andy Hardy meets Debutante*. Enough is enough!

July 18th: Called at 5.30 into a dull, overcast morning, not even the birds had bothered to wake up. After a cup of tea, I went down to the flight but there was no one there to authorise the trip so I wrote it out, got the aircraft to use and then at five to seven went along to Bracken's tent. He was awake and told me to get things moving so I took 'A3' again, for better or worse?

A flight sergeant led us without a trace of a clue. I hate checking an under-training pilot 'over the air' but he really was dangerously bad. We took off and climbed straight into mountainous clouds. Too late he gave us a 'turn-about' so we all drove into the bumpy mist while still climbing on instruments ... and so it went on. No collisions in the cloud which must have been miraculous and down we went in a stern chase, pulling in as close as we could when suddenly, at 2,000 feet, a slow roll! I had to call him up and told him not to be such an idiot or ever take such a risk again. He was rather sore when we landed but it might save his life and some others in due course.

Back to breakfast, wash and shave and down to the flight again, by 10.30. Mac led and after a bit of battle formation at 4,000 feet (just over cloud, now diminishing off the hills and breaking-up) we went down for some air to ground shooting with cannon. Both Mac's and mine fired low this time. Feeling bored for lack of real action, we went down to the deck over the Foggia plain which is like a billiards table. After some 40 minutes my windscreen had become too oily for comfort at that height and my eyes were screaming with pain augmented by tiredness.

July 19th: This morning dawned a beautiful day; we had all done our minimum 10 to 12 hours flying, according to previous experience, but most of us had one more sortie to do. I had an early lunch and took off at No 6 in the formation – much to Bracken's amusement. It was quite good fun and I was glad of the chance to make sure for myself that I could *follow*.

The news is excellent all round. Total enemy casualties since D-Day in Normandy are said to be 156,000, 60,000 of which are prisoners. 80,000 dead have been counted and 50 vehicles known to have been knocked out each day. It is a new attack which is going very pleasingly.

A very dark Labrador followed me about today; every day I find a different one. I gave him water which they all need so badly and rubbed his flea-ridden coat with AL69. He loved it and tried to lick my face the while.

At last, the news of my posting to 244 Wing came through, Mac coming along too.

July 20th: 'Signed-off'. Handed in parachute etc and strolled into town with Mac, awaiting our lift to 244 Wing tomorrow.

Spent a few minutes in the fine old church, the year 1290 carved into its portal stone, to give thanks and ask for guidance in all things. It's nice to know that you are *never alone*, no matter how much you feel you are sometimes. Back to the club for drinks and dinner. (Roasted almonds are much nicer than peanuts.)

CHAPTER NINE

Harvest in Italy

July 21st 1944: (*Happy birthday, Mummy*): A very still morning. A Catalina flying boat circled overhead waiting for its escort. Somebody or bodies must be in the drink. The day before yesterday huge formations of Forts and Liberators came streaming south one after another. I counted two lots of 24 so presumably they have been up to Turin or possibly the ex-British oil fields at Ploesti in Rumania.

Packed after breakfast and our Anson arrived at 9.00. Managed to get six of us into it with all our kit and off we went at 9.40. Climbed steadily north-west and turned left after fifteen minutes, round some very high hills, 7,000 feet at least. The gullies were full of snow or hail stones and ice. The storms of the day before yesterday had been really fierce to the west, and covered some areas thickly with the stuff.

Up still higher over the second range, then down hill over about three more. Above the tree line, the escarpments folded in pale green velvet, beautiful pasture scenery, as good as any Swiss postcard.

At 1.10 we were over Perugia airfield. Large, well cratered and thankfully well filled. All buildings demolished. Assisi, the home of the Saint, is a lovely little town overlooking the drome. It has two cathedral-like buildings built in honour of its saint.

We were taken straight to Wing Headquarters. The Air Officer Admin was visiting so we were taken round to 145 Squadron for lunch. It clouded over heavily and became very oppressive, all of us complaining of head-aches. 145 Squadron's dining room is a Jerry troop-carrying bus plus trailer, forming kitchen and dining room respectively. (Like his 'Jerry can', it just proves that the enemy has provided us with some useful bits and pieces; for who ever heard of the British army using a bus?)

Interviewed by the Wing Commander at 3.30. Forrow went in before me and he filled the gap in 145 Squadron, so I go to 92; Mac to 601. Two old friends are my flight commanders, Ben Garner has B Flight and Montgomery (ex Abu Sueir) has A Flight. Ben and the CO are on that which is called the Northern Detachment, to bag reconnaissance infiltrators. The Yanks have tried for three weeks without success and 92 (*me*!!) have clobbered one this morning, a Ju188. Every squadron is now bombing carrying one 500-pounder; there are three sorties a day usually, taking one hour per trip.

July 22nd: Awoke with a cup of tea in my hand! Such service! A solid night's sleep since 9.15 last night. A bright morning with 5/10ths strato cumulus which lasted all day, with a good 30 mph wind from the south-west. Had a few words with the Adj about photograph sets by the squadrons or the wing, but he says that he has never heard of it before. Gave him £5 for extra messing and he promptly *sold* me a bar of free-ration chocolate!

I spent two hours with Jimmy Longstaff, our 'spanners', working on the Spit Mk 8s we fly. We are the only squadron with all 8s; the others have the slower Mk 9s. (It seems that the advent of the FW190, with all its extra speed over the Me109 necessitated the rushed production of the bigger engined MkV which was called the Mk 9 but once the crisis was overcome, the earlier design of the Mk 8, also with the bigger engine and retractable tail wheel was allowed to go ahead.)

Ninety-two Squadron is the second highest scoring squadron to date; 459 is the first, then us, then 73. We have 315 confirmed so far. The flight at Cecina got a 188 yesterday morning. Spent all afternoon over at Wing operations room with Flight Lieutenant Smith who shares my tent. He tells me that Ben Garner is shortly to leave so that he, Smith, may get the flight, though he too is off shortly, tour expired.

'Toothy' brought an Ensa girl to tea (Wot no song and dance? shame!). Six were scrambled to bomb goods trucks. All squadrons now bombing and no one seems to like it. Still no news of the revolt in Germany opening out.

23rd July: The CO came over from Cecina and I nattered to him at 10.00. Saw Monty before he and the Adj went over to the other half of the squadron, now based in a vineyard on the west coast, and he fixed some flying for me. A good lunch of bully, salmon, cucumber and potatoes. Plenty of tea always, and at least one egg for breakfast.

Smithy gave me a map and at 2.30 I toddled off west. Got down to the coast and saw Elba in the distance shrouded in haze, but Monte Christo too far out. The cloud base was 4,500 feet and I stayed below it to see the countryside. It took a bit of getting used to. Two dromes there, covered with DC3s (Dakotas); one landed here today with black and white markings of D Day. Our proposed landing in southern France is due any day now.

Flew up over the mountains to Ancona, a lovely sight, for the cloud had risen steadily to 8,000 feet. Then I flew back to base, low alongside Assissi to have a closer look and landed at 4.00. The machine I used was one of the youngest Mk 8s I had flown – nothing in its trim or engine power had been stretched as yet so it felt incredibly responsive to every breath, let alone manual movement. Telling Smithy how readily I thought the engine had started, he told me that the fitter had come straight into the flight tent when I had left saying, 'He's a good pilot, sir, isn't he?' judging as they do by one's ability to assess the amount of Ki gas petrol injection required, direct into the inlet manifold. We learned this at OTU; it is quantified by the ambient and engine temperature, usually 1½ to 3 full pumps of the plunger.

It's one of the things that one always tries to do – Double Top with your first throw: a three point landing within twenty yards of the beginning of the runway; complete ignition of your engine within a 90 degree turn of the prop ... these are the little things of no importance at all except to the person who makes it his job to do his best at all times.

An oil pipe had burst, luckily just before I landed. The wheels would not come down fully at first, the hydraulic pump had jammed and the flaps would not come up, due to a leaking valve.

July 24th: A very quiet day for the squadron had been released. Had a party last night over at Wing. The Desert Air Force Swing band – first class – gave us a show. Steve Lee-Hardy, whom I had met at Coccumello and Sorrento, had brought his crowd with him today. Monty was with him in North Africa when he was a flight sergeant; now he is squadron leader. I walked round the kites hoping for a trip, but all the ground staff were also off duty, so there was no one to operate the starter battery trolley, or remove chocks after the running-up test.

'T', my kite yesterday, had no oil in the tank at all when checked, so I was very, very lucky.

Went to an excellent lecture at Wing Ops on the subject of Escape, and as we came away a lad with nearly 200 hours on Spits was coming in to land when he stalled, quite 20 feet up. The nose dropped and on nose and wheels he ran for 50 yards or so when the starboard leg collapsed and he started cartwheeling. The wings came off, then the tail, and the fuselage ground up-side-down to a halt after some further twenty yards. The pilot – whom everyone thought at least dead – scrambled out and brushed off the dust. Another lad from the same squadron did exactly the same thing yesterday, but he got his head pretty badly bumped; neither plane caught fire.

After lunch, Monty, Smithy and I went up to Assisi in the Lancia, a fabulous little car which seats six, and has the finest suspension I've known, which is highly necessary on these roads. It is a lovely old town; the ecclesiastical murals have been left alone while the rest of the walls have been renovated.

Had tea and cold bath at officers' club, Lambergo Grotto. Every house has lots of potted geraniums and other plants in iron hoops around every window, a heart-warming sight. A VIP arrives tomorrow and the paper says that General Alexander is to be his ADC-in-C from the 20th, while still retaining command here. We live in hope ...

July 25th: Called at 6.30 to be *off* at 7.00! Dressed in a flash and galloped over to Ops with a mug of tea. I was the first to arrive, so I donned overalls and Mae West and *then* drank my tea. Our target was a rail-over-road bridge between Cecina and Forli. As Monty started up, so did I and we went off in perfect formation at plus 2 lbs boost, 2,600 rpm. As we turned over the hills, the rising sun was a bit tiresome despite my spotless canopy.

Soon Ancona loomed-up and when we were about twelve miles out to sea, and 13,000 feet up, we sallied north-west. We swung in north of Cecina and round to the railway, there running west. Throttled back, pulled back the revs, fused the bomb and down we went. Monty's bomb fell a bit short so I swerved right, then a little to the left while doing about 470 mph at 5,000 feet. Let the stick come back a little and away went the bomb. Curled up again from about 3,000 feet looking at a very complete 'table cloth' of light flak shell bursts I was to fly through. Quite impressive afterwards, looking back at the hundreds of little grey puffs.

Then home again, over the mist-filled valleys; breakfast at 9.00. We had just finished when the next bridge's number came up, so off we went. Not as good as last time, and got back by 11.20.

Polished up after lunch and the King arrived at 2.45. He drove round all the squadrons and our previously parked aircraft. He is holding his pukka inspection the day after tomorrow.

July 26th: I was not on the early show this morning, and glad of it because I was rather late to bed last night. Smithy and I went down to Wing to gen up on the bomb line and mentally fix some of the more obvious land marks. No tea was forthcoming so we walked back. On the way met Monty and we brewed some Ovaltine with tinned milk and water; not bad at all.

The awaited call came through at 11.45 so we dashed down to Ops, a rail-over-road bridge north of Rimini. Almost as yesterday we climbed to our intended height while flying out over the sea and went past Ancona – now well in our hands. The Poles are doing very well in that sector of the front.

Up at 12,000 feet the haze was pretty thick, and a few clouds were drifting over the mountains inland. The target was superb, the road under the railway in a very narrow letter X. Smithy went down and his bomb fell very wide. I, close on his heels – expecting flak – went through rather fast but mine landed in the apex of the angle, some ten yards off the bridge itself so it is called a 'near miss', and evidently – according to the army at any rate who see the results at close quarters – a 'good thing'. Since there was no opposition, Nos 5 and 6 were told to take their time and No 6 got a direct hit on the bridge, sending up showers of black cinder dust from the track: And so home, a very pleasing op.

July 27th: Called at 4.45 instead of 4.30 so it was a bit of a rush. We bundled down to Ops at 5.10 and got our target. On our way to the bomb line we had to patrol as far as Ravenna, then across country looking for motor transport, before heading south again for our target. A record for a scramble since we were off and away within four minutes from arriving back at the flight from Ops.

Overalls have to go on, the Mae West with all its strings, parachute and dinghy, weighing half a ton, to be humped out to the aircraft, all the straps to pull and the knobs to push, then off we go ... Very dark still, but a pale green light coming up over the mountains in the east. Exhaust flames a lovely blue (dead right mixture) and instruments almost invisible. Slowly up to 12,000 feet heading NW.

Over the radio telephone we heard 145 Squadron chasing the two Messerschmitt 109s which come daily on reconnaissance. They caught them both; one crash-landed and hit a house, and both went up in flames just inside Jerry's lines.

At 5.50, at 12.000 feet, the sun rose above the sea, blood red in 6,000 feet of black haze. There was very little shelling going on, and no motor transport to be found. We turned south and six 88-mm guns fired at us from one little town but we soon found our road junction target in a 'punch-bowl' of a crescent-shaped hill and down we went, the four of us. Three of us got direct hits and the fourth unfortunately 'hung-up'. A battery of three 88-mm guns in the crescent put up three rounds each at us which were uncomfortably close so ... 'Home, James' in the still of the early morning and landed at 7.00.

Back to breakfast when four were called for 8.30. No one else was up yet so we pushed off again. This time to the west. The army is now fighting ten miles south of Florence and heavy battles are being fought. It's a lovely little battlefield – for us, anyway – very compact like a slogging match in a boxing ring, so much so that nobody bothered about us at all. Jerry was far too busy shelling our hilltop positions. Lots of fires burning, buildings and houses mostly.

We flew up to Prato, just north-west of Florence and turned right, onto our railway target. All our shots went to the left mine being the closest but still too far, about 20 yards off the track. Still no interference, just a grandstand view of the battle.

July 29th: One of the Mess orderlies, Eagle by name, came to wake me at 7 a.m. carrying his gallon of tea in a jug, but finding that my mug was missing, went to fetch it from the mess so I was left sleeping until 8.00 without knowing. The weather looks very thick to the north just yet and I shall not be on a show until later, if at all.

HM King George VI at Perugia, inspecting 92 Squadron, Desert Air Force.

After a double breakfast (two eggs and two sausages) I drove the flight pick-up over to 417 Squadron to see the Doc; my toes are rotting. He gave me a formaldehyde bath for them for about ten minutes, then I went back to the squadron. Nothing doing, so I went to wash-down 'S' for Sugar, and she really is just that sweet, bless her. A good fast aircraft which I am sharing with Warrant Officer Newman until we get our A Flight kites back again.

We have lost half of our squadron for the time being, it being necessary to locate enough experienced fighter pilots and planes on the west coast to catch the Jerry recce machines which daily fly down to witness our forthcoming plans for the invasion of southern France. The choice of location sounds excellent, the mud runway lies between grape vines and is close to a useful beach near the town of Rosignano.

The CO came over from there yesterday and is going to swap us over ... but when? No one seems to know. There does seem to be a lack of spark in the way the squadron performs at the moment, possibly something to do with our enforced disunity.

July 31st: Late last night the gen came through that six were required on stand-by at 7.00 and, sure as nuts, Mike woke me at 6.50. On my way down to the flight, we were recalled because the weather over the target was still duff. During breakfast, we learned the form from Wing to the effect that only four of us were needed and the cloud base, (now at 2,500 feet) was rising and the cloud breaking up, so we set off.

Well tucked in, we formated up through the cloud and were suddenly borne into a shining white world with a cotton-wool floor. The sudden change of light – though half expected – is always a shock, particularly when you feel so acutely silhouetted against the white floor below you for any one looking from above. The sun was still low enough to hide the ever-expected Hun, but he is hardly ever around now, except for his badly needed recces.

The hills were quiet, and seemed untouchable by war; nothing moved on the roads. We went north, leaving Forli and its deserted aerodrome behind on the right, swung left-handed to Bologna, then north and onto our level-crossing target; a tricky thing to find.

Monty got pretty close but the other three of us put a beautiful group together, like three complete Bulls. Regrettably we were miles off. Feeling somewhat disconsolate we flew home *under* the cloud, in the hope of being able to put at least something on the scoreboard. The very fact that we had no opposition made us think that the Jerries are already in their buses on the way home; lucky chaps.

Nothing for us all afternoon, the weather growing thicker again which prohibited dive bombing using a fighter since the depth of dive controls your accuracy as does a rifle over a pistol; the length of the controlled trajectory being all important. Suddenly, at 5.00 we were given a long job, looking for motor transport 135 miles north!

We set off west, then north-west from Florence, seeing heavy shelling going on everywhere it seemed, and passed some of the highest mountains in Italy, as they lay below us at 9,000 feet. The roads and rails were empty as usual, and though we flew over and down to be alongside numerous power stations and large, useful looking factories, we found no motor transport. (After the very empty morning trip, we did hope to find at least a few buses!)

We plodded on, to our main target, the main road to Bologna. Monty undershot, and I overshot, by the same amount. Mine must have landed in a mine field or ammunition dump for it burst with explosions most prettily. Being a little short of gravy, we had to come back with throttle well closed and revs down to 2,000. (Personally I would have preferred 1,800 at which your prop no longer roars, it simply purrs.) We had flown for 1 hour 55 mins, just about the limit of these Mk 8s.

August 1st: Same weather this morning, low cloud. At 8.30 we were suddenly called out to bomb a heavy field gun which was holding up the Poles, north of Ancona. The cloud was terrific, if not horrific. It lay in layers of stratus from 2,000 to 10,000, with huge knobbly cumulo nimbus towering up to 16 thou, with lots of little cumulus everywhere. Understandably perhaps, it took us some time to find the place, then down we went.

Luckily the gun fired twice; once when we saw the place then again just as No 1 went down. I was flying No 6, and No 5 – whom I had to follow – is a very poor flyer, let alone leader. Result? All our bombs went all round the spot target, one of them luckily falling between two houses where the gun crew would live, while not tending their gun. No 1 had a hang-up so No 5 led us back.

We went *way* south as our leader seemed to *Bradshaw* his way. As his Number 2, I kept my eyes skinned skywards, until I too looked downwards, where I saw a magnificent water-fall from about five lakes. Smith had talked about them as being at this foot of the valley of the Perugia Plain so I told No 5 to turn north over the RT, but he didn't. We were about fifty miles south of our drome and *miles* inside our territory. Finally, after somebody told him he was short of petrol our 'leader' called home for a 'homing' to put on his compass. We landed after 1 hour 15 minutes.

A show went off after lunch, but not being required I took the flight pick-up over to Wing to collect my photographs. Sent off the negatives of the three fitters at the ASU at Sinello; 'Sorry; no prints, no paper available.'

At 7.00 we took off on another 'armed recce' way north, but we never saw more than three lorries at a time. The cloud was very thick and heavy, making it very tiring to fly due to the inherent bumpiness of air below cloud. We bombed the road north of Prato again, and since we had been free of any opposition we enjoyed a line astern chase all the way home in a golden world of cloud and sunset blend. As a 'thumbs-up' to the troops, we banked over those in our bomb line so that they could witness our silhouettes through the cockpit canopy, in a wide-sweeping turning-climb so that no one could harm us, we hoped. Behind our lines we dropped to hedge-height and our tail-chase had taken us to watch the cows being led from milking to their pastures, when suddenly the drome appeared immediately in front of us. Since a quick response is expected of us, we vectored slightly right, and still in formation, slowly rolled into our spaced positions for landing a few seconds later. (Later reports indicate that it rather shook the ground crews waiting to prepare their aircraft for the morning stint; a battle formation approaching at 20 feet might have been a Jerry raid. Nonetheless, we enjoyed it, all of us, air and ground-staff alike.)

August 3rd: I went down to Maintenance to see how my 'S' Sugar was getting on. They had not been told about the right rudder pedal so I got them to work on it. After dinner I went down to give her an air test; she's been losing power a lot recently and now gives only 9 lbs boost at 12,000 feet whereas she should give 12.

The job took a long time so I cleaned up her paint work with dope thinners. One of the fitters knudged his mate saying, 'That's unusual, Harry, ain't it?' nodding towards me. Very quickly, three others with nothing to do got cracking with me. She still looks rather old and shabby, and though not as fast as most, I shall be the first to get a replacement aircraft, in about twelve days, all being well.

At North Weald, we always reckoned that a good waxing gave the kites an extra 5 mph, and was well worth the trouble; that sort of action does not seem to have sunk in out here; perhaps it's not necessary. If the 190s arrive, it most certainly would be.

Now, she looks very spick and span, the white letter S shining out of the dull camouflage. Taxied her back to dispersal at 9.00.

August 4th: After lunch I took the wireless out of its cupboard behind the seat of my Sugar, and took out about a pint of oil sludge from its belly, together with bits of locking wire, plus nuts and even bolts. This action was prompted by rolling off the top the other day, and waiting to see my bomb-burst while inverted. A click on my earphones made me look up – or *down* as it happened to be at the time – and there was a ¼″ x 5/16″ Whitworth spanner lying in the bulge of my cockpit canopy. I pulled it down and tucked it into my Mae West, for real fear that it could so easily jam a control cable when I least wanted it; needless to say, no one I could find had lost that spanner, so I kept it.

The men are too inclined to wash out bellies with petrol; one did the other day and spilled it over the battery which promptly blew up!

August 6th: Our ground party got away yesterday afternoon, taking my bed-roll with them so I slept in the CO's bed last night, he having gone to Rosignano late in the evening.

Monty and I did the evening show, which passed without incident so after our – almost usual now – cup of tent-brewed Ovaltine slept like a top till 8.30.

Lieutenant Man (a South African) brought his kite over to change his compass and told us that no kites were on their way to exchange the three of us left behind. He took off at 10.30 with instructions to let the others know of our plight.

A Lockheed Lodestar landed and dropped a very inebriated Group Captain. He telephoned us immediately saying, 'Where's all the gin?' We hadn't any but the Adj told him that the CO could get some from Malta and the GC gave him 36 hours to get it! So, the

Adj has to set off for the 'other side' to tell the CO tomorrow.

We had quite a party in the mess till 9.00-ish, when we settled down to cheese and biscuits (quite like Desert days). Our mail has come through at last including a letter from Valerie. She tells me that my goddaughter has arrived. '8 lbs at birth, platinum hair, blue eyes, long legs and fingers, what more could a girl want?'

August 7th: Ben set off at 7.50, taking the Adj with him and we hoped he would catch the two exchange pilots and let them bring the Auster for us to return. Not necessary; the two Spits landed at 9.30 and Condon and I set off. The cloud base was down to 3,000 feet and interminable storms raced from the north, but, as we approached Leghorn through thick haze, the cloud ceased to exist. It was a lovely day, the sea looked most inviting. We landed after 35 minutes flying and collected our lorry-transported kit from the mess and set up house again.

August 9th: At 7.45 last night, Warrant Officer Lane and I went off on the dusk show. We had planned the thing in strategy and damn nearly caught the fellow. We beetled up to 34,500 feet indicated (which, I am told was 42,000 feet in fact) and there at 120 mph were some 2,000 feet deep in cirro stratus ice-crystals, making the biggest vapour trails I had ever seen. Flying the thing was almost like putting your horse at a six-foot stone wall, for, being the sensible creature I knew her to be, she tended to shy off. Try as I may, and did, once in the thickest part of the cloud the altitude slipped back to 32,000 feet, yet if we moved into a thinner layer, she climbed happily at 1,500 feet per minute.

We followed the patrol line twice when Lane suddenly peeled off into thick cloud, and I lost him; there was no warning over the RT. Control had said, 'Two 109s over Leghorn' so I shot after Lane as best I could. We always patrolled about two miles apart to give the best possible coverage of the area, but when he went into the cloud, I had no hope of finding him, better that I find the 109s!

There was no point either in losing too much height so I aimed at the hoped-for point of contact and gave her full throttle, but not through the 'gate'. By 28,000 feet I was doing 275 indicated i.e. about 395 computed, towards the cloud base which hugged the coast. The 109s turned northeast and Control called in the CO and his No 2 who were waiting over Spezia to catch the true recce coming out after the 'feint' by the 109s. They joined up with me streaming east as hard as we could go but the 109s had been alerted and dropped off our plot.

I was recalled, leaving the CO to catch the recce which he just saw in the distance by Spezia, going like the clappers due north. He caught up with it but not close enough to shoot. By this time he was down to 11,000 feet and the recce fired a 'double red' Very cartridge, which was probably the correct colour of the day for friendly aircraft, so they had to call off the hunt.

This morning I came on stand-by at 5.30 and fell fast asleep in the cockpit. The fitter woke me with tea at 6.00 in case we were needed. The early birds landed at 7.10 having seen nothing so I got ready and through it came at 7.20. We rocketed up to 15,500 feet, only to be called home again. The 'bogey' on the plot turned out to be a USAAF Aerocobra not using his IFF (Identification Friend or Foe) radio signal.

The CO returned to lead the dusk patrol so I missed the trip. Chezinski failed to bale out when his engine cut, over the sea; I'm afraid he's had it.

August 10th: The CO decided to split our patrols and put two Mustang fighters with two of ours. (We have borrowed six of them from No 260 Squadron). The reasons behind this is that Mustangs have a faster downhill speed than we do. I had always heard that they fly like bricks so they must fall likewise!

When the recces start to dive the Mustangs can catch them while we cannot. *C'est la guerre?* Result, my trip was cancelled.

August 11th: Hackett arrived back with the mail, late last night. Very happy letters from the family, and all around. They were the first letters addressed to me at 92 Squadron.

Still a little cloud left this morning and the drome very patchy. We were to take off only in emergency. Smith and I went on 'call' from 8.00 to 12.00 but nothing turned up. I got Flight Sergeant Moore of the transport section to send over his roller. The Beaufighters who have dropped in occasionally have made deep ruts in the soft bits, but it is the high ridges of squeezed-up mud which would set like knife edges if left up in the sunshine. The soil has a deal more sand in it but the colloidal content is still very high.

The place is lousy with refugee Itis. One type came along this morning saying that he was an accountant in an English rolling mill in Piombino. The place was bombed and all hands ran for their lives; this type had his pockets filled with Lire!

At 12.30 a dirty great 155-mm gun opened up 500 yards away, the shells furring overhead. We went along to investigate this new caper. The Yanks were new and did not know of our landing-ground over the hedge. The shell explosion took 42 seconds to reach us by the sound of the firing. I reckon that is about 35 miles away. Even so, it sounded like a 2,000-lb bomb going off. It fired every two minutes from 12.30 to 3.30, about every eighth round sounded like a blank cartridge (to clean the gun perhaps?). Some shells sounded like delayed action fuses since some of the crumps were not forthcoming 'on time', yet at other times several crumps came to one shot fired.

Smithy and I did the last light patrol from 7.40 to 8.55, landing on the flare path.

August 12th: Nothing to do all day. 260 Squadron are now doing the 30 minutes readiness, so we are freed, greatly. We all went swimming from our new beach. It's delightful. A little shingle and rock beach, half a mile long between two outcrops of rocky cliffs surmounted by summer chalets. We always take two K-type dinghies (inflatables) and great battles take place.

Several Iti girls, all beautifully made and dressed, help to decorate the beach. Stevenson – having lived twelve years in Rome – knows the loose customs here and breezes up to them and chats; so that we are now all getting on very well.

Group Captain Brian Kingcombe came over this evening. Last time I saw him was at Biggin Hill and I didn't know he was over here. The CO went off on the evening show, onto a Ju88 at deck level, having chased it down from thirty grand; he had forgotten his M blower and so couldn't catch it. (These Mk 8s have a two-stage super-charger. The drill is to throttle back to about zero boost at 18,000 feet, then engage the H blower for high level work. The extra speed of the charger takes another 50 hp out of the engine, but gives the extra boost needed at high altitude. If left in 'high' at low altitudes, it can be most unhelpful!)

I entertained the GC until they came back and we settled into a very interesting evening. He tells me that the 'Doodle Bug' is nothing like as bad as people make out. We have a squadron, No

616, operating the Gloster jet jobs, more for publicity than anything else, yet they have not been mentioned in the papers. All fighters now in the UK have gyro gun sights. Deflection, bullet drop, skid and yaw, every damn thing is taken care of. All Pilot Officer Prune has to do is to keep 'Wobbling Willie' – the Red Dot – on his target, and press the button!

August 13th: Called at 5.15 by a brilliant torchlight in my eyes. Dressed and staggered down to ops at 5.30. I was amazed how quickly the mornings are shortening. It was only ten days ago that we took off at 5.30, but now have to wait till 6.00 for that much light.

We went west to Gorgona Island, then north-west to Spezia, haze and light restricting our view but the mountains north of Viareggio were clearly visible. Wright was my No 1 and he flew up at 1,000 feet while I went ahead of him at 2,000 feet, and so I could keep him in view just behind the trailing edge of my wing. From 5.55 to 7.30 we cruised up and down, turn-about after turn-about with no word from Pyrex, our ground control.

Feeling bored, we called him, and he told us we could 'pancake' i.e. return to base and land. We hung about until 8.00 when the others came on readiness, should anything of interest come up on the plot.

Breakfast and down for a swim, while the CO, GC and Neville Duke (ex-flight commander 92 Squadron, now CO of 145) – over for breakfast – and the CO of 600 Squadron went off for a conference. A peach of a day, no cloud, hot sun and a fresh breeze.

August 14th: Last night on dusk patrol Young and Stevenson went off and soon saw an aircraft heading off for Corsica. Pyrex had reported nothing. Steve being the No 2, yet having the faster machine, caught it first. Young went down to the side to identify. It was a Me210 but without side markings of any kind, nor top markings; only very dim crosses on the underside of the wings. By this time Steve was right up its chuff and let fly.

The port engine caught fire and the flames shot back at him so that *his* engine gushed oil and glycol. The 210 fell away skidding violently in an effort to blow out the fire. Young went in and caused another explosion in the same engine; by now, they had come down from 30,000 feet to 10,000. Smithy and Jonah had come up from the deck led by the two smoke trails but when the Jerries saw them coming, they baled out.

Steve did the same and all three landed in the drink within a mile of each other. An air sea rescue launch raced out from Pomilano but by midnight had still not sighted them. Beaufighters continued the search but had to be recalled due to the formation of low cloud. A number of Bostons landed here for the night also, their drome being blotted out with the fog. Leghorn became very excited at all the aircraft in its vicinity and let off hundreds of rounds of shells in sheer panic.

I was called at 5.00 to search for the dinghy. Set off with Jonah at 6.00 and sighted the launch but my receiver on channel 'D' was not working. I plotted its position by timing the flight on course to the coast and pinpointed myself there. Pyrex gave me a rough vector onto Steve, and off I went. Just came down through a layer of low cloud again and there was Steve immediately below. Circled him for 35 minutes when the launch came alongside and picked him up, all OK. He gave me masses of parachute silk and cords – no use as a brolly again after being ditched in salt water.

CHAPTER TEN

Keeping Up the Pressure

August 15th 1944: D Day: the troops are now well established in Southern France. They landed at 8.15, the first landing to be made in broad daylight. The Mustangs from here went in to beat up some troublesome gun posts. They arrived on *our time*, i.e. one hour ahead of the invasion force from Corsica who were briefed to set off on *French Time*. How shall we ever win the war like that? Happily the Mustangs have tremendous range, and when they saw the gliders arriving on their way home, they turned and went alongside as escorts. Only one glider of that bunch of about 50, bent its nose on landing, but everyone scrambled out unhurt.

We were woken at 4.45, had a cup of tea, then waited for the CO who was late. Anyway, we got away at 5.30 (first light being at 5.55 these days) in double-quick time, formed up and away. Up to 18,000 feet past Spezia. There was low cloud about 7/10ths all the way and every valley was full of cotton wool almost to the brim. We went inland over Genoa and then turned left up towards the Alps. Our patrol lay to the west of the Alps to the coastal strip in the hope of catching any fighter Jerry might send out from his northern airfields.

The sun rose at 6.15, at 18,000 feet, but the haze so thick that Nice, almost at our feet, was invisible. The mountains of Corsica stood out just above the haze horizon. Back at 7.40 and there was no tea for us, even when we landed. All of us were feeling a bit narked about this sudden lack of an established procedure so I was not all that surprised when the CO ticked me off for falling into line astern of him as we flew over Leghorn, rather than out on the wing. The GC had called to learn of anything we had seen of interest and grinned heartily when I told the CO that we had direct orders not to fly over Leghorn, which he had done, as all harbour installations were out of bounds. It made the CO look somewhat stupid, I'm afraid, though I was in the wrong for having moved out of my allotted formation position.

We went straight off again, same patrol but not a sausage in the air, no flak, only cloud on the deck and haze all the way up. Back to breakfast at 10.00.

August 16th: D + 1, and still they meet no opposition. I went on a full squadron show this morning but we did not have to use the flarepath. Took off at 7.15 and having formed into three fours, started the long climb to the north-west. As we looked down onto Spezia, into sun, the haze was very thick. The two little islands at the end of the 'Great Orme' (it looks a bit like that from the air) looked like a double dot on the end of an exclamation mark.

The docks there are embraced by a man-made wall built out from the cliff, making them very extensive indeed. By 7.30 we were passing over the orderly rows of red roofs of Genoa; not a shot fired at us. We turned to '10.00 o'clock' and went up to Turin where the cloud started, in highly concentrated cumulus low down, but the Maritime Alps to the south were clear.

The air was cleaner looking down sun, and from 20,000 ft flying towards the west coast again, Monaco and Nice lay off to the right. The coast swells slightly south there, looking west, and I could just see the beginning of the Marseilles bay. We turned left to Genoa again, up to Nice and back again, and then on the way home we went down to the deck and flew just skimming the wave tops; it helped the time to go more quickly.

Thanks to our long range 'slipper tanks', specially fitted for the trip, we had been up for 2 hours 25 minutes.

The invasion of southern France safely accomplished it looks as if our job here is nearly over. The B party got its orders to move back to Perugia and before lunch, they were on their way. Smith and several other pilots, leaving nine of us here, went back after their afternoon swim. Dundas has a cold so is staying here 'to get better'! No joy for those on dusk patrol. Very high fracto stratus from the north-west; a storm soon, I'm afraid.

August 19th: Woken at 7.30, the beginning of a busy day. No time for a shave, just a wash and then over to breakfast. Down to Ops and dress up in Mae West, kit into the cockpit and stand by to scramble by 8.30. Monty arrived back from Corsica about 10.00

having had a wonderful evening with 263 Wing with whom he flew last summer. Fisher was over there and wished me well, which was good of him, though there was no sign of Roy Kingsford.

There is quite a flap on today; four of us had to be on readiness all day. Condon and I had to patrol over the drome at 8,000 feet from 12.15 to 1.15, so we had a quick lunch of bully cheese and bread between 11.00 and 12.00. Ben landed in the Auster at 1.30 with Squadron Leader Dyson. I was back on readiness by 2.00 with Monty.

At 3.34 we were scrambled to patrol over Leghorn. It was quite good fun, but though the little amount of cloud had gone, the haze into sun was very tiring to look into. No matter what happens in this new 'push' – in which the wing will play its full part – this anti-recce kite is just as important. In the last week a 177 has been over three times yet has dropped neither flares nor bombs. It is my belief that he picks-up short range transmission by local Jerries and Itis still here in hiding.

I have more or less adopted 'C'-for-Charlie – though that is not what Dundas called it – and tonight its wireless packed-up, a glycol leak developed and I find that the root of each propeller blade has been bored by woodworm! Checking the glycol leak, I found that I had landed with a dry tank, and just a spot left in the pipes; after 'T' and its dry oil tank, I suppose it'll be dry petrol tanks next time?

August 20th: Called at 5.00, so sleepy and snug; it was far too dark, so I stole ten more minutes in bed, then with a rush jumped into horrid dew-damp clothes – one of the curses of life in a tent.

I took my kit out of 'C' Charlie girl, just helmet, gauntlets and parachute and put it into 'B', our third Silver Spit; no need for camouflage any longer.

The crew had not changed the burst flap control diaphragm last night and became rather worked up when I told them that I wanted to take off at 5.45: it was done by 5.50. There was a little oval of light over the hills to the east, though the stars above were brilliant.

We took off and climbed straight up towards Spezia and by 6.12 we got a vector. The Jerry, a Me410, was heading due south, but west of us. We turned onto 270 degrees then Monty's wireless auto switched off. We flew over the devil, and about three miles *behind* us, but it was still so dark we would never have seen him beneath us.

Then we turned east, then north to Genoa to lie in wait for him. We covered the 110 miles in eight minutes diving flat-out to 3,000 feet. About two miles off Genoa the place looks very like a large scale river Conway estuary, looking from Deganwy on its northern shore. Anyway, he didn't come our way, so we climbed back up to thirty grand, to no effect.

My port wing tank would not come on and pressure dropped off – which can allow the petrol to boil at that height; then my wireless packed up and we came home after 1 hour 20 minutes.

Ben and the Wing Doc came over; no mail. Sunbathed, and cut a 40 gallon drum into a bath, as per 70 Squadron and desert days. Excellent.

August 23rd: A 'scrounging party' went into the nearest demolished houses yesterday for a piano, and found one, needs a lot of work but someone might enjoy playing with it.

My team was placed on 15 minutes readiness all morning, so I got cracking on the piano, bending a few wires straight; then spent two hours getting a piece of iron rod, drilling its end and trying to square the hole round the tag-end of a file to make a tuning key. Couldn't get the iron hot enough with a blow lamp, but the square is reasonable and seems to work. Tuned all the Cs, Es and Gs, then the As before lunch, since I was on readiness all afternoon.

We were called to stand-by, but halfway to our kites we were recalled. Relieved at 4.30 for 'dinner' and after a quick wash, and equally quick meal, went back on readiness at 6.00. Got fully dressed and into the cockpit by 7.00, largely because two Me109s have been appearing frequently at the time of the dawn and dusk patrols so we wanted to be ready for them.

We took off at 7.10, up to a leisurely 1,500 feet, then peeled off into the bay where the others – lucky Bs – were swimming. 'Riding the waves' till the last split second, then up the cliff face and house fronts, with vapour trails from our wing tips due to squashing, we sailed over the roofs and got on with the job. That was to climb to 30,000 feet, and hope to see the intruders.

After about fifteen minutes I suddenly felt very dizzy, so went down to 27,000 feet, but felt no better even with full emergency oxygen on. My legs and arms were suddenly full of pins and needles, indicating lack of oxygen so I told Con I was going down to the deck.

My chest first, then my whole body felt as if they were being crushed by some invisible force so that I could hardly breathe let alone speak. Gradually I lost control and tried gripping the stick with both hands, but had no strength in them. I tried to raise my arm to jettison the hood in order to bale out, but I could not lift it high enough, so I simply had to hang on, and get down fast.

At last 10,000 feet was indicated, and I knew I was safe if the problem were lack of oxygen. (Of course one never knows it – if that is the case – for one is supposed to feel hilariously drunk and happy before passing out for good.)

I was down to 3,000 feet, feeling very loose and floppy, flying mechanically with whatever pressure I could bring to bear, when my fingers started twitching and my face was being inflated like a balloon. I pulled down the mirror, having managed to open the hood to see my lips purple and pouting like some ghastly caricature; they too started tingling like fun. Coming up towards Leghorn, I took off my oxygen mask, in the hope of scooping gales of fresh air into the cockpit with my hand over the side. Suddenly the dizziness came back and the terrific force crushed me again. My whole body and my hands started jerking uncontrollably. This time I felt that I would simply *have* to bale out, willy nilly, for I was in no fit state to land the plane safely if at all. I slammed open the throttle and wallowed up to 3,000 feet using the trim tabs, when some instinct told me to put on my oxygen mask again.

Up at 3,000 feet, or so I thought; I tried to lift myself in the seat, but had no strength. Having made that little effort, I felt sure that had I rolled her onto her back in order to drop out, once in that position I would not have had the strength even to pull out the harness securing pin.

By this time I was approaching the landing strip and feeling relieved to be 'home', did a very careful 'wheeler' landing which came off better than expected.

Taxiing in, I overshot the turning to my dispersal point and half ran up a bank of bull-dozed earth; feeling very drunk.

I was obviously relaxing too soon. I switched off and took off my mask, started to undo my harness and collapsed. By this time my crew had rushed up and slapped the mask on my face again, undid my harness for me and lifted me out of the cockpit. Feeling such a fool I told them I was perfectly all right, and promptly fell in a heap. They lifted me up and propped me over the wing so as to apply oxygen again and I gradually came round.

Later, I was told that I went on breathing oxygen for 12 minutes and my breathing rate was 90 per minute. Every time I stopped, to breathe normally, I collapsed again. Virtually carried to bed, as weak as a kitten, I lay there panting and sweating like mad in some sort of coma I do not recall.

August 24th: Al Taylor flew 'C' last evening but was up at 30,000 feet for only about five minutes; even so, he complained of feeling dizzy. They dived onto a Jerry almost immediately; just their luck!

Woke at 7.00 feeling pretty fit, rather drunk more than anything, giggling at nothing and very watery at the knees. Very dry mouth – soon wetted with hot tea – and still light-headed. Doc has put me off flying and will take a blood test tomorrow (by which time I am sure all traces of whatever it was, petrol or carbon monoxide, will have gone).

My tummy has a pretty empty feeling and does not like being relaxed; it prefers to be tightly belted, i.e. under pressure from without, rather than from within.

The piano tuning key gave out at 10.00. I found a better square for it and this time got it really hot using the earth and blow lamp as a forge. Bending down hammering the square into it, brought on great nausea, weakness and dizziness again, so I sat in the mess for a while and soon felt better. The tuning went well and by 3.00 all was fine. All notes played freely and smoothly, repeating the faster the more they were used.

Corporal Brooks went off into Leghorn again to collect some more panelling sections for the Mess; he's making it very smart. Unfortunately he found them shattered with shell splinters. Even the piano has one splinter through its side, but having passed through the case it hit the iron frame so no harm done.

A new sergeant crashed after a flight to thirty grand. He undershot on landing, hit a bank of bull-dozed earth and rolled into a ball. Not much hope for him; he 's very badly smashed.

On patrol this evening Monty and Al ran into two 109s. Monty's spun off before he could get in a shot, and Al got a head on cockpit strike, very nearly confirmed, but could not see it hit the deck.

August 25th: Sergeant Sellers died this morning so Lobby and I went through and sorted his kit. Warrant Officer Sanderson, acting Adjutant, this side, dashed off to the Yank hospital to represent the squadron at the burial. The Yanks led him all over the country then decided that they could not find the cemetery. They brought the body back here so we'll bury it tomorrow. I shall take the burial party and so will have to set off later than planned on the Naafi run.

Some time ago, after that stooge flight for the radar spotters, I had gone to the radar site to watch the plotting. The airmen there had had a beer ration, something unknown to me here at all. This piqued my curiosity and by chance found that the man on the tube was their Naafi wallah. He told me that the place was down at Piombino, so that is where we'll go.

Feeling a lot better today but hundreds of pussy pimples on tummy and legs, and digestion very windy. Monty says I can fly tomorrow so I might, if we're not too late back.

August 26th: Woke fairly early and cleaned buttons and shoes before having breakfast. There was nothing to do but wait for the Padre. He arrived at 9.50 and we set off.

I had sent Warrant Officer Sanderson on ahead in case a grave had not been prepared. The service was very straightforward in a beautiful cemetery of about 2½ acres, three quarters full, on a slight slope. The sky was so blue that the white cross on the orange coloured earth had a violet collar, some freak of light transference I suppose.

The Yanks, who run the place were incredibly disrespectful, wanting to rip open the blanket shroud to take finger prints! I was so sickened by the very thought of it that I told them that he had lost his hands in the crash, which I am sure was not, in fact, the case.

Because of the possibility of a queue at the Naafi we went straight to Piombino, a grand little spot, but no Naafi to be found anywhere there. At last I got its location from a Scotty driver in the artillery, the only British type I had seen. It was 1.00 by then so we pulled off the road into a farmyard and brewed-up a good cup of tea. Off at 1.30 and got to the Naafi at ten past two to find that 'they don't issue on Saturdays', e.g. today!

All the staff were away off-loading a ship except for the sergeant, who was stocktaking and could not be disturbed. Space does not permit the line-shooting I had to do at HQ to get the stuff but after waiting till 4.30 we got three bottles of beer per man, twelve bottles of whisky, twelve of gin and twelve cordial for the twenty-four officers and senior NCOs.

I came straight back and everyone was delighted when they got over the shock: they did not think it possible. Now, after the piano effort, we are all set for a party.

While landing off the dusk patrol, Monty had had to land off the runway, wheels up; his engine had cut, presumably out of gravy. Only a small mark on one eyebrow, maybe from the gun sight? But it looks like cerebral haemorrhage and there is little hope. The shock of this has stunned everyone; nobody had heard of anyone getting hurt from a belly-landing before.

August 27th: Woke early as usual but lazed there listening to the crickets. I wish we had some birds here, but all we get are a few silent swallows.

Had a pretty rapid breakfast and down to readiness at 9.00. The phone rang at 9.30 to tell us that Monty had died at 6.00 this morning. We spread the news as quickly as we could. Sid Young, being the most experienced officer, took over the flying side of things, as much as it is, i.e. writing out the programme on a daily basis, which we arrange among ourselves. The rest he left to me. The Doc arrived back at 10.30 and told us of the funeral arrangements.

Our two Candians took over, freeing Sid, Condon, Franky and me, together with Lobby and Evans to have an early lunch and set off for the cemetery. The RC Padre read the service in Latin, then when I told him we were mostly C of E, he said a few prayers in English.

We set off back again at 3.00, had coffee at a Yank Naafi, and were home by 4.45. Jones and I did the evening patrol off Spezia. We spent one hour and ten minutes at thirty grand, indicated, and my fingers nearly bought it; I thought they would drop off with frostbite any moment.

Ben arrived with our new equipment officer. The signal about Monty had not arrived so he was naturally knocked back a bit. The flight sergeant has taken the only glycol pump we have from the stores to fit it to 'C' so I gave Ben a list of things technical and otherwise to collect from Perugia.

The new CO arrived at 6.00 and I introduced him to everyone present, a few of whom he had met before. We had a huge party in the mess till after 1.00. The very first party in fact since the squadron split into its two halves. Piano in great form and much appreciated.

August 28th: Woken at 5.00 but dozed till 5.15. Got dressed and went down to the flight with Jonah. We were to do 'stand by' till 6.30 while the others were airborne. They took off at 6.00 just as one 'bogey' came up on the plot, east of Spezia and coming south. As they climbed to meet him, the *one* turned out to be four! We were scrambled immediately but by now it was 6.25 and all the fun was over.

The 109s were above them when sighted, and instead of taking a squirt into their soft underbellies, they climbed up to them for a dog fight. One of the 109s got a few shots at Hackett and then dived away under Frank Newman. The latter peeled off after him and later shot him down. Hackett was told to follow and protect Newman's tail, but stayed up top to 'mix it', three to one! For God's sake why? The other 109s must have been very newly fledged for they didn't even attempt to attack.

We went up to 30,000 feet and patrolled off Spezia. The haze was held down rigidly by patches of cloud at 8,000 feet and the glare from the sun was terrific; a wonderful morning for spotting aircraft. We were vectored onto a Jerry who was hovering over Florence, so we tooled after him but he had gone long before we could get that far.

Coast to coast visibility ... marvellous. The whole country, lit by the early sunshine, was exactly a velvet green-grey relief map, a lovely sight. Very cold after an hour up there.

I sorted Monty's kit this morning, and moved into his tent this afternoon on readiness at 5.00. The CO left at 6.00, leaving me to take over completely. Smithy may come over to give us a hand, and he'll certainly send over any aircraft he can. The South African Jew boy brought 'H' over for us.

August 29th: The B ... Bostons were practising night landings till heaven knows when, so I took an aspirin which worked wonders. I woke this morning having completely forgotten that I was 'on'. Cloud had formed early and made a blanket over us so the morning was pleasantly warm and still. Con and Mosedale set off at 5.50 but returned at 6.00 to say that they could not contact Control on channel A. Al and I took off at 6.10 and the same channel was still duff. I told Al to try channel B, which was alive, and away we went.

Up through patches of cloud, fracto stratus at varying heights up to 34,000 feet. We levelled off at 28,000. At 7.15 we were vectored north (being down by Leghorn at the time), then east, then north almost to the coast, were told to lose height to 26,000 feet followed by a turn-about to put us up-sun of two 109s. They were still a thousand feet below us when they saw us coming and peeled off east but parted, so Al and I went each to 'our own'.

They started to climb when we were nearly in range so I tried a very short burst of cannon with wide deflection; no hits. From then on it became a diving match as we rolled over keeping G on to maintain full power to the engine. Surprisingly I had gained on him enough to be within range when we were down at 3,000 feet and to get under his tail I had to graze his slip-stream. The kite I was flying I'd never flown before and she was a bastard to trim at that speed. Luckily the Jerry flattened his dive a little which enabled me to pull up into range, whereupon he aileron-turned left giving me a chance for longish burst from just below his port side to just above. I saw some twelve strikes in the wing root which would normally be fatal, but nothing fell off so I won't claim it. Almost into Viareggio he was still spiralling down into the cloud-covered valley, so I left him.

August 31st: Corporal Brooks woke me at 5 a.m. this morning, everything very cold and damp. Down to ops by 5.20, got dressed and then just waited. It really isn't light enough to be of any use if we go Hun-Hunting before five past six now. We took off and climbed to 28,000 feet when they vectored us north, then south, then told us of a bogey at 9,000 feet off Leghorn. (An obvious decoy we thought, if it were a Jerry, making us lose all our precious height.) Anyway, they sent us after it, but as soon as we got down to his level, they lost him off the plot, and so we had to climb all the way up again.

The sun had risen at 6.18 at 25,000 feet, over the sharp horizon, making a magnificent spectacle, and making me feel smaller than the smallest thing in its sight; if there are Jerries about, I hope I'm that small, or should I be that attractive? So, we had our climb up again, and another view of that magnificent sunrise.

Sid was flying 'H', our only Silver Spit left, a starlike sight for anyone looking! My engine started to run exceedingly rough, but I could find nothing wrong with her, plenty of fuel, mixture right, but then the revolution counter started to show some ill in the engine. Suddenly I noticed silver lights in my vision again, the first time since February, when I knew that my liver had had a rough time. Also, after every breath of oxygen, a stabbing pain caught me under my heart, like a 'stitch'; it did not leave me feeling very happy.

At 7.15 we were recalled and I was very relieved to emulate the Lift Man by saying 'Going Down', while peeling over into a vertical dive. After a boring and freezing patrol, little gives more pleasure than doing just that. For an excuse (which I felt I had to have) I was doing an aileron check. The cables stretch – but not under our present form of warfare – so that the ailerons get sucked up too much in a high speed dive, causing instability; ⅜" at 445 mph at 3,000 feet is the maximum; after that, they have to have their turnbuckles adjusted.

Mine were as tight as owls when doing 440 indicated, which was around 570 actual, at 15,000 feet. If we *have* to carry bombs at that speed, those wings will not change for the Angel variety just yet, unlike the poor B ...s who have to fly 109s at that speed. My itches have all gone, thanks to Doc's Calamine lotion.

Sid and I did the dusk patrolling for three quarters of an hour over Spezia at 25,000 feet. My oxygen supply was leaking, so when told of a bogey steaming north, we did not bother to follow him, but came home.

We entertained a Colonel Walden of the USAAF and three sergeants to lunch. They are moving in eight Thunderbolts and a squadron of night-fighting Beaufighters. We shall be moving out, back to our main party with 600 Squadron so I let the news get around to encourage everyone to pack what they could, collect laundry etc.

September 1st: Called at 5.30 and went down to Ops, dressed up and went out to stand-by. The flarepath had just been turned off when we started off at 6.05; the stars were still shining.

We headed west to Gorgona, then north. We had patrolled till 6.25 when Control told us to steer 320 degrees, which we did for miles after miles after miles. Low cloud was hiding nearly all the ground and we could gain nothing it seemed from this trek. At five to seven we called Control to let them know we were still on 320 but our gravy was running a bit short. *Then* they told us to return!

On landing we asked why the unusual procedure? 'Oh,' they said, 'we've been told that Jerry has been commanded to intercept anything which goes north of Genoa and we wanted to see if he did!' Blimey, we thought, are we supposed to be that good? Checking our track, we would have been just about over Milan when recalled.

There were rolling patches of stratus at 20,000 feet on the way back with the sun and the cloud and ourselves all on one level. Every cloud made a spectacular colour picture, a truly glorious sight. Landed at 7.20 and stayed on readiness till 9.00.

Seven of the eight Thunderbolts have arrived, all new silver ones with vast balloon hoods, Squadron Leader Musson came over during the morning from Perugia, but had no news of our move. 600 Squadron are moving though no orders have come through for them to that effect. A New Zealander has joined us, named Meagher; personally I cannot tell them from Ausies.

Made up log books and flying time sheets. Amiens released last night we hear; forty-mile advance in one day. Field Marshal Montgomery well into Belgium.

September 2nd: Our dawn patrol went off and, as I expected, we were released at 8.00. Still no orders to move. Our telephones were taken away and Moru B (our general control unit) were losing theirs too, but since that would have put us completely out of touch I persuaded them to leave them till 6.00 tomorrow. The CO came over again, but still no gen. If we get moved tomorrow we shall probably go to the centre, Arezzo way, to weave behind the Tac R boys; they are putting in a four-day push.

If we don't move I think we shall go straight over to Loreto; those are my ideas, nobody else has any. Squadron Leader Musson told us that we might be needed in the centre.

The push goes well there, and on this side, Pisa is now wholly in our hands, after a month of stalemate. So, maybe we will not be needed here after all. High stratus coming in from the north and cumulus forming in the hills behind us; I'm afraid we are in for a storm.

The CO and Smithy went over to 234 Wing in southern France. They are living in tents still, but eggs and chickens, vegetables and fruit are being poured into them in an unceasing stream. They are still on the coast but expect to move up shortly.

The FFI are well up towards Annecy now, and our troops are on their heels. Vichy, Lyon and Bordeaux in control of FFI. I think I'll win my bottle of beer (European war over by 7th October).

We went over to Moru B to see Squadron Leader Musson at 8.00. No news. They are packed up also, but have no orders to move *anywhere* yet.

September 3rd: The sky was clear this morning after a night of terrific thunderstorms. It started raining at 1.30 a.m. and my guess was 2.00; I was not far out at that. Our drome is OK but thinking that Perugia could well have become a bog, I got 'Bluey' Meagher to fly up high enough to contact 'Commander' on the RT. Now that we have lost our telephones, it is the only way to contact base, and it doesn't take long. Told not to leave, and this at 10.00.

Since 7 a.m. we had been completely packed. My bed-roll (blankets and bed frame) fits snugly into the locker still known as the Desert Tray on which we used to store all the rations required for a 100-mile hike, if lucky. Next time I'll carry high flying kit and at least one change of clothing in the wings since all such stuff was buried in one of the lorries this time.

The cookhouse was unpacked again and we sat round in the sunshine, killing time. All we have heard, and this unofficially, is that as soon as we join the squadron, the whole will move north. I reckon that with this hold-up we'll both move together and form up again on a new drome. The advance is terrific, the Poles and Canadians have taken Pesaro. Belgium is being overrun and by this evening Brussels was liberated.

News reporters are unable to keep up with the advanced troops so all news is way behind, which they frankly admit.

The American push in the centre is being kept quiet for security. Yesterday they were doing at least one mile an hour and were 24 miles from the German frontier. Doc gave us a lecture on VD to pass away the evening.

CHAPTER ELEVEN

Bomb Racks to be Fitted

September 4th 1944: The sun woke me as it rose above the hills at 6.50 but I slept again till Doc woke me with tea at 7.30. How often have I blessed Kinglake (was it?) for his glorious phrase ... 'I woke and then slept; and awoke and then slept, then awoke once more for the sake of sleeping again!' How right he was, and still is.

Got up, bed-rolled and ready. Had breakfast of pork sausages and fried bread, toast and marmalade. We hung about waiting for a signal, but none came. Bluey went up but got no joy on the RT so, they must have left, and *forgotten us*.

A South African lieutenant called Lawton landed after a bombing raid and told us that the ground party was already moving from Loreto to Fano. Pesaro was taken yesterday, so we'll be about fifteen miles behind the lines. The convoy pulled out straight away, so we sat and lay about till 4.00.

We took off for Fano in two Vics, with one in the box and climbed to 8,000 feet. The visibility was wonderful, Florence, just off to the left, was like a relief map and the hills were green velvet. I called the team into echelon port and climbed perhaps fifty feet above them, telling them to formate on my No 2 and tuck it well in. As we flew east, and with the sun now well west of south, the formation would have graced any Hendon display, and I slid back the hood and took as many shots as my camera film would allow.

By 4.15 we could see the far coast line all the way up to Venice. Very surprised by the bumpy air of mid-afternoon flying but by five to five we had swung in and landed. The drome had been extensively bombed and the graded strip, running east to west, of some 2,000 yards had been ploughed. The graders had done a fine job, and apart from intensive dust, there being no wind to bother about, all was well.

We were the first kites to arrive. The GC greeted us in his car. The ground party were well established and after tea the sky was full – for an hour or more – of the squadrons coming in and dispersing. All buildings have been demolished. Grass is very long among the tents, so we'll have to have it cut. Met B Flight commander for the first time, one Bob Sarl.

September 5th: Called at 5.15 into an incredibly cold morning. I dressed over my pyjamas having no battle dress or any warm clothing. Al and Moose – our two Canadians – went on cockpit standby while Jonah and I stayed in the Ops trailer. Why is it 'Al'? not Alan or Alun, or Alfred or Alfriston perhaps; he is very touchy so I've never dared to ask, perhaps I never will.

By ten past six the world had colour again after the black and white of the full moon light. The sun rose at 6.35, about fifteen minutes earlier than on the other side. Drove out and collected Al and Moose at 7.00, but Jonah and I stayed in the ops trailer while the others went back to breakfast.

Slowly the morning warmed up but even by 10.00 it was still chilly; oh for that Mediterranean life rather than this!

It makes me remember a day not so long ago, having done the dawn patrol on the west coast, then a swim after breakfast and going over to some camp on the east coast for something or other we hadn't got. While my package was being organised I was invited to stay for lunch, then after it, for a swim in the cold green Adriatic. Not wanting to seem ungrateful to my hosts, I swam as best I could in that which seemed like ice water from a glacier. Happily I was relieved by a member of my host's squadron flying his kite so low along the shingle beach that the pebbles came at us like buck-shot, from the thrust of his prop. That gave me enough excuse to leave, saying, 'Thank you, that was most refreshing!'

No wind, and a blue sky soon warmed the day. 145 Squadron by luck found two 109s yesterday, climbing from a straff and got one of them. Neville Duke, with his incredible luck, was on a weather recce when the first of three 109s seen on this East Coast side came by quite close. He was vectored onto them and got two. (His score is now up to 29, I believe.)

We now have to keep two on readiness and two on thirty minutes until our bomb racks are fitted. The two on readiness were scrambled onto twelve 'snappers' over Trasimento, but were pancaked again when it was seen that they were heading north too fast. Really looks as if we'll see things. The Canadians on this side lost 25 tanks yesterday, in a heavy battle. 87 of them parked here for the night and pushed off at dawn.

All the NZ tank types came back here today, presumably on rest. Back on readiness from 11 a.m. to 1 a.m. and 5 p.m. to 7.30, the last hour in cockpits.

September 6th: Called at 5.15, not knowing why I felt somewhat annoyed – perhaps the interruption of a dream not to be missed? – anyway, it started a day of intense activity. We were called to thirty minutes from 6.00, but nothing came through till 7.00 and Al and I were the only one to get a trip. Over to Wing where we were given our target, and the area to sweep.

We took off at 8.00 but not all that smoothly. I was to have been the CO's No 2 but Blue Section's No 2 was unserviceable, so I took that position. Then on our way out, No 5's RT packed up, and I took over that section. We went up the coast out to sea and in just north of Rimini. The Jerries had some 88-mm guns which were very clued up. Al got a spent lump of shell case in his radiator flap.

We were shot at madly, north of the river, then orbiting the target (guns) just south, the air was ours. Nonetheless, we couldn't find the guns anywhere. The CO went down and raised the thickest carpet of 40-mm shell burst I have ever seen. Having decided that our gun target just was not there after all, we went north again and attacked a railway bridge. I hit the embankment.

Then we split up to do a Rhubarb. Lawton went off with his No 2, and the other three followed me. Lawton saw just one lorry in the whole area; it was a petrol bowser and went up well. We searched for half an hour at 1,000 feet. Bluey got separated from his crowd and went off north, having followed us for a few minutes. He has not been heard of since.

From a nearby farm house, we got a lot of 40mm tracer, but we couldn't find the gun position. Came home along the beach past an RAF pilot's dinghy amongst a lot of other boats. Sergeant Smith got two 40-mm balls through his port wing and one through his rudder, plus a .303 through his sump, but he brought her home safely nonetheless.

At 1.15 we were off again, and the CO put our bombs slap on the bridge west of Rimini, the only two out of the six. I was flying as his No 2 and followed him down. Very accurate and heavy flak and a bit of light stuff accompanied us, Jerry is a bit touchy about his bridges just now, but if we don't blow them, he certainly will as we advance northwards, so why doesn't he save himself the trouble and let us get on with it? (Just part of the idiocy of war, or is it just me?)

Wonderful view from as little as 1,000 feet, south of Rimini; could see Venice in the distance as a pink mass on green and grey water and land. Very intense artillery inland of us tonight, bang after bang, not a second in between.

September 7th: Covey woke me at 7.15. It was a quiet cool morning, but with steady, heavy rain. He was wearing his anti-gas cape and hood, so the water just streamed off him. There were ten of us on thirty-minutes from 7.00, so we might be busy. It finally stopped raining at 9.00.

I dressed in a *blue* shirt, collar, tie and battle dress; caused quite a sensation in the mess but the air was cold and fresh, i.e. damp, *very* damp, so it was really an excuse to wear a shirt I could not feel. A heavy drill bush-shirt is a particularly clammy garment in a damp climate, and far from flexible, particularly when one's hemmed in by overalls, Mae West etc.

The drome was sodden, but under about eight inches of top soil lies a deep bed of gravel. The trouble is getting the top very loose soil and stone mixture to dry, but we were assured that by 1.30 the drome would be operational.

Neville Duke and Cox came over to lunch; I had to hurry away for we had a Rover Jimmy to do, rather like Cab Rank, we circle just behind the lines, tuned in to the army radio frequency, and wait for them to tell us where they want the eggs laid. As soon as we were up, the cold front was crossing the mountains and layers of cloud in patches swept fast out to sea from the hills just north west of us.

These patches persisted from 500 to 15,000 feet so tried to weave our way through the gaps to 8,000 feet from which to bomb, but even so our targets were covered. The sky was full of other aircraft formations, fours and sixes, sometimes within 100 yards of us, quite exciting when one realised that they too were looking for some dot on the ground and not at us! We had to jettison our bombs out to sea. Two destroyers were still shelling the land from close in shore and about six mine-sweepers apparently in a line-astern circle.

It was raining heavily when we landed. The Mess is flooded,

literally a mess. With the thunder and guns booming incessantly we have nowhere quiet to ponder on anything. The news everywhere is excellent, and we hear of an offensive which has been in progress for a week, with Tito's Yugoslav liberation forces.

Also news that the flying bombs are no longer hitting London. 1,900 out of 8,000 sent were brought down by fighters and in the last phase – the 'battle' lasted 80 days – only nine out of every hundred got through.

September 9th: Nothing much doing today, so it might be worth recording the facts Captain Brown made known to me; we rarely see or hear of the actual fighting, which is all done by the 'Brown Jobs', a somewhat lurid nickname for the Army. The centre is very 'stiff', he called it. Yet, the Canadians and Poles to the right, and the New Zealanders to the left could move fast if allowed to ... it meant really nothing to me so I asked about the showing of our films. Yes, they could be shown at Wing tonight at 7.00.

'C' for Charlie was in for inspection, and I spent a lot of time being the 'mate', I know they liked it, as did I. She is a fine lady, so we christened her 'Charlie Girl', knowing full well that she will respond to my every action, as every good girl should. (Our Wing Commander, 'Cocky' Dundas, uses another extension of the letter 'C' when using it over the RT, I didn't know why, but someone said he must be thinking of the old adage that 'one into one, can make three'.)

Our state for tomorrow is 'All available aircraft from first light'; they must be throwing everything in as a final thrust. 231 Wing, flying from Jesi's Pressed Metal Strip (PSP) runway were hard at it all day on the thirty-six Marauder sorties.

September 10th: A glorious morning like one in early June at home. The GC put the drome unserviceable until 11.30, so after a lazy breakfast I took the 12 bore and ten cartridges for a walk through the long grass to the sea. I was surprised to see so many skylarks; they sang prettily when made to get up and fly but one never sees them flying of their own accord these days.

There are no partridges at all, only skylarks. I met a SAAF captain at the watch office from 185 Squadron, who told me that when they were 'in the middle' i.e. around Perugia area I suppose, they bagged quite a few pheasants. 'Hardly in season,' I thought.

It was the smell of gun-oil which reminded me of my days in Norfolk, when I paid for the lodgings and cartridges with the rabbits I shot 'for free' on nearby farms. My landlady told me that the old lady who ran the post office stores loved a rabbit, but could not afford one these days, some 10d a lb, so I told her I would give her one as soon as I could. It was a Thursday, which meant that I had only that evening's shooting to cover my expenses for the week, and I needed at least seven rabbits to break even.

My friend God, to whom I spoke – and still speak – frequently, knew of my miserly thoughts for I had already decided to break even before giving anything away. 'Thou shalt not tempt the Lord thy God' my guardian angel kept telling me, for which I thanked her, but pig-headedly went my own way. I learned my lesson, for I never saw a single rabbit that evening, and when I said my prayers that night I *promised* that the next one I shot, would go to the old lady at the post office, willy nilly.

The following Monday I shot ten, within about fifteen minutes, using the ten cartridges I usually carried; the place was swarming with them, but I had got the message and have tried never to tempt my Lord God again. I like my guardian angel; we get on very well together so when she pressed home the teaching of Christ that whatever you truly *give* away is returned ten-fold, I believed her, and still do. ('Let down your nets', He said, and they were filled to bursting.)

I walked back roughly the way I had come, the other side of the runway being too covered with aircraft. There was a pile of bull-dozed earth, grass and stones, hard by the runway and I thought I might find the odd rat or even rabbit behind it so walked over. Suddenly from behind it a peewit got off with incredible rapidity; it would have done credit to a snipe. I had already cocked the gun and was about to fire when I recognised it and was just lowering the gun when another got up, and before I could stop myself the bird was spinning in from the four feet of altitude it had gained. I felt pretty rotten shooting it but tried to console myself by the fact that these large and clumsy birds are definitely a menace to aircraft.

A formation of six was sent off at 1.45, 8/10ths cloud at 6,000 feet so it wasn't much good. A B Flight four went off at 3.45 and found five trains, all electric. There was no opposition so – very unwisely – they strafed. Many of these passenger and cattle truck trains carry our chaps as prisoners, surely they have been told that much? Kill the engine with pleasure, and give any captives on board the chance to escape, but rake the cars with gun-shot, and somebody might get hurt. Made myself a scarf out of the silk gore from Steve's parachute.

September 11th: Woken at 7.30 into yet another glorious spring-like morning. After breakfast we sat about in the sunshine, outside the mess waiting for Jonathan Blow, our Army Liaison Officer at Wing. At 9.30 the CO called me across to his trailer to tell me that John's pick-up was u/s (unserviceable). This was a day many of us had been greatly looking forward to, going right up to the front line to see the battle from the ground, for a change, but more importantly to show the flag, as it were, and sympathise with the chaps on the ground and wish them well in their arduous task.

I collected our Doc (you never know, do you?), Al Taylor, and rations for the day, and went over to Wing. There we picked up Jonathan Blow, Ben Garner, Bentley and 'the dim one'. We set off at 10.30 through the other side of Pesaro where the suburbs are literally *flat*, then through the Gothic Line defences, with their notices in German on the barbed wire etc.

We went up to a small village and parked the pick-up and walked forward to our latest ridge, captured eight days ago. A nearby village was taken in the same rush but was relinquished under counter attack.

We ran over the ridge and into the remains of a house where we watched the battle through field glasses at 4,000 yards range. Our guns fired continually, each shell passing overhead making a sharp 'crack' as it went. No troop movements, or tanks, but several squadrons of Churchills and Shermans were waiting, ready behind (just ahead of our guns) for any Jerry counter-attack.

Nearly all the fighting is done at night, we were told, since both sides have such terrific artillery to call upon. Two Shermans had been knocked out just over the lip of our ridge; the dead crews had been buried alongside though their bloody clothing lay in the sun, swarming with flies. The smell of dead bods on the whole ridge was pretty thick, though all bits found had been burned.

A Stuka dive-bomber had killed 150 last night in an attack on a laager which we presumed was a not very well dispersed collection of motorised infantry. The shock of learning of that loss was enough to dissuade us from asking any questions.

We had seen and *been seen*, so with our lesson over, we went sight-seeing to a Borgia castle. We got back by 6.15 to learn that Lawton had been shot up and baled out into the sea half a mile off Rimini.

September 12th: Lawton arrived back after an interesting trip. He was picked up at dusk after twenty minutes in the drink by the Air Sea Rescue Walrus, which could not get sufficient revs to achieve a take-off. Two motor torpedo boats on anti-E boat patrol had been told that any other surface craft than theirs would be Jerries. Hearing the Walrus, they opened fire and promptly hit its petrol tank, so illuminating the whole area beautifully! Taken on board the first launch, they continued patrolling until 5.00 and then made for their base. In so doing the second launch had its stern blown off by a mine, killing three of its crew.

September 13th: The weather much about the same this morning, ten out of eleven of our aircraft are serviceable but the push starts today again with thousands of guns and we'll be hard worked. The CO led off at 7.30 with a formation of six, they bombed Monto Scudo as '300 plus' rocket shells from Jerry's 'Sobbing Sisters', the multi-barrelled Nebelwerfers, poured over the ridge onto our troops. B Flight's four went off at 8.00 on an armed recce. They found two trains between Forli and Bologna. Going down to straff, Mannie's kite got hit in the glycol radiator and he had to bale out only four miles south of Florence, just in the foothills so he may get away with it.

Bob and I, Jake and Steve went off on a similar show, sweeping Rimini-Bologna, Modena and north to the river Po at Ostiglia, then past Ferrara. Bombed a road-over-rail bridge at Lavezzola. Our dive was much to shallow, and mine fell about twenty yards short of the bridge and ten yards off the road; the others undershot badly.

Down past Ravenna and home again. Bob picked up a bit of flak in his radiator flap; a near thing. We landed at 11.50, we now have only five aircraft, so they have put us onto aerodrome defence, two on readiness, and two on fifteen minutes. That leaves us ten out of our proper establishment of eighteen aircraft to work with.

September 14th: Yesterday we put up a new record for the Wing: 257 sorties in 47 missions, and I don't think we lost anybody. We shall move to Rimini aerodrome on the 20th, if the town is taken by then in this push. Things are going very well now.

Overcast morning again which keeps the air rather muggy, but on the whole it's pleasant enough. Six of us went off to bomb some guns just ahead of our troops. The grey world beneath was dotted over about 200 square miles with fires, some forty miles long by five deep. Every farm house and its straw ricks were burning with rich red flames, each its own plume of pale blue smoke.

It takes time to find your target when they are so heavily camouflaged, and their position only roughly known. We flew up and down the lines and watched Jerry's Nebelwerfers send their spiral of pale blue smoke about 5,000 feet high where it ends in a little puff, or quite often in a true smoke-ring when the propellant is exhausted. (One of 417 Squadron was hit by one and got blown to little bits.)

Eventually we spotted the place, and we went down. Four out of the six got direct hits on the gun pits. As the battle intensified, so did the haze, and visibility came down to a thick brown cloud of dust and smoke, rising to some 4,000 feet. Mitchells, Baltimores and Marauders were attacking in sixes. I never knew Jerry had so many 88-mm guns, but though he let hell loose on those boys with them, none was shot down.

At 3.00 another show was on, for which the Wing Commander had asked me to fly as his No 2. I was the first off of the seven of us and we soon found the battery of Sobbing Sisters, four of them, which were doing a lot of damage to our chaps on the ground. We went in to strafe following our bombing runs but at 50 feet one could see less than half a mile through the dust which smothered the place. I put everything I had into the nearest farm house, where the crews would naturally live.

Quite a party in the mess to celebrate our record! Everybody was there so small wonder that we got through £35 worth of hooch.

September 15th: A very pleasant cool morning again. B Flight were on first, but a show came through for us also. I went off in 'X', but couldn't get her to give more than 2,500 revs which would not have been enough to get her airborne, so I shut everything and pulled up just at the end of the runway. Taxied back and got Jimmy to look at it. He ran her all the way up and she vibrated like hell, and gave 2,650 revs at full bore – not surprising when it was discovered that she was still in fully coarse pitch!

So she was taken down to Maintenance to change the constant speed unit on the prop. Several of our newest Mk 8s have automatic settings for throttle adjustment so as to give us maximum efficiency and economy, in both engine life and fuel consumed.

Another show came through and I took Hackett's place since he had flown once already, and my trip was a flop. I flew as the CO's No 2 this time on a Rover Paddy. He sent us to look for some gun pits in San Marino, but they were empty. We went down together to some 50 feet to make sure, leaving the other four of the formation above cloud at 6,000 feet, as top cover.

The opposition did not exist at that time, so we went exploring. The villages were smashed to piles of spikey rubble, the odd hay stack or rick of that which was once straw still glowed and lazy smoke drifted up and away.

The CO asked me to identify an armoured car and since it had two Jeeps beside it I told him they were 'ours'. Then there were two tanks, 'Whose are those?'; they were Churchills so we went further north and in a gully in the hills found three big jobs, naked of any kind of camouflage. Under the trees and undergrowth nearby there were lots of suspicious looking objects so we pulled up to the cloud base at about 2,000 feet, and bombed them well, strafing as we went in. Then we called down the other four onto another bunch of motor transport that we saw pulling into a tunnel; the CO and I poured bullets and shells into it to show them the way. They bombed well, and blocked the tunnel.

Under my wing tip a farmer was trying to control his terrified bullock and some refugees, pushing their hand carts for all they were worth, and backing away from the tunnel. I hope there weren't any hit *in* the tunnel.

September 16th: Called at 7.30 after a good night's sleep; we were on the first show, thirty-minutes from 6.15. Got up straightaway and decided to have breakfast for it was far too dark to be called to action at that time of morning. The show came through for a briefing at 8.30: another Rover Paddy (close support bombing controlled by our ground observer in the front line).

Off at 9.15, climbing through patches of cloud from 3,500 to 5,000 feet. The plain east of San Marino was clear of cloud but Rover Paddy put us over the hills onto four guns. We went down through the clouds and dropped all our bombs neatly within the area required, not one more than twenty yards from the pits. Then they told us of transport in the Free State of San Marino.

I found a staff car and left it smoking, then Bob found two despatch riders and wrote them off. It reminded me of a search of mine about a week ago perhaps, following a winding road at about 100 feet when a despatch rider suddenly appeared in front. I flew over the 10 foot high stone wall which surrounded some estate, but the poor bloke on his bike couldn't, and I never fired a shot; it was rather a steep bend now I think about it.

Just as we crossed the lines an Auster flew right through us, the silly clot, but behind it was a most unusual sight. Austers are dangerously like sitting ducks to anyone on the ground and we quite thought that some new sort of flak was being used against it. Like a cubical balloon, some 200 yards across, 'ripened' like blossom before our eyes. There was no way in which we could avoid this silvery mass of ?, what the hell was it anyway? The penny dropped, as did the *leaflets*! (I should not have maligned the Auster pilot, for we must have been the culprits for crossing tracks; at his speed he couldn't avoid us anyway.)

The whole afternoon went by without further ado, and the weather clamped right down. We got four more aircraft tonight, putting us up to sixteen and that now, under a fresh ruling, is our full complement. Almost forgot, a new experience. No hydraulic power when I came in to land so I had to drag out the locking pins to release the undercart – which took some doing – and then blow the emergency supply bottle of CO_2; it was only just enough to lock them down. Examination proved that pipes and filters of the hydraulic system were *blocked*, which rather surprised me.

September 17th: We went to bed at 10.45 last night and put our clocks back one hour, naturally we hoped for the promised extra hour, but fate held us otherwise. The army, last night, took the last hill commanding the plain just west of Rimini. We were to strafe like fun today, sending six aircraft every ten minutes *all day* until our troops had dug in, but Jerry drove them off with a counter-attack during the night. This fight is now nothing but spite. 'Take that, you bastard,' we say, and Jerry hits back in like manner.

Anyway, the first six were called at 5.30 and since this yesterday was 6.30, I was awake. Ten minutes later, feeling in need of tea I put on flying boots and Irvin jacket to collect some from the cook-house only to find that the next six had been called for also. Dressed in a flash and after waiting for Bob we set off for Wing. They gave us a Rover Paddy.

We were airborne by 6.15. The cloud over San Marino as bad as ever so Bob and I went down to look. We found the two field guns at last and we all had to bomb in a 20 degree dive under the cloud base which was at 2,000 feet. The later bombs fell badly short which is understandable really, for some of the new boys feel terribly exposed in such a shallow dive, looking as you do down the barrel mouths of too many guns and rifles for comfort. The natural thing to do is press the tit to release the bomb and 'Get to hell out of here', albeit far too early sometimes.

Back by 7.45 to a good breakfast. The earth still warms quickly in this late summer month, so I washed and changed into shorts and shirt from battle-dress.

At 11.00 we had another 'do'. Briefed at 12.00 after an early lunch and set off at 12.45 after machine guns in someone's back garden at a cross roads. The cloud was 10/10ths all the way from 3,000 to 5,000 feet, so we 'tucked well-in' so as to keep together and hurtled along the table-top smooth cotton wool when we got there. The cloud ended abruptly by Rimini – just like a table cloth I thought – where we were heartily greeted by 88-mm flak.

We found two cross roads, and Bob bombed the wrong one. Luckily as his No 2 the others followed me and bombed in my bomb-burst, which itself was slightly over-shot, owing to the shallow dive I made, following Bob who I thought had merely misjudged his run.

Nothing happened later as the cloud was 10/10ths and low. Later it thinned a bit and we went off to destroy four 88-mm guns. Four of our six bombs went slap into the area, which was good 'shooting'. Bob, this time, came straight home so the whole trip took only forty minutes, and ten of these were lost due to a hang-up; it sometimes takes that long to dislodge a bomb caught in its toggles; one might have to climb to great heights in order to get the necessary thrust at the bottom of a dive and violent shaking of the aircraft to finally tear it free.

September 18th: Mike woke me at 5.10 a.m., when it was still pitch dark. But I was really awake, having tossed and turned for two hours trying to find a warm spot in the bed into which I could snuggle. Briefing was at 5.50 when we were put onto the northern side of the Il Grazie Ridge. The whole wing is on it, and 239 Squadron on the southern side. The army location map shows defences – machine guns and field guns – every fifty odd yards!

Six aircraft every ten minutes was the order of the day till Jerry had been softened enough. We had to bomb at 0515, and strafe the houses, and yet be out by 0619. It was terrific; every house a stronghold. I finished all my ammunition into hedges and houses where any heterogeneous object caught my line of sight, two bursts went through bedroom windows, which certainly warmed up *those* beds on a cold morning.

We formed up out to sea and sped back. Two destroyers were heading hard for Ancona and three motor torpedo boats were hard astern of them. The little air-sea rescue launch was bobbing about; it gives one a warm feeling inside, always, just to see it, though I hope we never have to use it.

I did some laundry during the morning, as the cumulus clouds had formed heavily over the front, but our pounding had done the job and the whole front is advancing well. Sat down to lunch at 12.20 and the phone rang for a show at 1.15. We gobbled our lunch, beetled over to Wing and got our field-gun target, and set off. No time to lose when that sort of thing turned our chaps into cats'-meat – come to think of it, I haven't seen a cat since I've been in Italy. Perhaps that's why there is so little spaghetti around, no cat-gut?

I took 'J' again; she's horribly rough. Bob led us, badly unfortunately, and we had to bomb more or less in cloud. Out to sea as we arranged, then he said, 'Rendezvous over target at 8,000 feet.' We were all at 5,000, so as we went inland we got in the way of dozens of aircraft on their own bombing runs when he called us out to sea again. What a waste!

Nothing to do all afternoon, but Jimmy told me that 'C-Charlie Girl' was almost ready. (Bless him, he's adopted my name for her already.) At 3.30, she was ready so off I went to twenty-five grand so that she could show me what she was made of. She's wonderfully smooth, and pretty handy, though only a fair average on speed (not really necessary for bombing anyway).

The army guns are now so far away that they are only flashes in the sky. We rarely hear their rumbles. Too hazy to see far even at 25,000 feet though the clouds were indescribably beautiful, the sun setting beneath their western horizon.

Shell damage: spare cartridges and pitot tube punctured, rear spar and flap shattered.

War as we saw it. Rimini was blasted, but not demolished. Other towns were much worse hit.

September 19th: The war this morning swung west so as to bring the central troops up in line with those close to Rimini. The town north-east of San Marino, that of Verucchio, also stands on its own little cliff. This was said to be full of Jerry troops, so we pranged its northern half, and the hill slope on that side, which was said to be holding heavy mortar positions. Having planted our candles in this funeral cake – for some we regret – we hoped to light them, or their ammo dumps, by using all our cannon and gun ammo into the hillside also.

Al Taylor was sent to recce the road north. Jerry had left his rear guards in the town we were told, but no flak guns. Seeing some of the troops 'escaping' in a truck Al went down to strafe them and got a bullet in his engine. Hearing the fuss it made after being treated so brutally he went south like a bomb, and managed to bale out just south of Monte Colombo, now well in our hands. He 'took to his brolly' at 7.50 and was back to lunch! The rest of us landed at 9.00, so we had some more tea and toast.

For the rest of the morning I got to work on Charlie Girl. She is in a filthy condition. We rather left it to the army to slog away all afternoon and, as somewhat expected, we were not called upon to help them and I was able to finish all the rubbing-down of the paint-work. She's due to go in for one of her inspections shortly, in a few days in fact, so I'll get cracking on her with our spray-gun. I think I'll mix-up a pale wood-louse grey for her, all over, true Rolls-Royce that she is, (with a little help from Supermarine!).

After tea, the CO led off a six formation, and we – about six of us – went into Rimini for badly needly (and atrociously executed) hair cuts. We mooched round the town to see whatever there was to see. There were hundreds of refugees with hand-carts covered with pillows, even chests of drawers, trying to find rooms. Many shopkeepers back today, trying to clean up what's left. A huge pile of rubble in one corner of the Square must hold a large number of people; the sour smell of very dead humans nearly made me vomit, and I had to hurry away. Three more Jerries were found in the rushes by the river which skirts our camp; the doctors say only three days old, all shot through the head at close range. Probably prisoners?

September 20th: A lovely night's sleep, and as yesterday, woke at 6.50 knowing perfectly the time and happy to dwell on 'thoughts for the day', 'thanksgivings for yesterday' while semi-conscious. Holmes came round with tea at 7.00 and told us of a show, take-off at 8.15. There was no time to spare, so I got up and shaved hurriedly, a quick breakfast then down to briefing at Wing.

Started up, taxied out, and took off. I had just got airborne when the engine cut, at about thirty feet. Already in rich mixture, I thought the butterfly might have stuck so pulled back the throttle a fraction. (With a live bomb under my belly I could not do more than a little of anything.) She picked up and coughed again to a partial stop-start staccato, but remained flying, thankfully.

Some terrible mixture seemed to be choking her, but with throttle back to plus 2 lbs boost she picked up a bit, so I whipped up the wheels and told Bob over the RT that I'd have to take her back.

She was hardly firing at all, and it seemed to take a year to cross the drome, scrape over the housetops and at last reach the beach and the sea, where I jettisoned the bomb forthwith. Relieved of that weight she almost bounced skywards, but sounded horribly sick at heart, particularly when I opened the throttle to coax her along a bit. Suddenly she responded like a clay pigeon and soared towards the heavens above; so immediate was it that I was loath to pull in the reins while gaining the height I desperately wanted.

The runway was clear of aircraft by the time I was at the bottom of the down-wind leg, so I left her to glide down and relieve her aching heart, or was it her tummy, suffering from indigestion? Yes, it was, indigestion. We found that the air-intake cowling was half full of grass, congealed with oil drops which carried above it half a pint of neat petrol swilling in a pond. God knows how much there was there on take-off, but as the drain hole was blocked the in-rush of air had carried that ultra rich mixture to the pots and wetted the plugs, poor things. Nothing so soaked – internally particularly I have noticed – can have much spark, if any.

Nothing else came through till an eight-aircraft show at 12.00. It was a bridge way north of Ravenna. There was 3/10ths cloud at 3,000 feet so Venice was just out of sight. The bridge was a beauty, three-span (convex arched job) and luckily we didn't hit it. Lots of barges on the canals, but these were forbidden fruit; they don't want the canals blocked with sunken barges.

CHAPTER TWELVE

A Roof over our Heads

September 21st 1944: All morning the rain scudded down, from cloud at only 300 feet, which stretched across the drome and far out to sea. Wasn't able to do much to Charlie over which we erected a tent – for want of a better word for shelter – but we did adjust the tappets. Two of these were tight shut the whole time, thereby leaving the inlet valves permanently open and losing a good fifty horsepower off those two pots; this could well make 10 mph difference. Perhaps that is why I felt she lacked speed?

I would like to have had the flame-traps changed, after all the muck which had gone up them but Jimmy doesn't think it necessary; we clean them pretty regularly with long 'bottle brushes'.

Practically everybody went off to the officers' shop in Fano, but I was duty pilot, in case the drome became serviceable. The CO called me into the trailer and tore me off a strip for saying what I felt last night. Evidently he chewed it over for a good four hours before retiring and intended to get rid of me but this morning has thought better of it.

I told the Adj how sorry I was that I had hurt his feelings, since he had taken what I had said (as a joke) as a reflection upon his running the squadron. Such a pity that these South Africans can never understand our sense of humour (any more than we can understand or stand their Africaans language, which they seem to use when we, the British, are not supposed to hear that which is being said. It really makes us sick).

Jimmy, Duffy, Warren-Hastings and I went to see *Rosie O'Grady* at the Desert Air Force cinema (theatre, they call it), and it was excellent. All the Wing were there. Back to dinner to find a chicken apiece! I decided to have a glass of vermouth with it to celebrate, and everyone joined in. It started a party – the CO being away. Divided costs came to 16/- a head.

After such a well-filled tummy, and hilarious chatter it was difficult to determine which had made my tummy ache so much, was it the unaccustomed over-filling, or endless laughter from which the muscles had grown exhausted? In any event I could not fall asleep in my usual fifteen seconds flat, i.e. after four or five complete lung-filling operations, with a pause at the top end, followed by complete deflation and utter relaxation of every muscle and again a pause. It is usually after only four such attempts that I remember no more.

Between the CO and myself, there was a barrier, undoubtedly, but nothing I could think of would warrant his obvious ill-feeling towards me, so I puzzled over it, instead of going to sleep. Obviously I would be incapable of running the squadron myself, but perhaps the innovations I had effected after Monty's death at Rosignano before the squadron was re-united as a whole here at Fano had given me an inflated opinion of my ability in that direction, who knows?

It had not cost us anything out of the ordinary to obtain the beer for the messes after Monty's funeral, and its arrival had been my goal anyway; the men needed some uplift. They had been used to seeing the squadron's score mount in ones and twos for many months, but we had lost Neville Duke to 145 Squadron, as their CO, and the news that fighter-bombing was to be our role in the future seemed to dampen everyone's spirits, just as the filthy weather had done to our drome, and our ability to fulfil that very purpose.

The outlook of fighter-bombing did not occur to me as in any way detrimental to the fine history the squadron had gained for itself, either in this war or the last. Perhaps I was hardened to flying through flak which my colleagues were not, and the very thought of flying below 25,000 feet was abhorrent to the majority if not all of them.

'It's bloody hot down there,' I had heard several of them say, when being interrogated after their trips, something to which they were utterly unaccustomed, particularly since the demise of the Luftwaffe they had known so well hitherto.

We were all fed up with wet clothes, wet bedding and having to struggle with bogged vehicles in snow-covered knee-deep mud; this was not, and never had been, our life to date and I felt strongly that there was no longer need for it to continue. Rosignano, on its sandy-gravel vineyard air strip, had been bliss compared with the cold and utterly different Adriatic climate. Our drome here is virtually a bog, surrounded by streams north and south and all of it practically at sea level.

My argument with the CO was quite simply that we *must* find dry billets before the winter sets in, and the sooner the better. 'You can be a stick-in-the-mud if you want to, but I don't know of anyone else who does.' He was furious, not, I like to think, because of his own vision of the squadron's situation (with regard to getting petrol, ammo, food and water to the men over rutted muddy tracks which was important enough surely?) but because the Adj had been with the squadron since the year dot – 'Right through the desert,' as he so often told us.

'Mobility, that's the thing. How can you get the squadron on the move at two hours' notice if they are scattered all over the place in billets?'

It was never my idea to *scatter* the men at all, just house them in their normal and natural groups with one man appointed in a roster at all times to be the 'runner', night or day, so that if Group called for a move, then everyone would be alerted within a few minutes. After sleeping well and *dry* for a few nights, we would all be better off. Why the CO and the Adj took it so badly I could not tell, for they, of all people, enjoyed their creature comforts as much, if not more, than I do.

September 22nd: This morning I was woken by the warm autumnal hum of threshing machine tackle a few hundred yards away. Chickens were crowing their praises of new-laid eggs and the sun shone into a perfect blue sky. I felt like a new man. I still regret the barrier which exists between myself and CO but still feel that if he wants to get 'stuck in the mud', he will have the good sense not to keep the rest of us stuck with him.

I was still not satisfied with Charlie's performance, so we changed the whole air filter, which was quite a job. She is now being completely re-painted by a cellulose expert from High Wycombe. That will encourage my crew to follow my Nannie's very strict instruction to me: 'If a thing is worth keeping, it is worth keeping *clean*,' – to me, she meant less material things such as firstly one's soul – which can be so easily damaged by taints from many sources, one's mind, for similar reasons, and one's body.

Jerry's recce came down at 11.15 this morning, making vapour trails, but no one bothered him. Also one bomber went over at 9 p.m.

September 23rd: Went up to Maintenance to see the finished Charlie girl in broad daylight. She is very beautiful now and we'll keep her well scrubbed.

The boys had quite a good time pulling wrecks out of houses in Rimini. Lunn got himself a camera, wireless and electric fire, (roll on that day when we have a house to plug it into!). The Greeks were mad with delight, blowing locks with the Sten guns. They got a safe into the road and blew it open with an anti-tank rifle, only to find it empty. The CO released us after lunch and about 14 of us went off. The sour-sock smell of dead bodies, now considerably reduced in the towns.

The army reports that the central sector is going well, fifteen miles from Bologna.

September 25th: Again a brilliant morning. The Wing Commander, Cocky Dundas, rang up to say that he would take the first show, so I, as his No 2 led out. We took off at 10.00 and climbed slowly going north up the coast. Past Pesaro we flew over huge clouds, or rather through gaps between them in some of the roughest air I have ever experienced. Eventually the Wing Commander found our target which was very tricky to find from the photographs given us. I had not positively identified it myself as yet, so stayed aloft while he went down, and I dropped mine where his bomb had fallen. I hope it did some good.

Then we went down to strafe the valley where our mortar targets were supposed to be hiding. In these light flak came from just north of the area and as the Wing Commander broke away, his kite was hit by a small arms stuff, one through each wing. I had seen it coming up at him; some of it was tracer so I headed for the guns which were invisible to me, and they stopped firing. Those nuisances out of the way, we broke onto our proper targets immediately followed by a hard swing to the right over the flak guns, so their shooting would be inaccurate when they picked their heads up again.

Then the Wing Commander screamed that he was hit, and was he streaming glycol? He wasn't, but we went home fast. Once over our lines he asked me to see the holes from underneath, and despite our props almost tangling, I couldn't. He kept saying, 'You *must* see them, come closer' but the blackish mud splashes on the under side of the wing and the wheel spats made it impossible. He made a peach of a landing on one wheel, the tyre of the other being punctured, with not enough ground-loop to cause damage.

We followed him in when his kite had been pushed out of the way and after a quick lunch we were off again to bomb and strafe the cemetery of San Giovanni di Galilia, which we did in no mean manner. The cemetery is on a ridge where the village lies, and it overlooked our troops swarming up the hill towards it. The walls of all their cemeteries are about six feet thick, with pigeon holes (or should it be coffin holes?) throughout the inside lining containing photographs or other memorials, and they are virtually impenetrable without overhead bombing.

Reports later told us that we had killed an important General and some 250 Jerries; I believe it took three 3-ton lorries to collect them all for burial.

It rained again this evening, but Cyril Wells and Olive Del Marr, plus Marius Sellars of *Eve on Leave* made quite a party after the show in town.

September 26th: Aerodrome again a bog, but we may be able to get off at 12.00. We had two guns to bomb and then a recce up north. We did get off. When going north, round Ravenna, Control called up and asked us to stop a train going east from Bologna. We hurried off but couldn't find it, but in its place about five miles east of Bologna were sixteen cars. As there was no likelihood of them holding any of our chaps as prisoners, we strafed them; no problems.

Going from west, back to the east, we saw a stationary train and engine about three miles east again. It looked a cinch so we all spread out and waited our turn. A lot of 40mm flak had been waiting for us too, but it wasn't very accurate. The train load comprised about eight open trucks and eight flat-tops, with motor transport and two tanks on them. I concentrated on the engine and on my third run every shell went right home; it really was perfect air to ground firing. In air combat, the deceleration effect of the cannon is so short-lived that one's automatic tensing of muscular control – to aim and fire accurately – tends to pull the stick back just that fraction to compensate. In this prolonged air to ground firing the deceleration effect is so much more marked that the nose drops quite fast, and has to be corrected. Perhaps I have got used to it by now. Anyway, the film should show it.

The CO called us up into formation again so I was the last to strafe. He congratulated 'No 6' on his gunnery, but since it was I, and it was my luck to have a 'buckshee' strafe, I did not acknowledge. It should do Moose some good since he was the true No 6 of the formation.

Started a head cold and my cheek sinuses very painful coming-down; merely full, not infected very much. Inhalations have not done much so if it gets worse, I'll stop flying. Olive and Marie came round to tea. Very nice to have them. Cyril is bringing the whole cast for a party after the show tomorrow night.

September 27th: My cold today has developed into that pendulum state wherein for half an hour one feels grand, then a heady dizziness swoops one into bleary stupidity with much nose-blowing. No blockage of sinus, DG.

The weather is clampers again on the front so there is only a little practice flying for the five new NCOs we have. The Squadron was released at 4.00, so we bundled into the flight pick-up and had hot showers at the portable unit in town. Unfortunately it moves to Rimini tomorrow. Came back and 'smoothed-up' into new blue shirt. I altered two collars on Jimmy's sewing machine this morning, and they've turned out quite well. The standard collar has its points too close, almost under the tie knot, so I cut off $\frac{5}{8}''$ at the tip of each, and stitched in the raw edges with a tiny hem.

Adj and I got cracking on the sandwich cutting and egg mashing from 7.00 to 9.30. It was a terrific spread. Unfortunately, someone who ought to know better is very drunk, having been knocking it back with another of the same sort all afternoon. The two of them brought quite of crowd of others with them for the party and luckily sobered up enough not to spoil everything by the time the ENSA types arrived.

The Adj drove and I escorted them back at 12.00. We had to rush them away before the chap who brought them could get hold of them again. 'Never again, please!' they pleaded; so who are we to deny them?

We got back at about 12.30 when battle commenced: 'Piggyback'. This started to smash furniture and glasses like tinsel in a matter of seconds, far more quickly than anyone would have suspected for the rules of the 'game' had not yet been decided. John Blow, Jimmy, Duffy and I rushed the tables, crockery, and all available glasses off, out of the mess. Everything very quickly stopped when Corporal Brooks broke into tears at the sight of his broken mess. Never before has 92 ever let its guests smash up its mess.

I went to bed last night leaving Brooks still weeping and telling the CO that he was applying for a posting. I thoroughly agreed with his point of view, for I had seen something of the way some of our 'tough guys' liked to show off in public, and the more carnage and splintered wood they left about, the more they seemed to like it. The feeling of most of us was simply that the war had brought about enough carnage and misery, so why add to it? It was a great come-down for us and we felt very ashamed that this thing had ever happened; it often does in other messes but we've always kicked rowdy people out before.

Jones went off on a weather recce to Bologna very early. Cloud base was down to 300 feet everywhere, and because of this every road is packed with Jerry transport. He clobbered an engine, which blew off steam like a geiser, and two cars, before getting a 20-mm ball through his wing which cut his air pressure pipe (for flap control) and his aileron control.

Churchill gave us some figures of the north-west Europe battle to think about. Out of every 3 fighting men, 2 are British, and 1 American. Of the fighting vehicles, we represent 4 out of every 5½ yet we keep our casualties down to 9,000. The poor Yanks have lost 140,000; some battle!

October 1st: An odd morning of quite *blue* cloud, pastel shade, at 10,000 feet. Ops went by steadily as usual on a fine day. The CO pranged when he landed off the 8 o'clock show, badly cut about the head and an ear lost, but he's been taken to the head-mending hospital (83rd) near Rimini so they ought to find him an ear to match off some stiff. They were put onto a Jerry pontoon bridge which he defends better than he did his aerodromes. Four got hit altogether. I spent the morning making up my log book and the CO's.

Mannie is now in Naples being interrogated having been

'brought back', but Don Wright came through on Thursday and got a signal to us from a South African Squadron. Jonah flew over for him in his Spit, discarded his parachute so that Don could fill the gap, and Jonah sat on his lap to fly the thing home. Grand to have him back. He told us of his treatment and experiences, with the Partisans who found him and brought him through.

The Jerries are really terrified of the Partisans and rightly so. Jonah's party caught three Jerries on the way back and just knifed them, time and again in the guts until they fainted; then they shot them. Evidently that's the sort of treatment we can expect, and the way we'll go, if we fall into the hands of the Fascists who are drawing back with Jerry in the Po plain.

October 2nd: My cold is streaming heavily, but we're so short of people that I'll fly if necessary. Low cloud over everywhere again today, so no Ops as yet. Sat playing with the piano in the mess most of the time. Johnny Gasson, a SAAF fighter pilot – said to be a first class type – is on his way back to our wing; he was a flight commander, so will probably take over as CO here, everyone who knew him certainly hopes so. (The present CO has been made Station CO).

Adj went off today to get some more hooch for a party on October 10th, our birthday!

At lunch-time, a squadron leader type from Public Relations came down from DAF headquarters to say that the day we bombed that cemetery at San Giovanni di Galilia we killed the colonel – not their general as we had believed – and his staff at the observation post. The body count of 250 Jerries was accurate, it seems, but more importantly our chaps were able to storm the hill-top position with their heads held high! So highly was the army delighted that Al, Steve, Sergeant 'Red' Smith and I had to give our own stories, photographs 'an-awl', just like film-stars we were! *Ever so*!

Just because he learned of my time on 'twins' and other 'Desert' activities he wasted yet more of my time. (Hey-Ho for Public Relations!)

Finally after that deplorable delay, I managed to get to see *You Were Never Lovelier* with Fred Astaire and Rita Hayworth; I was delighted to learn that 'Our Fred' is English – I never knew!

Very wet and sloshy back at the camp; it's all wrong to be here at all.

October 3rd: It rained steadily all night and this morning everything is mud, leaving us all bad-tempered. Bob is aggressive this morning. He came across while I was shaving at 8.15 and told me that we had to do 'readiness' from 9.00, so I took the first pair. Had a quick breakfast and off to Ops. Due to the impossibility of getting to our briefing point and back to our aircraft in reasonable time – no one thinks of our comfort it seems – they have kindly moved the Ops trailer to the edge of the runway. The bomb line now is more or less the Rubicon.

Our ten mile bridgehead has been wiped out and Jerry has more artillery than that. A big scale attack was to have been made the night before last, but this perpetual rain has put paid to it.

At 9.45, we were called upon. 145 Squadron had sent out four aircraft, two of which were shot down, one over the sea. I took off with Sergeant Smith (a new Aussie) as my No 2 and we went straight to it. Easy to see, just at the thick end of an exclamation mark of oil, from the sunken aircraft. He was not being shelled, nor were we and at 10.50 a Walrus came along to pick him up. After four overshoots he landed; they picked him up and back we came rejoicing – for him at least if not for his mate. The Wing Commander rang up when I landed and said, 'Jolly good show': what else could he? It was a grand morning, and a very pleasant little trip.

October 7th: Called at 7 a.m. and told that briefing was at 7.15! Why the rush? Such is the salt that Abe (our briefing officer) is made of. We got down to Wing Ops by 7.45; it's quite a distance, and he let everyone know how late we were. We were supposed to be on thirty-minutes availability from 5.45. Naturally if it's a normal patrol one can get dressed and airborne comfortably within the thirty minutes of being called, and now, with briefing at Wing, we expect to get there by the half-hour. Abe has other ideas, he thinks we can get up and over there in fifteen minutes, then back and away by another fifteen. He's nuts anyway.

We took off at 7.10 and went up to Cesena. Heavy guns two miles south were our target. The flak was the heaviest yet. 88-mm followed us everywhere and 20- and 40-mm shells bursting formed a cloud blanket we simply had to fly through. As I went down in the bombing dive, a 40-mm burst just below me and a splinter about 2½″ by 1″ rattled into the starboard elevator at the trim tab box. It merely steepened my dive a bit (having nearly knocked the stick out of my hand).

She seemed to go very solid when I tried to pull out, but she came up quite nicely using the trim tab control. The canvas flapping about disturbed the air flow a lot but after five minutes all the canvas had gone and control came back to near normal.

A quick breakfast then off again, the Wing Commander leading. Two 250-mm guns we were told were waiting for us way back behind the lines. Guns as big as that must be worth seeing we thought. About 160 rounds of 88-mm were fired at us on the way in, and out, judging by the rapidity of the shell bursts and the duration of the time involved. I made a dummy run, as I was too steep, but even on the second attempt I overshot by about thirty yards. The Wing Commander called us up on the way out, each in turn, and when No 6 had said he was OK, he replied, 'Amazing'. He told us afterwards that he had never seen so much stuff thrown up.

October 9th: Surprisingly enough the water has drained away quite well this morning, 601 Squadron are bogged down so we were put on aerodrome defence. Lazy morning reading the *Countryman*, which arrived yesterday.

Down on readiness at 3.00, into the cockpit at 4.00. Just having a sandwich and cuppa when scrambled. The Yanks had been doing close support with Thunderbolts and one of them baled out just off Cervia. We circled and searched from 4.45 to 5.25 but saw nothing. The Walrus arrived and thought they saw a submerged body. Huge storms were blowing over from the west and as it was growing dark, we called it off and landed at 5.35.

Another Yank, having had his port aileron hit and jammed, intended baling out off Rimini, then like a clot, instead of baling out over land, or crash-landing, went all the way down to Ancona, and then baled out into the sea. Luckily he got away with it and a launch went out to pick him up though there was a hell of a sea running.

Went over to Wing after getting horribly stuck in 18″ of drying mud – now almost solid – and I'm amazed our truck clutches stand such treatment. I brought the film people over and gave the mess a half hour show of strafing films.

October 10th: Today is sunshine and showers; in fact storms really.

I'm delighted to see a flock of about 150 sheep on the drome. The ripened grass seeds, scattered by slip streams and bull-dozers have made a wonderful carpet of the richest green grass after the rain.

An old woman has been round collecting the snails which still climb up our tents, boots, suitcases etc every night, I suppose they eat them?

Airtests only this morning, but we may get the odd show later on.

Some days ago I was approached by one hungry-looking youth of about sixteen who could speak a few words of English. He told us that we had killed his parents and destroyed his house together with all his belongings. He had nowhere to live and I decided that he could be useful keeping the camp site clean, carrying water and taking our washing to the ladies in the village. We fixed him up with a tent, and I introduced him to the cookhouse, telling them that he could be useful to them if they wished, and please feed him.

His help was most welcome to us, though some chaps loathe the Itis as much as the Huns. His name is Enso; someone said it ought to be Eno's, 'These Iti's give me the shi ... vers'.

This morning one of my films had obviously been stolen from my camera. Never had anyone suffered theft of personal or other goods once we were out of North Africa, so I immediately had to suspect Enso. I always mistrusted his shifty eyes anyway. I got him to clean my boots while Corporal Brooks and I searched his tent. My film was in *his* camera, wound, exposed and onto a 120 spool, mine being a 620. I told the Adj, and Duffy (who was with him at the time) slanged me right, left and centre, saying that I was degrading myself terribly by accusing the lad so I let it rest.

Tubby discovered that £10 had gone from a pocket in his clothes so the search of Enso's tent was resumed afresh. Everything came to light, even Steve's diary which he feared might have fallen into the hands of the Germans. We grilled the lad thoroughly but with sympathy and it came to light he had stolen stuff and thrown it away or destroyed it simply from his personal need to destroy everything he could, belonging to those who destroyed his life, or so he put it.

My exposed films he had burned, even my cherished echelon port exposures I took while flying over from the west coast, and not yet developed. Three cigarette lighters were found and all sorts of stuff. We then went into town where a friend of his lived – he could have lived there too had we known – and there we found Tubby's gloves which he had bought in Florence. There'll probably be a lot more yet, but we handed him over to the Carabinieri; Heaven help him now!

Eric Mannie turned up with Captain Gasson, who returned, after a wash and brush-up, as *Major*. Quite enough excuse for a party, which went excellently. Group Captain Paddy Green, ex-flight commander, brought Pat Burke along from Naples or somewhere; the airmen loved it.

October 14th: Corporal Brooks called me at 7.00, saying that take-off was at 8.40. I dressed in battle dress, black flying boots and long socks. Toast was being made on the stove when I came in for breakfast. Down to Ops at ten to eight. Rover Paddy work, like Cab Rank, when we fly off to pre-arranged rendezvous with photographs of the area, criss-crossed with grid line and wait for the observation Johnny to tell us what he wants flattened.

Just as we returned to the flight, the trip was postponed. In any case, I thought I would put in my kit, (helmet, gloves, 'chute etc). Then just as this was done we were told to take off as arranged. It was a grand trip. Patches of cloud – stratus – at 2,000 feet. We flew up to 9,500, and I pulled my seat up to its full height, feeling like a king; the world looked very beautiful.

We flew up to Cesena, half covered with cloud at 5,000 feet, no flak to greet us today. Then orbiting Gambettola observation post, we were given a cluster of houses, eight in all about half a mile north. Funnily enough four of the bombs fell in the gaps between the houses, which were pretty close together so they may have bulged their walls somewhat. Only two direct hits. It was Major Gasson's first trip, so we didn't go in to strafe, which was a pity. I felt fit for anything this morning, and Charlie was as sweet as ever.

After lunch we were briefed at 1.00 to bomb a jetty loaded with ammo north of Ravenna which would have been fun, but all afternoon the cloud was 10/10ths at 3,000. At 5.00 we bogged off into town to have a shower.

October 15th: We were on the first show this morning, being at thirty-minutes from 5.45. I got up and made some toast on the stove but we were not called upon. As arranged – if nothing came through – we went along to Wing at 7.30. They gave us a target each, two sixes. Our second six took 417 Squadron's show (Ops had forgotten that they held twelve of *us* on!).

We took off at 8.15 to bomb on the dot of 8.42. The air was horribly full of aeroplanes, two squadrons of Mustangs, and about thirty-six Spits, all just south of Cesena. It was made all the worse by the very thick haze; either into or down sun you felt you could see only as far as your wing tips. The guns were located just north of the army's 'sound-located' position and we bombed them well. I got a direct hit in the pit, and the others were almost as close. We re-formed well south, and after orbiting for quite a while in case required for a strafe raid, went home.

The weather clamped a bit and though I was in the next team to take off, we never did. The REs have now completed our up-graded strip of gravel, and now want the PSP from the old one, putting us out of action for some 48 hours. Went to a party at 145, and fixed for Ken Noyle to bring the cast of *Ensa Pie* along on Thursday.

October 18th: It rained very solidly last night for two hours so the work on the drome is held up again. Took Doc and Warren down for a shower. The Adj and CO, have arrived back from inspecting our proposed new camp site. They have found a magnificent spot where everything can be included. Major Gasson is truly an excellent fellow. He has now detailed me to find the local Admin Officer of the new site tomorrow, to set up a housekeeping party etc.; ought to be rather fun.

The heaviest barrage I have ever heard started at 3.20 this afternoon, probably no more intense than that at El Alamein but we are much closer to this one. When I went to bed the roar was louder and more consistent than a heavy sea breaking on a rocky shore.

October 19th: Having collected my 'house-keeping' party, together with rations for the day, we tried to make an early start. It rained gently all morning but we got off at a quarter to ten. At first the road was clear, but towards Rimini we were held up for half hours on end, nose to tail for miles.

We arrived at the proposed spot at 12.45, so we got a brew going immediately and took a stroll round the four buildings. The owner is a dapper little chap with long white moustachios, struts like the proverbial peacock and received us with cold resignation. He speaks English and French without much hesitation but tried to put us off from our intention of billeting ourselves here for he explained that forty people already occupy it, seven families in all.

I saw the Town Major after lunch, a French Canadian, and he was very difficult indeed. He wanted us to go south of the drome, so to butter him up a bit I went down to see them with him. The buildings he suggested we use had been shelled to pieces yet he expected us to have the Royal Engineers to put new roofs onto them etc. He was quite shocked when I told him that they could not do that sort of thing; they had better things to do keeping the roads and bridges usable.

After a lot of hard working diplomacy I got permission to occupy all the buildings we want and a chit signed to that effect. Large forces are moving through and will be there, possibly, for a fortnight. The drome (sand) will be ready for us in about six days, but we shall probably have to live under canvas for a few days, or until the army moves out. Got back at 5.45, very tired.

October 20th: A heavenly day, but we didn't get a show till 8.00. The labourers were still working on the runway when we taxied out but they soon scattered! Formed up quickly and up we went to 7,500 feet, so clear you could see for ever!

We had an old target, one heavy gun quite well north. Every time we bomb near a pit, it makes them move the gun which stops them firing it for about a day. Its new pit was about 50 yards from the old one. The north wind was very strong and, bombing from north to south, we all overshot. Another six went after it, when they heard of our abortive attempt and clobbered it well and truly. Tubby hit their ammo dump a few yards away.

The weather clamped down at 4.30; we got our release and went down for a hot shower. At dinner we heard that our forward troops had occupied Cesena after house to house fighting. The CO told me to take a party out there tomorrow so I selected a crew and turned in early.

October 21st: Woken early at 7.00 and got up straightaway. Had breakfast and laid on a 3-tonner. Corporal Brooks, Cliff Hackett, Warren Hastings and Sergeant Doyle came with us. We got off at 8.45 and were in Rimini by 10.15, very good going. Then we turned down 'Lincoln' track south of the river and eventually crossed it into Santarcangelo, finding it very badly smashed. On through Savignano – also smashed beyond repair.

From there on the dust flew off the tarmac roads so that visibility was down to 50 yards at times. Still the road was very clear of traffic. Five dead horses still lay on the roadside approaching Cesena and stank to high heaven. Going into the town we discovered that no one but Iti's were to be seen.

We drove gaily on till we found tanks half-hidden between houses; I hailed one of them and asked how much further we could go? We were told that Jerry had a nice little machine gun nest just 200 yards ahead! Everything was quiet, hardly any shelling. We went east to the residential area only to find all the residents at home! We went into several small houses which Jerry had ransacked but found about fifteen odd glasses and five cups. Looking round for something a little more promising I found a better class row of houses and when we approached the best-looking one, found a notice pinned to the front door, 'Reserved for the Town Major'.

We had split up slightly to save time, and were walking round to the back to find a way-in when a shell exploded slap on the front door step; 'Open Sesame' said someone. So, with blatant robbery, we walked in and helped ourselves to glasses and odds and ends for the Mess. One drawer had about twenty kitchen and table knives ground to fine points, like stilettos, highly vicious; I wondered for whom those were intended?

Set off again at 1.15, and had tea with the aerodrome advance party who had just arrived at the drome but soon pushed on again through drizzling rain and got back at 5.30. 43 out of 46 glasses arrived home safely.

CHAPTER THIRTEEN

Near Catastrophe

October 22nd 1944: The weather was almost on the deck all day and we hoped for a release around about 2 p.m. so that we could go to the cinema, when the phone rang ... a funny little tingling feeling just above the navel and an indrawn breath from everyone, showed something of our tenseness, but all done with calculated nonchalance, we hoped. Low cloud like this can only mean two things, that Jerry is using the cover to run for it and there should be plenty of game on the roads and secondly that our losses from such concentrated ground fire could be severe – as well as I knew from 222 Squadron days.

Lander was on the blower to say that there was a likelihood of a show coming off. I rounded up the types and we went down to Ops. A Rhubarb it was to be (i.e. bomb a particular target then scour as far north of our lines as possible, shooting up anything Jerry has left of value to him. The further north the better, for he then thinks that the country is over-run. All this, after bombing, has to be done at hedgetop height, or lower ... or else!).

Four pairs were called for. Everyone's face was taut and looked a bit grey when we heard it. The Adj described the rather frightening penetration of a fighter pilot's eyes, which, he says, look so old, in such a young setting! I think we did all look rather like that as we motored down to Ops in the drizzle. Originally it had been six pairs, for we normally operate in sixes these days, but now four of the twelve were released; they were youngsters who gathered, I think, that they had probably been reprieved from what they took to be certain death (again remembering North Weald on Rhubarbs, they could well be right).

All feelings were easily subdued when we started dressing and we planned our attacks. Jerry was suppposed to be pulling out hard to straighten his line, east to west from Bologna. Met said 9/10ths cloud at 9,000 feet so we took our bombs. We went off to find 10/10ths at *3,000* feet from Cesena to the north, a solid blanket, so we went out to sea and dropped our bombs.

Steamed up the coast to just south of the canal into Ravenna and in we went, all along the deck. It was infernally bumpy and very dark after the brilliance of above-cloud flying. All was disappointingly quiet, no transport to be seen anywhere, not a soul could be out working in those water-logged fields. Farmers' families were standing in their house porches watching us pass by, and regarding the atrocious weather. Bob went along the canal leading slap into Ravenna. It's true that we might have seen convoys there but we never glimpsed a thing.

Suddenly we were the hub of a wheel, the spokes being dotted lines of slowly moving golden drops – my old acquaintances of long ago, those gorgeous Dingleberries, but never had I seen them at such close quarters. Bob was way up at about fifty feet so naturally they saw him coming first, and those ahead of him fired head-on. He dived into them immediately and I thought he had *had* it. I pulled up – in order to aim *down* – and pushed everything, throttle, guns and cannon, knocking out three guns in separate pits in echelon port from where I was. That stopped them but a single 40-mm gun put a long yellow finger up Bob's starboard quarter. He turned into it, but was over its top before he could get in a shot. We were now heading even closer to Ravenna, being about half a mile out of the town.

That fellow's shooting was damn good, and Bob was so high again that I thought he would cop it. I was a bit further south than he was so my chance of pulling round onto the gun was better than his. Naturally one turns hard and fast on these occasions and even as I started I saw a winking yellow light off my port bow, which made me pull all the harder when there was a *plop*, like the noise of a paper bag being burst. I saw a piece about 14″ by 10″ in my port wing, just aft of the cannon bloomed with metal petals, like a conjuror's paper flower from a pot.

It seemed to decelerate the wing rapidly but an immediate feeling of relief came over me. Flying through that stuff, and feeling like a duck in a fair-ground shooting gallery we were very much the centre of attention and I knew I would be hit. Once it had happened, I felt safe. Nonetheless, I couldn't get the nose down and round again onto the gun before I had overshot him. Down under the trees again, I had a chance to check everything. We were flying up a shallow valley, and having told Bob that I'd been hit I looked for, and saw him, a little ahead but at least 200 feet up, while I found myself flying under a span of high tension cables.

Seeing him up there – too dangerous for both of us – I pulled Charlie up into the merciful blanket of cloud at 1,200 feet. Checking instruments, I had pushed the revs up to 3,000 and throttle up to plus 6 lbs boost, speed, 165 mph. All seemed well.

As the stick became lighter – in my uphill pull – I eased gently forward to take the air speed into safer regions (with a damaged wing which could stall way below safe parachuting height) and nothing happened! After about eight seconds of blind flying in that helpful cloud cover, I popped out into blinding sunshine like a salmon from a pool, nearly vertical, and right on the point of stall – as indicated by Charlie shaking with natural wrath; they don't like being treated like that.

Then, and only then did I realise that while I had an accurate altimeter, the pipe from pitot head to air-speed indicator had been cut, leaving the needle set at 165. I headed south and Bob joined me over Rimini and from there we sailed south to the drome, always wondering if oil or glycol had suffered from the bombardment from below, but all was well. Bob asked me to formate on him for landing. Kindly enough, he flew at well above landing speed (in case my left wing caused me to stall into the deck at low flying speed which would have been fatal), so I waved him away, flew another circuit and knowing that my flaps would be useless – the hinge was shot away – felt her down very gently, flying – as the Yanks love to tell us – 'flying by the seat of my pants'.

Poor old Charlie. On inspection, that exploding 40-mm shell had not only cut my air speed indicator pipe line and flap control, it had severed the rear main spar and – most surprising of all – had actually punctured the few rounds of 20-mm cannon shells remaining in the magazine without exploding them and me to smithereens!

The CO had a 20-mm ball through the rear of his fuselage which shattered his accumulator and his No 2, Warrant Officer Doran, had to crash-land, about a hundred yards inside our lines. The aircraft broke up and he was lucky to get away with a whole self. Three aircraft almost written off. Shame!

October 29th: The weather 10/10ths again this morning after a night of intermittent rain. We all pushed off into Fano at 10.00 in search of billets. We found three houses on the main road, just perfect for ourselves and the NCOs. We put about a hundred men in straightaway and then had a look at the Count's house – our moustachioed gentleman – where we hope to move soon. Actually for us, the few officers concerned, it is not what we want. The whole palace, as it must have been once, housing those seven families that he had told us about had been too long the domain of those family retainers for us to intervene, conquerors or not; hence the search for the bulk of the squadron's billets, while ours, had to have a telephone link; tapped or not, it little mattered.

There are only about three rooms in which we could sleep, being ante-rooms or drawing rooms off the ballroom, which means eight to ten persons in each. The ballroom we decided to use as our Mess, and once decided, his Grace swept us into it with more than one would expect from a well trained butler. His motto was not in evidence, but *Noblessė Oblige* would have been adequately apt, I thought.

His coat of arms is everywhere present: a Maltese cross at the head and a unicorn plus three stars blazoned occupy the bottom half. My guess that this is very early indeed, almost certainly going back to the Crusades. Our Mess 'hall' must have been over 50 feet long, for it had four huge murals in relief plaster along each long wall, each measuring some 12 feet by 10 foot high panels.

The staircase itself is a national monument, pretty wide with shallow steps of brown mottled marble, in six-foot flights between the pillars, with a four-foot landing between flights. The whole gracious assembly spirals widely from the central courtyard of the house. It's the oldest house in Fano, I was told. (As a footnote to this transcript of my diary notes, I would mention that our Adj, Lawrence Travis, who was such a perfect caricature of Colonel Blimp, though much more lovable, actually fell in love with the Count's daughter, and married her not long afterwards, and had a son. It gave me much pleasure to see this confirmed bachelor so subdued after such a short space of time. Such is the force of a woman's attraction; long may it be so.)

October 30th: The morning appeared clear in the north but heavy low stuff crept relentlessly up from the south. A team of six went off at 10.00 to bomb the store park and landed at 11.00. The weather was pretty low but hoping for the best I went over to Wing maintenance in the 15-cwt pick-up to air-test my newly winged Charlie girl. My parachute had slipped off the seat into a quarter inch of water, so I hurried back to get another. On arrival, Bob asked me to take four new types on a show to let them see the battleground, and try their hand at bombing.

I nipped back for lunch and intended taking off at 1.15. Unfortunately most of our aircraft are bogged down *behind* the impassable taxi track, where those on Readiness have to stand, so our take-off was scrubbed. The weather closed in and it started to rain gently. The drome was wonderfully quiet. A few larks gaily chased one another at high speed and a 12-bore cracked away up the valley every now and then. Partridges, I expect.

Despite the difficulties of low weather and the boggy drome, I was determined to have Charlie doing her intended job in life as soon as possible, so I took her up: whereupon she refused bluntly to tuck up her legs. Put her down, over to Maintenance and jacked her up onto tressels. (She still has a petrol leak and a very gentle oil leak.)

While checking the undercart we discovered that the adjustment of the manual controls was very badly out of alignment, and somehow their electricians had put my navigation lights up to my undercart so that when my wheels were not locked down, my red lights came *on*. Same thing happened when the wheels were not locked *up* ... quite a puzzle and I let them know what I thought about it, for such mistakes could be lethal!

We went on a show which was a horrible bore. We sat over Rover Paddy for 55 minutes, then bombed slap over Forli, trying to avoid it for flak there is very intense as a rule so I made my dive very steep. We were up for 1 hour 25 minutes altogether. Came down and made out log books etc. 14 hrs 45 mins ops last month. Even that low score was above the average. On early recce tomorrow, so early to bed.

November 1st: Corporal Brooks called us at 5.00. Got up into the bitterly cold night, the moon shining its fullness upon us with more than its due frigid beauty. Tea and toast then down to the aircraft. I took Bob's 'A', a beautiful kite. Took off as the CO's No 2.

It was very dark at 6.10 and we used navigation lights up to

Pesaro. There, 10/10ths cloud lay beneath us at 3,000 feet. We turned out to sea then due west till we spied a clear patch just south of Ravenna. I have never seen a more inspiring sunrise. The clouds out east had their horizon suffused in peach-gold and crimson.

10/10ths above, at 9,000 feet gave the blinding sun a momentary flame. Its soft red rays poured and hung on the top layer then as the sun seemed to rush at us between the layers in its full face, the lower carpet grew red in a fantastic stream, ourselves being the centre of the fan. Had we been shot or blown to pieces at that moment, I felt that it would have been a perfect ending.

Funnily enough, after one stretched look into the clouds and sun ('You never know, you know!') a terrific flash appeared quite close. You don't often see the flash from an 88-mm shell burst; it has to be that close. They pooped a lot of stuff up at us after that. We were running along the Po and must have flown over a bridge which was still whole.

We swung south, 10/10ths still holding over the whole valley, the cloud forming a perfect water-line round the hills, in and out of valleys and crags.

Way beyond Florence – hidden by the hills – the 9,000-foot hills next to Spezia have a good 4,000-foot cap of snow, such a glorious sight. A clear patch revealed Faenza beneath us, so we headed home, the sun now being well above the 9,000-foot layer. Cumulus was building up through the stratus to the north.

How it occurred I do not know, but the refracted sunlight through the top layer of cloud flooded those cumulus with an exquisite duck-egg green, so pale yet so clear that one looked several times to ascertain its presence. Way south-east I noticed a minute hole in the carpet of cotton-wool cloud and then as we approached, it was the little cliff-top town of San Marino; its warmth had dissolved the quilt of 'glass-wool' and the three little points just poked through. What a wonderful sight from the church tower that ocean of cloud must have been, yet there was nobody visible to enjoy it. At last, after one otherwise uneventful hour exactly, we landed: the most perfect approach and landing I have done on this field.

We came back in close echelon starboard, and I don't recall ever flying so close as yet; the closer I got, the more I liked it, my cannon just off the wing tip of the CO's machine. (Open praise from the ground observers is a rare blessing.) Something about the stillness and lack of turbulence at that hour of the morning here helps a great deal. It reminded me of the 'Bull' fly-past we always did over Chelmsford, when going out to the coast from North Weald; going out and coming in, we always tried to put on a show; for the people down there had had enough of 'sneak raiders'.

And so at 9.00 we moved into our billets. It was a strenuous two and a half hour's work, but the Count had lent us a lovely 'upright', the worse for German wear but I'll fix it in the morning, if I can get some glue. Five *Tatlers* arrived, terrific. A pen and ink portrait of Robin Johnston by Olive Snell is excellent. He is now a Wing Commander of a Mustang wing, it seems.

November 3rd: On the team of thirty-minutes stand-by from 7.30 so I got up at 7 a.m. and had breakfast. Huge storms were blowing all the time and giving really heavy rain. I went round to Wing and drew out £10 which I gave to Adj for extra messing. The piano this morning is grand – how I wish it were just one of those! The keys have stuck wonderfully. At 11.30, Abe rang about a show.

We went up to briefing, the Wing Commander leading one six and the CO the other. A sugar factory just south of Ravenna is now a strongpoint of resistance. We returned to lunch hoping that the weather would lift a bit. It did, shortly after 1.00 and we went down by stand-by. The recce was done by 145 Squadron and as fast as they gave us the all clear, we were off.

Our take-off and formation was the best yet. In one half circuit we were all in position, all twelve of us, and that takes some tight turning and great concentration, straight off the deck. We climbed slowly, flying at 180 mph but stayed below the heavy raining cloud at 6,500 feet. Just south of our target the storm ended and we wheeled out to the coast and in again at 8,000 feet. The Wing Commander went straight in, much too shallow and undershot by the 100 yards. Being No 5, I waited and went in from almost on top. Gave the bomb four seconds to drop, counted eleven seconds for the delay and watched. Up came a great red-brown cloud of building dust from the centre of the factory group. We formed up straight away and set off back to base.

Hutch had lost all his air pressure and on landing overshot; not unexpectedly since he had no flaps or brakes. The kite turned over onto its back, but he's all right. Cut sandwiches after dinner for the SAAF Concert party.

Too many men and too little work. *Hooray*, I'm off on leave in the morning.

November 4th: Corporal Brooks woke me at 5.30. Needless to say I did *not* get up. At 6.30 it was half light and I dressed, packed my few needs into a parachute bag and had breakfast.

At 7.30 we were under way, batting down the bumpy road to Jesi. From there on, we wound through low foot-hills with the same dull flooded countryside all round us. Jesi aerodrome was literally packed with aircraft; the Thunderbolts have moved in as well as everything else from the look of it.

Suddenly we started to climb, the sky was as blue as it could be. (Odd that the first day in weeks that we could *possibly* have flown the journey, we find ourselves going by road!) The first range of hills showed us just what we miss on the coast. Full poplars along every stream, hundreds of feet below, all yellow and shining like polished brass. Little mountain-ash trees and low shrubs turning copper, but it was the elegant height of the huge trees along each valley which commanded all eyes.

We went over three ranges quite quickly then slid down the zig-zag passes into Foligno; the high mountains to the north were just dusted with snow. Riding behind the cab in our 15-cwt pick-up, with woolly coat zipped up tightly, I felt the sun and wind burning into me though in some of the passes, out of the sun, the wind and our forward motion nearly froze us to death. It was a long hard push (after sandwiches and tea at Foligno) to arrive at Albergho-Reale at dusk, 5.20. Shampoo, haircut, and into Blues for a delicious dinner; we're here. Rome at last, and I love it.

November 5th: Today we walked in the morning, having woken early and *tea* arrived at 7.00. (This was a wangle by the man who occupied the room before me. Enquiries tell me that it is not to be repeated as a practice. Shame!) The sunshine was heavenly. We toured the town south of here, along Umberto Street, then across to their 'Bois de Boulogne'. Had coffee on the terrace of the restaurant 'reserved for British officers only', then slowly, through the trees and fallen leaves back to the hotel for lunch.

The number of civilian cars outnumber the military ones by about 30 to 1. We enquired as to how they got their petrol and were told that the Yanks, Negros especially, ran the black market. At first, the police used to check up on the cars using military petrol, and confiscated any they found using it. Now, they have used up all possible space to house them so let the whole matter slide. It hurts a bit when the people at home can get virtually none, and even when you consider the ending of so many men's lives, having to bring the petrol across the Atlantic, and having to be fried alive, floating on a sea of burning oil when a U-boat finally catches them.

After lunch I lounged in a really hot bath for an hour; had a wizard shave and then had tea. I settled down to write some letters but found that I could only write one letter home. It must be some reaction or other which will surely pass, but somehow I'm rather disappointed with the place. Half the streets have no pavements and those which have are never more than four feet across, so movement is sticky.

Steven went off to see his popsie, while Warren and I went to see *Thousands Cheer* at the ENSA theatre; quite a good film in this vast theatre called 'Super Cinema'.

November 5th: Today I practically walked my feet off, but enjoyed every minute of it. We set off for the officers' shop just before 9.00 and arrived before it was crowded; a good twenty minutes' walk. They had little RAF stuff, but hope to have shirts and so on in by Saturday. Bought socks, tooth brush, tits for 39-43 Star and a tie. We hunted a good many shops for Christmas presents, mostly scarves of Italian silk, so easy to post.

Found an ideal tie for father, but naught else. The scarves were £2 odd, and the very fine woollen ones even more. Practically all woollen goods apart from cloth contain 50% angora, cheaper than importations I suppose. Nearly every household has its rabbit hutch for the wool (whereas we at home keep a few chickens for the eggs!).

Rome is said to be full of beautiful women; as yet, I have seen but one, and she would pass unnoticed in Regent Street. She wore a lovely Glengarry suit, two silver fox furs, swept up the front and ending just behind her shoulders. Gloves, bag and court shoes of very fine pale brown leather (I disliked the colour but it is in fashion here at the moment). Her hat was a wide fur felt almost of sombrero proportions of the same colour. The others were small, over or shabbily dressed and over made-up usually with poor complexions.

Plucked eyebrows are still in vogue here.

There are plenty of the key-swinging variety around too, and they don't wait till dark to hawk their wares it seems. Having been brought up to learn and understand that a night with Venus could well mean a life-time with Mercury, that sort of pastime is not for me. Tragically enough, we learn that the Jerries have used the new Sulphanilamide drugs instead of mercurials to combat VD throughout their occupied territories. Either by intent or default, the doses given simply case-hardened the bugs which are now immune to that treatment.

We lunched early in the sunshine at the Garden Restaurant, but feeling unsatisfied, returned to our 'pub' and lunched there too.

November 8th: Up at 8.15, breakfast, then straight off to the Victori Emanuel Memorial, the 'Wedding Cake' as it is called locally. We found a caretaker and he showed us through its empty halls. The floor is of marble, but no clever intricate designs, just circles and rectangles like a public bath house.

In the basement we found three models made by the architects with various modifications on each. Model capitols, a bronze bust of the architect himself even! The gilt bronze horse and rider at the top of the pallisade weighs 50 tons, measuring 20 feet by 20 feet.

After that, we went through the various ruins taking pictures of the Colosseum etc. truly a huge affair, though the arena was quite small. (With my sister on the stage, I begin to sympathise with the importance of large bookings and sufficient seats to accommodate them, no matter how little important is the performance on stage.) To give us some idea of the seating capacity, we were told that the surrounding wall was, at the top some 180 feet high.

Back to lunch, followed by a walk round the walls. Passed the Pyramid to the Castel St Angelo, a most interesting place, built about 1500. A bust of Cicero and one of Hadrian stand inside the keep. Popes lived there till a king was besieged in it; then he very wisely turned it into a fort. Models of catapults and machine cross bows stand on the battlements, together with original ball amunition.

November 10th: Had a lazy breakfast for a change, collected our sandwiches and set off to call for the nursing sisters we met touring

St Peter's. We ran south and soon rose up the hills to the little town of Frascati, where the famous wine is made. It was one of the bitterest dry days I can remember. Snow clouds tore themselves to shreds on the mountains as they came in from the east, and soon our faces became set so that to smile was difficult: years since I felt like that.

We passed Lake Albeno, a crater from the long extinct volcano. The hillsides were wonderful, stippled, mottled, yellow-brown. The chestnut trees giving the loveliest of colours then Oak and Ash all blending. We turned up a dirt track till we could go no further, then walked for two miles to a monastery. We filled our billy-cans with water and sat there under the walls working like crazy to get a fire going.

Rome, about fifteen miles away, and fifteen hundred feet below, looked exactly right, a hazy yet glittering white bowl set centrally in the hills which lie behind, and the Tiber flowing down the gentle slope to the sea, which itself looked no further than a stone's throw away.

At 3.30 we wandered down the hillside picking wild flowers and trying to absorb the smell of wet earth, leaf-mould and trees all at once. There wasn't a bird to be seen. These Itis are worse than the French for shooting anything feathered.

After dinner, Warren and I went to a variety show across the way. Apart from the conjuror, it wasn't worth it.

November 11th: Slept till nearly nine this morning; the extra blanket on my bed helped a lot. At 9.15, we set off for the officers' shop. I saw the clerks and they told me that I needed an RAF stamp to buy the suit of blue. Dashed down to No 2 base area and flannelled the Adj into signing the form, back to OS and collected OK. Bought a pair of flannel pyjamas, the first I've ever had; must have been the effort on the Adj that made me think of such stuff to sleep in.

Then to Mussolini's Palace across the street, and saw a wonderful collection of Masterpiece paintings, from Naples, Florence, Venice, Milan, Turin and so on. The most lovely, I thought, was Grossi Grosso's Madonna, in a wonderful blue, quite unobtainable in pigments today.

After lunch we rushed down to St Peter's and climbed to the golden ball on the top.

This is nine feet in diameter, much smaller than it looks from the ground, and only just room for three people to climb in at once. It is quite illegal to take photographs within any of the basilicas we were told but I got a good shot of the square below by viewing through the tiny slit window overlooking it.

Coming down to the square, we found that the damned MPs had pinched our truck again, but I got it back without much trouble. A quick tea at our pub and then to a soirée held at the flat of Steve's friends. It was grand fun, just a collection or gathering I should say of young people, dancing, talking and drinking tea with lemon. We stayed much longer than we meant; then the long walk back to a superb dinner.

The fish entrée was cold, a huge beast four and a half feet long, delicious even so. We sat next to the quartet and they played me the overtures to *Don Giovanni* and *The Marriage of Figaro*, and loved doing it. It must have exhausted them, having put all they had into playing those vigorous numbers (when only four are playing the parts of an orchestra particularly) and other requests were answered with '*Domani*', and so to bed feeling wonderful; a half bottle of Frascati helped.

Sunday, November 12th: After such a delicious dinner last night we felt that an effort was necessary so when the phone called us at 6.55, we got up straightaway. A very brisk walk – it was freezing, just about – to the little English church, quite beautifully built of brick and imported pure white limestone. (The local limestone looks as yellow as Dutch cheese). It was a delightful service, but the sight of the massive brass eagle lectern, always with its highlights polished like distorting mirrors made my eyes water; not so much the polished brass, but that grey-white powder of dried Brasso cradled in the hollows, just too home-sick making at that time of the morning.

On the way back we climbed the steps in Spanish Place, the flower stalls empty as yet.

We had been advised to enjoy a meal at the So and So restaurant, but we should 'beware of Topolino'. Mr 'T' was the head waiter of this most august establishment and made sure that 'his guests' lacked nothing. Our tummies were still contracted to made do with the rations we gratefully received, so that enough was enough, despite the protestations of Mr T, whose chef would be most embarrassed etc. etc. etc. We had been warned that Mr 'T' enjoyed

92 Squadron Reunion, London 1956.

his farewell palm-greasing in a reversed cup of a hand, held behind his back.

Never a pudding eater myself, I retracted from the idea of placing a portion of Crème Caramel in the man's hand, for he would immediately think that the unwanted 'dish' was mine. We tossed for it, or drew for it, with broken straws, and I was 'out'. Standing in front of Mr 'T' and trying the European bow to match his, I am able to say that he deserved a place in Hollywood.

In perfect timing with his discreet bow – from the hips – his hand clenched the egg-sized lump of Crème, but as it trickled through his fingers, down his trousers to the floor, his face showed no sign of his emotions if any. All I can say is that he stayed bowed as we left, and we never saw his face again; it could have been blanched white, or furiously crimson, what ever it was, he was not prepared to show it to us, and we were grateful for that.

November 13th: Called at 6.15, up and dressed and packed by 6.45 and had breakfast. As we gathered in the hall, we felt that we must be very high dignitaries by the way the whole staff lined up to bid us farewell, and safe journey. I got the message eventually, (being a bit unused to this plush hotel life, I suppose) and doled out the tips in the icy hall until our truck mercifully arrived at ten to eight. We picked up the Doc at 8.15 and sped out of town.

The hoar frost glittered on every horizontal surface – so it was freezing after all – I knew it had that extra nip in the air. Sitting in the back, the sun came streaming in, and kept us snugly warm.

The roads were dry and empty so we arrived at Foligno at 12.00. A quick cup of tea and our cheese and bully sandwiches and off again. Soon we were climbing the snow-capped mountains, and way above, ski-tracks could be seen. Up the winding pass we turned a corner and there was snow, not six feet away! It gave me a most curious thrill, and quite a shock. Down into the lush valleys and up through the next two ranges but below the snow line (about 3,000 feet by now) making wonderful time.

Then, from Jesi, the bridges were still being washed away, even so, by 4.50, we were back in the mess. Approximately 310 kilometres, no wonder we felt dog tired. '*Toujours la politesse*', said some one, 'The ENSA party has been invited round, so do your stuff.' Unfortunately they came without escort, and did not know when to leave. Eventually the lights 'failed' at 1.15, and I was able to sleep; my room being one of the ball-room ante rooms to the present Mess was no help on this sort of occasion, which is rare enough anyway.

Jake and Aussie Smith did not return from a weather recce over Yugoslavia.

November 14th: Rained solidly all last night but the drome has learned to drain itself, so it rarely suffers. How long before it becomes useful farmland, I wonder? Rupert Mansfield used to tell us that farm land is just like a baby, to get the best out of it all you need to do is 'feed it, clean it, and *keep its bottom dry*'; on that basis this drome should soon be useful to someone!

A six went off but the weather was appalling and the whole trip rather a waste of time; we were released at 11.00.

I went over to Wing after lunch to air-test Charlie girl; her new engine has bags of guts, but on the straight and level her ailerons are all over the place. I have ordered a new starboard aileron; the new one on the port wing does not match its counterpart and sometimes one has to juggle with several to get a perfect match. Tomorrow I hope I'll get a fine day and really have fun.

The whole ENSA party came to dinner, they have been out here for six weeks and go back in two, before going off to Burma.

November 15th: Up at 7.30, but the morning was pretty duff so there was no hope of flying Charlie girl. At 9.00 I was reading a new batch of Tatlers etc when the CO called me over to him in the Mess, where he had just taken a telephone message from HQ. In effect, it was a signal from Air Ministry saying: 'Mother of Flight Lieutenant E.R. Henshaw White expectation of life a few weeks only stop. If operations permit request compassionate posting to UK immediate.'

Thank God, the shock was not as great as it might have been. My mother's letters recently had very gently warned me that the cancer she had suffered in one breast, followed by one hip – both of which had been cured it seemed – might just have gone into her liver, causing frequents bouts of jaundice. Asking Doc about this some time ago, he kindly suggested that it might be a case of gallstones, easily put right.

Nonetheless it was a shock, and with very mixed feelings about leaving my friends here, I knew that I must do *all* that I could to make the end as *easy* as I could, if the end it really had to be. I packed a suitcase and raced up to rear DAF HQ and got down to Falconara just after the plane had left. All later planes had been cancelled owing to bad weather.

I rang the Adj to tell him of my movements, in case any query came through from AM and he told me that I'm definitely on 'Posting', and that my OTE papers (operationally tour expired) would follow me. Another shock, for this meant that I would need more than a suitcase, and might even not be coming back???

I drove into Ancona and got a bed for the night. Phoned the Adj again to ask for my battle dress, Irvin coat and heavy suitcase. I'm allowed 100 lbs of kit which should include more than I possess so he'll send it down tomorrow, by 10.00.

November 16th: Didn't sleep much last night, trying to recount the number of times I must have hurt my mother desperately, by the things I had said, the things I had done, and particularly the promises I had made and therefore the things which I had *not* done, even after all those promises. This morning the weather was pretty grim again but the kite arrived OK from Bari and took us down to Naples in one and a quarter hours. My kit never arrived. Heaven knows why not and though air freight is safe from pilferage, I cannot imagine that Irvin jacket arriving at the Junior Carlton. I waited for hours for a lift out to 249 Wing. Had a coffee and sandwich at the Air Transit Camp snack bar while I waited. My kit ought to arrive today, 3.30 being the deadline.

All hopes hang on a 'special' coming in today and taking me to England at 7.00 tomorrow. Dashed into town and got a room at 414 Group's transit hotel, walked madly up to the officers' shop to buy some gloves. Thinking of home I suppose, I suddenly realised that all my house keys are in my suitcase!

Walked back to the hotel and had an excellent high tea; hoped to get a bath in town but they shut at 5.00. Had a very good haircut at the officers' club, but feeling filthy dirty and terribly tired; black half-moons under my eyes; I don't think I have ever seen them on myself before.

Rang up 249 to confirm tomorrow's plane and it's fallen through. The weather at home is said to be perfectly bloody, it rained throughout October. But the plane for the 18th is here *now*, and will definitely set off. Maybe my kit will arrive here by tomorrow night.

November 18th: Up at 4.45, a cup of tea, collected sandwiches and was driven up to 'Cappo' in the Yank bus. Hung about on Tatler's instructions to await our call. None came by 6.40 so I bundled my kit as best I could and went out to the waiting kite. There was Tatler fuming because we were not all present. I told him he'd better tell the other half dozen waiting for him.

We were under way by 7.15 but she took five long minutes of tree and roof scraping before she left the high ground and gained height. Cruising speed was down to 135 mph instead of normal 165. We had two badly wounded stretcher cases on the floor, and two enormous long-range petrol tanks which occupied about a third of the cabin space.

At 9.15 we flew over the northern edge of Corsica, the snow line being very strikingly half way down the steep mountains. Southern France was obscured by cloud but we could see the Alps way behind Nice ahead.

After Dieppe – the countryside quite untouched by war as we knew it – we flew into thicker and thicker haze. About mid-channel, the engines spluttered and stopped; surprising how much wind noise there is when the engines are silent. The petrol pump had failed and it took us a 2,000-foot glide before the other pump took over. We had been losing height anyway from the French coast and were little over 1,500 feet off the waves. Just got over the cliffs when the second pump failed, and by dint of very hard work by somebody, we crawled onto a disused drome on the emergency hand-pump; that too packed up before we could taxi to the perimeter track.

Just why my tranquility and contentment were absolute, as they were, I shall never know on this earth, but I just knew we would make the trip, come what may.

Happily for our stretcher cases, an ambulance had been alerted and was waiting for us on the drome at 3.00. By 4.15 another kite arrived and took us to Hendon where we landed in very thick fog. Cleared through Customs by 5.30, and then I got a lift from an Air Ministry driver going back into town to drop me off at our house in Hampstead, (now re-occupied by my sister, who was currently playing with the Old Vic company in London. My parents had made the trip to see her performance).

My father was at home when I arrived – and after a stiff drink together, he told me that my mother had died that morning at about 2.00 a.m. She knew that I was on my way home and that made her very happy. As soon as she heard the news she faded away quickly; drugged against pain, she died peacefully.

So, my war was over. So quickly it was hard to adjust. Some chap in Fighter Command HQ at Stanmore very graciously gave me a posting to Hawarden in North Wales, so that I could go home to be with my father at Deganwy within an hour. It was strange to see mufti on everyone after about 4.30 on a Friday afternoon, and the station deserted all weekend; the war here seemed to have finished *months* ago.

My old Singer 'Le Mans' was none the worse for being on bricks for the couple of years, and all it needed was a new battery, but despite this link with my much relished past at Hawarden, it was no longer the 57 OTU I remembered so lovingly, where I had first flown my precious Spitfires. Now, it was some sort of repair and maintenance unit, where they re-built them for use in other theatres of war and where they were still very much needed.

Knowing something of their future role, it was my pleasure to test-fly each of these machines after re-build and make sure that they were *perfect*, even to the aileron up-float, which had not to exceed ⅜ths of an inch at 450 mph. Diving down onto the River Dee estuary to obtain that sort of speed, it was not difficult to think of my colleagues of 92 Squadron doing virtually the same thing on an armed recce over the River Po; but, without a lump in my throat, it was:

> 'But they that wait upon the Lord shall renew their strength: they shall mount up with wings as eagles; they shall run, and not be weary; and they shall walk and not faint.'
>
> Isaiah, Chapter 40, verse 31.

Postscript

With respectful deference to the publisher, and the price-paying public, the advice of the 'Master' (Noël Coward) has been taken in as much that this script was 'Cut, Cut, and Cut Again' to some three quarters of its original length. Thankfully, Amy Howlett is an expert and I value her judgement greatly.

Being an agriculturist by profession, much of my written thoughts are, in retrospect, rather too Bellamy, perhaps; so much of my appreciation of God's Good Earth has had to be deleted. With them go the names and exploits of many friends and wartime colleagues, so few of whom have I been able to meet since.

During my six years of service life, there were many good times and bad times, but these would not sit happily within the confines of a few months' combat duty which this book tries to portray. I only hope that the structure (if I can call it that) is not just a pile of brick and stone with all the mortar withdrawn. There were so many friends who provided invaluable 'back-up' to my life in the Desert Air Force; space did not permit them all to be mentioned. But I would like them to know how much they were appreciated, both then and now. Anne Hope-Thompson, whose life underground at Stanmore as a WAAF in the Plotting Room had none of the glamour and fun we so enjoyed above ground; Valerie Spencer-Phillips, who honoured me by asking me to be godfather to her first-born; Frank Swann who worked with my father on the radio beam which guided Alcock and Brown on their first transatlantic flight, and went on to research for the Marconi Wireless and Telegraph Co, whose radar, asdic etc helped save more lives than can be counted; and finally the members of ENSA whose brave and comfortless efforts to entertain us can never be repaid.

My postwar career enabled me to meet such fellow combatants as Frierson in Australia, and Young in New Zealand; plus the family of 'Monty' in its North Island at their family farm, so much like mine.

I still see my guardian angel every now and then (and I am not being facetious). Perhaps increasing age brings with it increasing wisdom; she only appears when she knows I am in doubt.

Enslavement is something the British can be proud to have had abolished in many parts of our world, that is *by* others *of* others. Enslavement of ourselves in the service of our duty to our God, our Queen and our Country (our fellow citizens) is something which every serviceman and woman accepts as a weapon with which to fight all sorts of injustice, wherever he or she is called upon to exercise it. In these times of unemployment, I simply pray that those who have choice, serve their country; they will know what I mean, and it does not have to be in the military forces. My family motto happens to be *Persevera* (Keep trying), and more than mine can adopt it.

Appendix: Service Record

Unit	*Dates* *From*	*To*	*Location*	*Aircraft*
No.8 I.T.W.	Nov '40	April '41	Newquay	
No.17 E.F.T.S.	April '41	May '41	North Luffenham	Tiger Moth
No.8 S.F.T.S.	May '41	Sept '41	Montrose	Miles Masters & Hurricane I
No.57 O.T.U.	Sept '41	Nov '41	Hawarden	Spitfire I
No.222 Sqdn.	Nov '41	Feb '42	North Weald	Spitfire VB
No.1 M.E.T.S.	June '42		El Ballah	Hurricane I
No.73 Sqdn.	July '42	Sept '42	Western Desert	Hurricane IIC
No.2 M.E.T.S.	Sept '42	Dec '42	Aqir. Palestine	Well'n IC
No.70 Sqdn.	Jan '43	May '43	Western Desert	Well'n IC, III, & X
No.48 Gen. Hosp.	June '43		Tripoli (West)	
No.6 Gen. Hosp.	July '43		Canal Zone, Egypt	
No.5 R.A.F. Hosp.	July '43		Cairo	
R.A.F. Stn. Sorman	Aug '43	Sept '43	Tripolitania	Ferry Flight
No.71 O.T.U.	Sept '43	Dec '43	Ismailia	Hurricanes
No.13 A.G.S.	Dec '43	June '44	Ballah (Canal)	Lysanders
D.A.F. Training Flight		July '44	Sinello	Spitfire V
No.92 Sqdn.	July 21	Nov 15 '44	Italy Perugia, Rosignano, Fano	Spitfire VIII
No.41 O.T.U.	Dec '44		Hawarden	Asst. Adj.
No.41 O.T.U.	Dec '44	Feb '45	Poulton	Adj.
No.41 O.T.U.	Feb 18	April 3	Hawarden	Asst. Adj.
No.58 O.T.U.	April '45	Jun '45	Hawarden	Gunnery and test flight
No.12 F.U.T.C.	July '45	Aug '45	Melton Mowbray	Ferry
No.44 GP. T.C.	Aug '45	Dec '45	Gloucester	Records
R.A.F. Holmesley South	Jan '46	Mar '46	Christchurch	Ops. Officer
Cambridge U.A. Sqdn.	Oct '46	Jun '48	Cambridge	Tiger Moth, Oxford etc.

Aircraft Flown	*Engine*
D.H.82A Tiger Moth	Gypsy Major
Miles Master I & III	R.R. Kestrel XXX
Hurricane I	R.R. Merlin I
Spitfire I	R.R. Merlin XX

Miles Magister	Gypsy Major
Hurricanes IIB & IIC	Merlin XX
Spitfires VB & VC	Merlin XLV
Wellington IC	Pegasus
Wellington III & X	Hercules XVI
Lysander	Mercury
Harvard I, IIA & IIB	Pratt & Whitney Wasp
Hawker Audax	Kestrel X
Spitfires VIII, IX & X	Merlin 61, 63 & 66
D.H. Rapide (Domine)	2 Gypsy Major
Avro Anson	2 Cheetah
Air Speed Oxford	

UK Landing Grounds Visited and/or Used

North Luffenham	Rutland	17 E.F.T.S.
Sywell	Rutland	17 E.F.T.S.
Montrose	Angus	8 S.F.T.S.
Lossiemouth		8 S.F.T.S.
Edzell	Angus	8 S.F.T.S.
Stracathro's field	Angus	8 S.F.T.S.
Hawarden	Flintshire	57 O.T.U.
Wellingore	Lincolnshire	57 O.T.U.
Balyhalbut	N. Ireland	57 O.T.U.
Dyce	Aberdeen	57 O.T.U.
Sealands	Cheshire	57 O.T.U.
North Weald	Essex	222 Sqdn.
Fairoaks	Surrey	222 Sqdn.
Biggin Hill	Surrey	222 Sqdn.
Martlesham Heath	Lincolnshire	222 Sqdn.
Hendon		A.T.C. (Air Transport Command)
Poulton	Denbighshire	41 & 58 O.T.U.s
Melton Mowbray	Leicestershire	12 F.U.
Staverton	Gloucestershire	44 Gp. Comm. Flight
Filton	Gloucestershire	44 Gp. Comm. Flight
Swinderby	Lincolnshire	44 Gp. Comm. Flight
Moreton in the Marsh	Gloucestershire	44 Gp. Comm. Flight
Marshall's	Cambridge	C.U.A.S.
Shoreham by the Sea	Sussex	C.U.A.S.
Tangmere	Sussex	C.U.A.S.
Kenley	Surrey	C.U.A.S.
Woodley	Berkshire	C.U.A.S.

Overseas Landing Grounds Visited and/or Used

Lagos (Apapa Wf)	Nigeria	Pan American Airways
Maiduguri	Nigeria	Pan American Airways
El Genina	Chad	Pan American Airways
Khatoum	Sudan	Pan American Airways
Almaza	Egypt	Pan American Airways
El Ballah	Egypt	1. M.E.T.S.
Helopolis (Cairo)	Egypt	1. M.E.T.S.
Ismailia	Egypt	1. M.E.T.S.

L.G.Y.	Egypt	1. M.E.T.S.
L.G.89	Egypt	73 Sqdn.
Shandur	Egypt	73 Sqdn.
L.G.X.	Egypt	73 Sqdn.
Gianaclis	Egypt	73 Sqdn.
El Bassa	Palestine	73 Sqdn.
St. Jean	Palestine	73 Sqdn.
Lydda	Palestine	73 Sqdn.
L.G.100 (Wadi Natroun)	Egypt	73 Sqdn.
L.G.85	Egypt	73 Sqdn.
L.G.92	Egypt	73 Sqdn.
Abukir (Alexandria)	Egypt	73 Sqdn.
Aqir	Palestine	2. M.E.T.S.
L.G.237 (Kilo 40)	Egypt	2. M.E.T.S.
Yibna	Palestine	2. M.E.T.S.
L.G.77 (Kilo 8)	Egypt	73 Sqdn.
L.G.224 (Cairo West)		70 Sqdn.
L.G.140 (Tobruk)	Cyenaica	70 Sqdn.
El Adem	Cyenaica	70 Sqdn.
Benina (Bengasi)	Cyenaica	70 Sqdn.
Magrun	Cyenaica	70 Sqdn.
Gardabia East	Tripolitania	70 Sqdn.
Gardabia West	Tripolitania	70 Sqdn.
Castel Benito (Tripoli West)	Tripolitania	70 Sqdn.
March Arch (Trip/Cyr border)		70 Sqdn.
Kairouan Tamam	Tunisia	70 Sqdn.
Halwan	Egypt	71 O.T.U.
Abusuir	Egypt	73 O.T.U.
Luka	Malta	A.T.C.
Bari	Italy	A.T.C.
Capodocino	Italy	A.T.C.
Sinello	Italy	D.A.F. Training Flight
Perugia	Italy	92 Sqdn.
Rosignano	Italy	92 Sqdn.
Fano	Italy	92 Sqdn.
Falconara	Italy	A.T.C.
Habbaniya (Timbuctu)		2. M.E.T.S.
H.2 (Pipe Line)		2. M.E.T.S.

Index